Perfect Days in...
KRAKOW

Travel with
Insider Tips

D1003126

WITHDRAWN

Contents

 **TOP 10** 4

That Krakow Feeling 6

For chapters: See inside front cover

Not to be missed!

Our TOP 10 hits – from the absolute No. 1 to No. 10 – help you plan your tour of the most important sights.

⭐1 RYNEK GŁÓWNY ► 52

The Main Market Square, which covers an area of 200 × 200m (656ft × 656ft), is one of Europe's largest medieval marketplaces and Krakow's bustling centre (► photo left).

⭐2 WZGÓRZE WAWELSKIE ► 82

Wawel Hill, the nation's beating heart: in the castle, Poland's kings ruled over the country for hundreds of years; in the cathedral, many leading Polish figures have found their last resting place.

⭐3 KOŚCIÓŁ MARIACKI ► 56

On the hour the *hejnał* trumpet call resounds from the tower of Kościół Mariacki (St Mary's Church); inside, the real eye-catcher is the winged Gothic altarpiece by Veit Stoß.

⭐4 PODZIEMIA RYNKU ► 60

In the Underground Museum beneath the Main Market Square you get to the bottom of the town in all senses…

⭐5 FABRYKA SCHINDLERA ► 144

Oskar Schindler's former enamel-ware factory houses a multimedia exhibition about Krakow between the years of 1939 to 1945. Contemporary art is on show at the MOCAK Museum next door.

⭐6 SYNAGOGA REMUH ► 118

The synagogue named after Moses Isserles (Remuh) is still used as a place of worship by the Jewish community; the grave of the famous rabbi is in the cemetery behind the building.

⭐7 ULICA KANONICZA ► 90

Lined with medieval palaces, "Street of the Canons", which connects Wawel with the Main Market Square, is regarded as one of the city's most beautiful boulevards.

⭐8 COLLEGIUM MAIUS ► 93

The oldest building of Central Europe's second oldest university boasts a romantic, much visited, arcaded courtyard.

⭐9 PLAC NOWY ► 121

The market square in the Jewish district of Kazimierz is one of the nightlife hotspots. One good thing: night owls can fortify them-selves at the food stalls in the old market hall.

⭐10 MUZEUM INŻYNIERII MIEJSKI ► 123

The Museum of Urban Engineering, located in an old tram depot, showcases an impressive collection of historical vehicles.

THAT
KRAKOW

Find out what makes the city tick, experience its unique flair – just like the people of Krakow themselves.

A COFFEE ON THE MAIN MARKET SQUARE

Old coffee houses reflecting the style of the Habsburg period, trendy restaurants and lounge bars line Rynek Główny (➤ 52). When the sun shines, people crowd the terraces. It is not only the tourists who enjoy watching the colourful hustle and bustle on the square. The people of Krakow also like meeting in the city's "front room" for a coffee and a piece of cake.

WANDER ALONG THE BANKS OF THE VISTULA

In summer, the city inhabitants stream down to the banks of the Vistula. Families fill the promenade at the foot of Wawel Hill (➤ 82), where an iron dragon breathes fire to hoots of delight from the children. Young people sitting on the harbour wall enjoy the sunset. It is very crowded around the summer solstice. During the mid-summer Wianki Festival (➤ 106) young women float floral wreaths on the Vistula River.

ZAPIEKANKI ON PLAC NOWY

Those wishing to get through the long nights in Kazimierz need to

Watching the world go by in the cafés around the Main Market Square, the city's "front room".

FEELING

keep their strength up. Ideally with a *Zapiekanka*, an open sandwich made with half a baguette. It is to Krakow what Guinness is to Dublin. Long queues form in front of the old market hall on Plac Nowy (➤ 121). The classic choice with mushrooms, cheese and ketchup costs five złoty. Most people swear by the *Zapiekanki* from **Endzior**, which is available in 15 different variations.

RELAX IN BŁONIA PARK

In the nineteenth century, cows still grazed on the 48 hectares of Błonia Park. Hundreds of thousands of Catholics gathered on the grass here during the pilgrimage of Pope John Paul II. Large concerts take place in the Błonia, but it mainly functions as a recreation area for the city inhabitants, who go there to jog,

That Krakow Feeling

cycle, rollerblade, stroll or just take a little break from city life.

ENJOY OBWARZANKI

Wandering through the town makes you hungry, and to quell those little hunger pangs between meals you can always eat *Obwarzanki*, bread snacks sprinkled with poppyseed, sesame or salt that are for sale everywhere at street stalls. Made of rolled leavened dough and braided into a ring shape, *Obwarzanki* have been enjoyed since the Middle Ages: a crunchy fresh tradition.

MARKET DAY IN KLEPARZ

This market has existed since the 14th century. There you can find exotic fruits and spices, local vegetables, cheese, meat, bread and flowers, as well as wicker baskets, pottery and clothing. On seven days of the week, people crowd the market streets, compare prices and take time to chat to one another.

WALK THROUGH THE PLANTY

At the beginning of the 19th century, large sections of the medieval fortifications were removed. The Old Town could breathe again and acquired a new green look. The 4km (2.5mi) long Planty Park shields the Old Town from the traffic. Illuminated promenades pass through the expansive green gardens. Anyone wishing to get away from the hordes of tourists for a while, should take a leisurely stroll through the park and let his mind wander at will.

OFF TO THE DACHSHUND PARADE

Every year in September thousands of dog owners, accompanied by a brass band, parade along Floriańska Street with their colourfully dressed dachshunds to the general amusement of the many spectators. The *Marsz Jamników* (Dachshund parade) originated during the Socialist period – as a parody of the state-imposed parade on 1 May. In 1990 the Polish playwright Sławomir Mrożek revived the idea. At the end, prizes are awarded for the most original costumes.

This is how a winner looks at the Dachshund parade

The Magazine

THE **HEART**
OF POLAND

Poland's kings ruled the country from Krakow for more than 500 years. When there were no more kings and a sovereign Polish state had disappeared from Europe's political map, the town became a national symbol and place of hope for many Poles.

After the Second Partition of Poland in 1793, the majority of the country was occupied by Prussia, Russia and Austria. General **Tadeusz Kościuszko**, a highly decorated veteran of the American Civil War, set off to free Poland. On 24 March 1794, in Krakow's Main Market Square, he swore an oath to defend the nation and announced an uprising. With a small troop of regular soldiers and an infantry of poorly armed peasants, he scored a victory, albeit brief, at Racławice against the Russians, but was soon defeated by the superior forces of the Prussian and Russian armies. The Third Secession followed in 1795; and Krakow came under Austrian rule.

Hope for the Nation
With the exception of interim phases, the town remained part of the Habsburg Empire until 1918, becoming the intellectual centre of Poland

Tadeusz Kościuszko in the *Battle of Racławice* (painting by Jan Matejko, 1888)

after it lost its sovereignty. Whilst the Russians and Prussians were subject to very strict rule, the Habsburgs granted the Poles in Galicia a large amount of autonomy. Polish became the official language again, and the state parliament was dominated by Polish delegates. Krakow experienced a new golden age and became a cultural centre. The private Czartoryski Museum, the National Museum and the Słowacki Theatre were founded, artists of note carried out their work in the town and for the national cause.

At the beginning of the 20th century, this relative freedom enabled **Józef Piłsudski** to organise the troops in Krakow with which he would later fight for an independent Poland. Although Warsaw again became the capital of the new Polish state after World War I, the Jagiellonian University, the mining academy founded in 1919 and other institutions meant that Krakow developed into an important scientific centre.

Krakow's coat of arms

The Magazine

General Józef Piłsudski with members of the government (1926)

Persecution of Intellectual Elite

The Nazis regarded Krakow as the intellectual centre of Poland, and they did everything they could to destroy it. At the end of 1939, Hans Frank moved into Wawel Castle as Governor-General of the occupied Polish territories. As the "Butcher of Poland", he was later sentenced to death at the Nuremberg War Trials.

John Paul II visiting Krakow in June 1987

The arrest of 183 professors and employees of Krakow universities on 6 November 1939 marked the beginning of the systematic eradication of the Polish upper class. Besides the Jagiellonian University, many other higher education bodies, colleges and cultural institutions were shut. The German occupiers decided it was sufficient if the Poles learned how to write their names and understand a bit of simple arithmetic. However in Krakow's underground movement, professors resumed teaching their students. **Karol Wojtyła**, later to become Pope John Paul II, also attended an illegal seminary and took part in secret performances of a theatre group.

After the rapid advance of Soviet troops in 1945, Krakow was liberated from the Nazi regime without suffering any great damage but was then immediately under the yoke of another foreign power.

Whilst the new Socialist government initially met with favour in other Polish towns, it was rigorously rejected in Krakow. As early as 1946 thousands of people gathered in front of St Mary's Church, despite a

WORLD CULTURAL HERITAGE SITE
When UNESCO published its first list of world cultural sites in 1978, Krakow figured on it, with special mention given to its Old Town, the Wawel Hill and the Jewish district Kazimierz. The reasons given were that the town complex was an "excellent example of medieval architecture".

ban on demonstrations, in order to commemorate the first modern constitution that had been passed 200 years previously. In a tit-for-tat response, the political leaders set up a model Socialist housing settlement, Nowa Huta, on the bourgeois Catholics' doorstep. The irony of the story: during the 1980s, it was actually Nowa Huta that developed into a centre of the Polish opposition movement.

New Courage in Difficult Times

Some artists like **Sławomir Mrożek** escaped state domination by emigrating, others like the poet **Wisława Szymborska** or the composer **Krzysztof Penderecki**, made their own space and created works that cemented Krakow's reputation as a cultural metropolis. During the difficult political and economic times, many Poles looked again to Krakow. When in 1978 Krakow's Archbishop Karol Wojtyła was appointed pope, it gave the people new courage. During his first visit as Pope **John Paul II** to Krakow in 1979, hundreds of thousands of people gathered on Błonia Park to see him. His

trip to Poland acted as a catalyst for the fight of the trade union *Solidarność* ("Solidarity"), a resistance to the system which soon afterwards spread throughout the country and was responsible for the collapse of the regime in 1989.

It may be that the town's archrival Warsaw has overtaken Krakow in terms of cultural programmes, but in the hearts of most Poles Krakow remains the cultural metropolis and for most visitors to Poland the most beau-

Solidarność memorial in the Nowa Huta district

tiful town in the country.

Krakow and its Students

Although it is thousands of years old, Krakow is a young town. You will see a lot of students; around a quarter of the town's 750,000 inhabitants attend one of the many universities, polytechnics and academies.

"Student life here will not attract anyone who has read or heard anything about what it is like to be a student in Germany, and a cheerful poet, were he to spend eight days with his confreres here, would be totally depressed." That is how a German chronicler described the apparently once rather gloomy life at the Jagiellonian University in 1844. That has obviously changed in the meantime, since a lot of foreign students come to Krakow to study, keen not only to take advantage of the quality of the education but also to enjoy the Dolce Vita outside the lecture halls.

Studying like Copernicus

The Jagiellonian University founded in 1364 is the oldest in Poland and, with almost 50,000 students, one of the largest in the country. Nicolaus Copernicus and later Pope Karol Wojtyła attended the university. The Akademia Górniczo-Hutnicza (AGH University of Science and Technology) founded in 1919 is one of the country's leading technical universities and has around 35,000 students. Its range of subjects now comprises biotechnology, information technology and environmental sciences.

The neo-Gothic Collegium Novum is the main building of the Jagiellonian University

Costume parade during Juwenalia

A business academy founded in 1925 developed to become the Uniwersytet Ekonomiczny (Krakow University of Economics) and now with 23,000 students is the largest institution of its kind in Poland. There is also another Technical, and an Agricultural University as well as the Pontifical University of John Paul II. The new generation of artists are educated at the academy of fine arts and the music academy.

Colourful Parade for Juwenalia

One of the nicest events in Krakow's student life is the annual Juwenalia, which takes place in May. For several days, students from all of the Krakow universities get together for concerts and parties. The highlight of this traditional festival is a colourful parade to the Main Market Square during which the students from the various universities (www.juwenalia.krakow.pl) contend for the prize for the most original costume.

KRAKOW ON HIGH HEELS

Steffen Möller began his career with a language course in Krakow and, as a cabaret artist and actor, became one of the most famous Germans in Poland. This shows that it is possible to learn Polish. If you just want to have a go, you can attend a **Summer language course** at the Jagiellonian University or at one of the numerous language schools. The *Varia* language school offers an original programme for women. "Krakow on high heels" – with a lot of culture, shopping, health clubs and a mini language course (www.varia-course.com).

Insider Tip

CITY OF ART AND ARTISTS

Krakow lost its status as capital in 1609 when this role was passed onto Warsaw, but Krakow still confidently regards itself as Poland's cultural metropolis. Many important artists were and are connected with the city.

Maintaining its National Heritage

When Poland disappeared from Europe's political map as a sovereign state, it became art's task to preserve national spirit. It was during that period that Krakow developed into the centre of Polish cultural life. **Jan Matejko** (1838–1893) saw art as a weapon. His large paintings picked up themes based on major events in Polish history. His aim was to build up the national identity of his fellow Poles and help them shake off the yoke of oppression. Among his most important works is the monumental painting *Battle at Grunwald* of 1878, which depicts the victory of the Polish and Lithuanian troops over the Teutonic Order in 1410. His oil painting ***Prussian Homage***, which he painted shortly afterwards, is exhibited in the picture gallery in the Cloth Hall (➤ 53) and depicts the Duke of Prussia paying tribute to the Polish King Zygmunt I Stary (Sigismund I the Elder).

Centre of Glass Art

Two of Matejko's most renowned students are **Stanisław Wyspiański** (1869–1907) and **Józef Mehoffer** (1869–1946), who would eventually turn away

CITY OF NOBEL PRIZE-WINNERS

Czesław Miłosz (1911–2004) and **Wisława Szymborska** (1923–2012) are two Nobel Prize Literature Laureates closely associated with Krakow. The poet Wisława Szymborska lived in Krakow from a young age. She eventually turned away from the Polish Workers' Party to become a critic of the system. Miłosz, who took part in underground activities in World War II, spent most of the years after the war in exile, subsequently living part of the time in Krakow from 1989 and then all of the time from 2000.

Jan Matejko's masterpiece from 1882: *Prussian Homage*

from his perception of art. They became part of the art movement *Młoda Polska* ("Young Poland"), which picked up new artistic forms of expression such as Impressionism, Expressionism and Art Nouveau. Among the very varied works produced by Wyspiański and Mehoffer are the glass paintings inspired by Art Nouveau. They contributed towards making Krakow one of the most important centres of glass art in Europe. You can view glass work from Mehoffer in the Jagiellonian chapel of Wawel Cathedral or in the former bank building in Ulica Szpitalna (no. 13). Wyspiański created stained glass windows for the Church of St Francis of Assisi (▶98) and for the former building belonging to the medical society in Ulica Radziwiłłowska (no. 4). Many of the windows were manufactured in the glassworks founded in 1902 by **Stanisław Gabriel Żeleński** (1873–1914), now home to Krakow's Workshop and Museum for Stained Glass (▶103). There, visitors can try out some of the painting techniques for themselves.

ned glass windows by Stanisław Wyspiański in Wyspiański Pavilion (▶104)

Contemporary Art
Named after Jan Matejko, Krakow's academy of

In the Planty, near the Barbican, Jan Matejko sits inside a picture frame

fine arts (▶66) has produced many leading artists and sculptors over the years. One of its younger graduates is **Wilhelm Sasnal**, who was born in Tarnów, not far from Krakow in 1972. Sasnal is regarded as one of the most well-known representatives of contemporary art in Poland; his works collect very high prices around the world. He takes pictures from the media, comic strips and private photographs as his models, catching everyday moments or reflecting on social events in his pictures and videos. Some of his works can be viewed in the MOCAK (▶146), which has become a leading address for contemporary art.

Film Town Krakow

Krakow provides the stage for numerous films, but no other film has had such a lasting effect on the town as *Schindler's List* (1993). The American director **Steven Spielberg** not only commemorated the actions of the industrialist Oskar Schindler (▶144) in his film, but also made the former Jewish quarter Kazimierz known to people all around the world.

The director **Andrzej Wajda** (1926–2016), whose life's work received an Oscar in 2000, also had very close ties with Krakow. He studied painting there after the War before discovering film and later worked as well as a theatre director in Krakow. Wajda also sponsored the Manggha Museum for Far-Eastern Art (▶152).

He became a friend of **Roman Polański** (b. 1933) at university. Polański lived for a while in the ghetto of Podgórze (▶150) with his Jewish parents, but managed to flee. In the 1960s, Polański came under pressure from the Polish cultural authorities and emigrated to Great Britain, and then later to the USA. It was not until 2001 that he returned to Poland for his film *The Pianist*, and since 2015 he has been living off and on in Krakow.

From Classic to Klezmer

For people who love classical music, Krakow is the most important address in Poland after Warsaw. The Philharmonic orchestra has a good reputation, and many other ensembles perform in the city's concert halls and churches.

One of the most important contemporary musicians in the country is the conductor and composer **Krzysztof Penderecki** (b. 1933), who studied at the Academy of Music in Krakow and has since maintained very close ties with the town. He has composed symphonies, operas and film music and was awarded one of the coveted Grammy awards. His music is often played in Krakow, and from time to time he still appears on the conductor's stand.

Krakow also pulls in the jazz fans. Every day you will hear live music ringing out from many cellars in the Old Town. For over 60 years, prominent jazz musicians from all over the world have been coming to perform at the "Zaduski Jazzowe" Festival which takes place at the beginning of November.

The Jewish name for Krakow, **Kroke**, has been communicated to the world by the band of the same name. Playing traditional Klezmer music, which brings together elements of classical, jazz and electronic music, the trio began their career in the restaurants of Kazimierz and later went on tour with people like **Nigel Kennedy** (b. 1956). The British star violinist lives together with his Polish wife Agnieszka in Krakow for part of the year and occasionally gives live performances.

TOP 5 KRAKOW MUSIC FESTIVALS

- **Misteria Paschalia** is a top-class festival for early music that takes place at Easter (www.misteriapaschalia.pl).
- The **Wianki Festival** not only picks up the midsummer traditions but also attracts the crowds with top stars from the rock and pop world (www.wianki.krakow.pl).
- In August on the most attractive squares of the Old Town you can listen to classical music at the **Muzyka w starym Krakowie** festival ("Music in Old Krakow"; www.mwsk.pl).
- In Autumn the **Sacrum Profanum** (➤ photograph above) focuses on contemporary music, some of which is staged in unconventional locations, such as the Nowa Huta steelworks (http://sacrumprofanum.com).
- At the **Krakowska Jesień Jazzowa** (Krakow Jazz Autumn), the big names from the local and international scene honour the town with a visit (www.kjj-festiwal.pl).

The **Trumpeter**
of St Mary's Church

The Krakow *hejnał* is as dear to the Poles as the national anthem. On the hour the live bugle call resounds four times from the tall tower of the Kościół Mariacki (St Mary's Church).

A workplace with good prospects...

Zygmunt Rozem has one of the highest positions that the city of Krakow has to offer. There are 273 steps from the 40,000m² (10 acre) Rynek Główny to the small square tower room of St Mary's Church, in which he works. Rozem is one of seven firemen that take turns in the tower of St Mary's Church. Just before the bells chime the hour, he takes his trumpet, opens the window and after the last bell he blows his melody to the north, the east, the south and the west. Even at night, passersby on the Main Market Square will stop in their tracks to listen.

Legend of the Brave Bugler

Each time the melody ends abruptly as it reaches its climax. This commemorates the brave trumpeter who was killed by an enemy arrow as he was warning the town citizens of an attack by the Tatars in 1241. In actual fact, no mention of the bugle call appeared in historical records until 1392. During the Middle Ages, the *hejnał* was generally only played once in the morning and evening to announce the opening and closing of the city gates, or to warn of some danger. Since 1810, it sounds four times every full hour, and since 1927, the call is also broadcast on the national radio

INSIDER INFO

Insider Tip

You can visit the trumpeter room of St Mary's Church every half an hour. Although it is quite an arduous ascent, you are rewarded with a heavenly view (April–Oct daily – except on religious holiday – 9:10am–11:40am and 1:10pm–5:40pm, admission: 15 złoty).

Every hour, the Krakow bugle call sounds from the tower of St Mary's Church

at noon. For Poles, it is the second most important national melody after the national anthem. And it has to be the most-played live melody worldwide. It resounds more than 35,000 times a year from the tower of St Mary's Church.

On Duty 24/7

Were Zygmunt Rozem to see a fire today, he would call the emergency services or trigger a fire alarm. Otherwise his job is limited to his bugle call every hour. In the tower room, he has a little kitchen, shower and toilet. One shift lasts 24 hours, then he has two days off. He can take a short nap between trumpet performances. When asked if has every missed his cue, he admits haltingly that in 20 years it has occurred twice.

Zygmunt Rozem loves his work; he enjoys playing the trumpet and the dream view of the town. Despite the tiring shifts, he has a coveted job, one that is sometimes passed down from father to son. Until now, all of the trumpeters were men, but women are allowed to apply for the job as long as they are trained members of the fire brigade. Zygmunt Rozem believes that trumpeters will still be playing the *hejnał* live in a hundred years: "It is just part of our tradition in Krakow."

The Krakauer

For many Poles, there isn't another sausage to match it. The *Krakowska* (Krakauer) is an obligatory part of breakfast – and many people also eat it in the evening. The *Kiełbasa krakowska* is one of the most popular sorts.

Poland has been making sausages since the Middle Ages. During the 17th and 18th century it was a ubiquitous dish on the dining tables of the nobility. Even during the Socialist period, there were strict rules about the way it should be prepared. With the political turnaround, foreign products entered the market and, after joining the EU, the number of acceptable additives increased, although most Poles have remained true to the flavours they know. Traditional varieties of sausage are still very popular; they tend to be bought from smaller regional producers. And despite the rising number of vegetarians, the average Polish citizen still eats more than two kilos of such meat per month.

Top-quality Pork

Traditional Krakauer sausages have been produced since the 19th century in what was then called Galicia. They are now manufactured under this name all over Poland. Their common feature: they are mainly made of high-quality pork and produced with whole pieces of meat. Since 2015 the *Kiełbasa krakowska sucha staropolska* ("dried Krakauer old-Polish style") has been registered as a traditional speciality of the Polish agricultural ministry. It has to contain at least 70% first-rate pork with a fat content that does not exceed 15%, which is then cut into small pieces and salted. Then finely minced pork with a higher fat content is added and natural spices such as pepper and nutmeg. The thick, almost straight sausages are mainly smoked over beech-wood, which is how the skin gets its typically crinkled form.

It is worth taking a break on your city stroll for a grilled Krakauer…

Traditional Products from Liski

Comparable with the traditional Krakauer is the *Kiełbasa lisiecka*. It bears the stamp of the European Union for products with a protected geographical location and may only be produced in the municipalities of Liski and Czernichów located to the west of Krakow. Both places are renowned for their sausage products. There were more than 30 butchers in the area even in the mid-19th century. Since about 1930, Krakauer sausages have been sold there under the name of *Kiełbasa lisiecka*. Until 1989 the well-known sausage was produced by a cooperative; since then private companies have been continuing the tradition.

LONG AND THIN

Among the most popular sausages in Poland, apart from the Krakauers, is the long, thin *Kabanos*. It is registered by the EU as a traditional speciality. The meat comes from pigs that have been mainly fed on potatoes. The hot-smoked sausages are crispy and have a high fat content.

Krakow's
Underworld

Rich traders used to be based around Krakow's Main Market Square. They had their shops and showrooms on street level and stored their products below ground. Today, the red-brick vaulted cellars provide the venue for the city's vibrant nightlife.

Late in the evening when the streets of Krakow's Old Town have calmed down, the night owls swoop down to the cellars. Disco music blares out from one, rock from another, and in the third there is a jazz band on the stage.

Legendary Cellar Cabaret
Piwnica Pod Baranami ("The Cellar under the Rams"; ➤ 76) is the name of the legendary cabaret on the west side of Rynek Główny. For the last six decades, evening cabaret programmes have been organised here, ranging from jazz concerts to tango evenings. This "culture cellar" ranks among the trendsetters. However, Krakow's subterranean nightlife only really took off in a big way after the political turnaround when cellars dating back to

Klezmer live in vaulted cellars

Chill in Hotel Stary

In-bar Alchemia

"Cellar Under the Rams"

the Middle Ages were uncovered. Soon one new subterranean restaurant was opening after the other. In **Harris Piano Jazz Bar** (▶ 76) for example, which is right next to the "Cellar under the Rams" live jazz has been playing for almost two decades. Jazz musicians also play in other cellars in front of dense crowds of people, for example in **Piec'Art** (▶ 112) or **The Piano Rouge** (▶ 76).

Generations of students have been drawn to these unpretentious cellar bars such as the **Klub Kulturalny** in Ulica Szewska, where the beer is inexpensive and the atmosphere is good. At rock music or karaoke evenings, it is easy to forget that the next lecture is at nine o'clock the following morning.

Since the medieval buildings in Kazimierz and Podgórze also have cellars, places have opened there for partying and dancing. That is why live concerts regularly take place in the spacious cellars of the **Alchemia** (▶ 134) and the **Drukarnia** (▶ 160).

Elegant Enjoyment

In the elegant restaurants, such as the **Pod Aniołami** (▶ 109), the **Concept 13** (Rynek Główny 39) and the **Cyrano de Bergerac** (▶ 70), the atmosphere in the impressively lit medieval vaulted cellars is very welcoming. Guests at the two luxury hotels **Copernicus** (▶ 42) and **Stary** (ul. Szczepańska 5) can take time out below the ancient barrow vaults and enjoy total relaxation. Chic health club facilities have been set up there, which include a pool, sauna and exercise equipment.

You can immerse yourself in the history of the town in the subterranean rooms of Wawel Castle (▶ 82) as well as in the Underground Museum (▶ 60) beneath the Main Market Square, where the oldest traces of Krakow can be found.

... and in the Pod Baranami club

Jam sessions: in Harris Piano Jazz Bar...

Harris Piano Jazz Bar

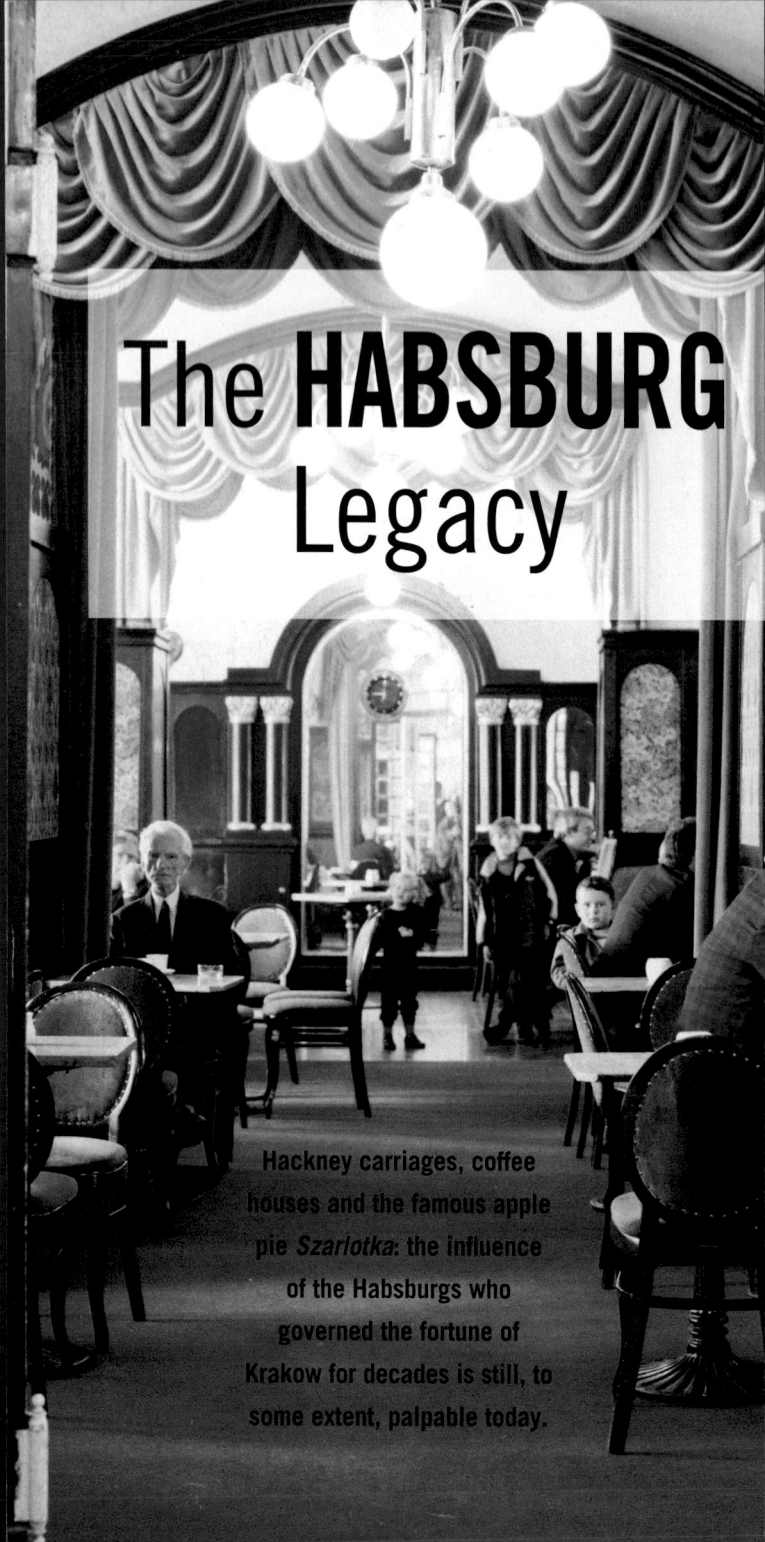

The **HABSBURG** Legacy

Hackney carriages, coffee houses and the famous apple pie *Szarlotka*: the influence of the Habsburgs who governed the fortune of Krakow for decades is still, to some extent, palpable today.

A difficult time began for the Poles at the end of the 18th century. The country was divided between three neighbours, Prussia, Russia and Austria. It was a very unstable period for Krakow. After a phase of repression, things became more liberal under the influence of the Habsburgs in the 1860s. Polish again became the official language, Poles were involved in the administration and were able to foster their traditions.

Many Austrian soldiers and civil servants lived in Krakow at the time, and conversely many of Krakow's aristocracy travelled to Vienna to go shopping or visit the opera. Young people from Krakow studied architecture in Vienna and transferred the architectural style from there to the city on the Vistula. As a result, Krakow developed a certain Viennese flair. That was particularly evident in the evolvement of the coffee-house culture. Although, it is a fact that the first *Kafehauzy* in Poland date back to the 17th century, they were mostly in very small, simple rooms. It was not until the mid-19th century that the coffee houses based on their Viennese counterparts were opened in Krakow, coffee houses in which there were newspapers and tables for gambling and playing pool, and where it was possible to buy cake. Austrian civil servants, Polish craftsmen, students and artists all had their favourite addresses. For instance, artists and journalists were regular guests at the **Kawiarnia Jama Michalika** (▶ 73), opened in 1895 (ul. Floriańska 45), where some of the penniless art students paid their bills with paintings.

Although in the meantime international chains like Starbucks are opening cafés here, the Viennese coffee-house tradition still prevails to this day. The best example of this is the **Café Noworolski** (photo left; ▶ 73) in the Cloth Hall. In 1910 its founder took his inspiration from the decor in the Viennese coffee house *Sacher*. At other traditional cafes around the Main Market Square, rolls, *kajzerki*, are served for breakfast and later on *sernik* (cheese cake) or *szarlotka* (apple pie) – just as they were during the time of the Habsburgs.

The history of the *dorożki*, the hackney carriage, also dates back to the time of the Habsburgs. Once the city's most important means of transport, these horse-drawn carriages are now, as in Vienna, just a tourist attraction.

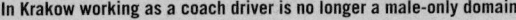

In Krakow working as a coach driver is no longer a male-only domain

Closing concert of the Jewish Culture Festival in Ulica Szeroka

New Life in the **Jewish District**

Once, more than 60,000 Jews lived in Kazmierz. Today the total number in Krakow's Jewish community hovers around the 200 mark. Yet by the time of Steven Spielberg's film, the memory of the city's Jewish history had been jogged.

Jews have lived in Krakow since the 11th century. Later King Kazimierz Wielki (Casimir III the Great) lured Jewish traders and moneylenders to the city by offering them special privileges, and many settled in Krakow. The Krakow Jews lived mainly around the area of what is now the Ulica św. Anny, on the west side of the Main Market Square, then also known as the *Judengasse* (Jewish District). When the university started expanding in the area around 1400, the Jews were forced to leave and they settled slightly further north around what is now Plac Szczepański.

After Pogroms a Designated Jewish District in Kazimierz

In the 15th century there were a series of pogroms against Jewish citizens; after the large town fire in 1484, many people claimed that the Jews had been responsible for the catastrophe. King Jan I Olbracht bowed to public pressure and banished the Jews from the town not long afterwards. They had to move to the then still independent town of Kazimierz and lived there separated by a wall from the Christian population. The Jewish district of **Kazimierz** (► 113) subsequently evolved to become one of the most important Jewish centres in Europe. It had numerous synagogues, temples and bathhouses as well as Talmud schools.

When the Jews received their full citizenship rights in the 19th century, and were allowed to settle anywhere in Krakow, many of them still opted to stay in Kazimierz. It was there that the poorer classes and the orthodox Jews lived. At the beginning of World War II, there were about 60,000 Jewish citizens in the city. Very few survived the Holocaust. Of those, some moved to the newly founded state of Israel shortly after the War, others followed them after anti-Semitic campaigns in Poland in 1968. After a while, the memory of Krakow's Jewish history started to fade.

Interest Reawakened by Steven Spielberg

Despite the fact that there are still seven synagogues and two Jewish cemeteries in Kazimierz, which were rebuilt in the period following the War, and although some of the houses still bear Jewish inscriptions and emblems, it was a long time before more than a handful of people showed any interest in the city's Jewish history. Nonetheless, an institute for the history and culture of the Jews was set up at Jagiellonian University back in 1986, and the first Jewish Culture Festival took place in 1988. Yet, it was not until Steven Spielberg directed his seven-Oscar-winning film *Schindler's List* (► 145) on the original site, that interest in the city's

Quite a few scenes for *Schindler's List* were filmed in Stajnia (► 135)

At the Jewish Culture Festival there is a lot of partying and dancing

Jewish history really saw a revival. The film, like the novel on which it is based by Australian author Thomas Keneally (*Schindler's Ark*, 1982), tells the story of how the German manufacturer Oskar Schindler (► 144) managed to save around 1,200 Jews from extermination by the Nazis during World War II. Since then, there have been guided tours to the sites that appear in the film, and a lot more cafes and restaurants have opened up that vie for customers with Jewish meals and Klezmer concerts. Foundations promote the work of the Jewish community and uphold the memory of Jewish culture. In 1993, the **Center for Jewish Culture** (► 129) opened.

Today, there is the paradox situation that there are hardly any Jews living in Kazimierz, although Jewish culture is visible throughout the district. Non-Jews such as Janusz Makuch and Krzysztof Gierat initiated the Jewish Culture Festival, which is now one of the largest festivals of its kind in Europe. It encompasses workshops, music, discussions and exhibitions. The large final concert alone, which takes place in **Ulica Szeroka** (► 126), brings in thousands of visitors. Many of the younger citizens of Krakow have begun to take interest in the Jewish traditions of their town.

PRE-WAR SCHTETL

Providing a bridge between Kazimierz in Kraków and the little artist town of Kazimierz Dolny near Warsaw is the private **museum** called **I remember**, which was opened in 2016. Shalom Goldberg set it up in memory of his father the painter Chaim Goldberg (1917–2004), who was born in Kazimierz Dolny and later depicted the life of the Jewish Schtetl before the War in his paintings (ul. Miodowa 19; daily 10am–5pm, Thu until 8pm; www.museum iremember.org; admission: 18 złoty).

A group of orthodox Jews planning their tour through Kazimierz

The owners of the Jewish cafés and restaurants, the waiters and also many of the Klezmer musicians are non-Jews, as are most of the sales people of Judaika and the tour guides showing the former Jewish quarter. Groups of young people with kippas are generally school classes from Israel that visit Auschwitz and Krakow. Former inhabitants of Kazimierz or their descendants explore the area. For visitors to Krakow, a tour through Kazimierz belongs to the standard programme. Whole bus groups meet up for Klezmer evenings as they eat *gefilte fish* in the restaurants on Szeroka Street (➤ 126).

Only a few Jews left in Kazimierz

The orthodox Jewish community of Krakow only has about 130 members, and only about a dozen of them are under 40. The community regularly meets on the Sabbath to worship together, they run a kosher canteen, a club for senior members and a traditional bathhouse, called a *Mikwe*. Even though the community organises a lot of things and occasionally acquires some new members, a leading community member Piotr Nawicki remains realistic: "There is no prospect of Jewish life returning to what it was like before the War".

The strictly religious Hasidic community *Chabad Lubawicz* has been represented in Kazimierz for many years. In the **Izaak Synagogue** (➤ 128) is a small shop with kosher dishes. The reform movement *Beit Kraków* founded in 2009 mainly appeals to the younger generation. Its members meet on Saturdays in the **Galicia Jewish Museum** (➤ 128), organise theatre shows, concerts and exhibitions. Tanya Segal, who was born in Russia and is the first female rabbi in Poland, brought the group together. She began with a few students, today her group has 40 active followers.

OPEN TO NEW IDEAS – KRAKOW'S MODERN ARCHITECTURE

Until the political changes of 1989, the contemporary art gallery Bunkier Sztuki was the only modern building in Krakow's Old Town. In the meantime, the city fathers are being a bit more adventurous and open to new ideas.

Built in 1994, the **Manggha Museum of Japanese Art and Technology** (► 152) was the first important architectural structure to be erected after the political turnaround. It was designed by the Japanese architect Arata Isozaki together with his Polish partners Krzysztof Ingarden and Jacek Ewy. The flat building is discreet enough not to compete with the nearby Wawel, its organic lines harmoniously moulding in with the surroundings and the wave-shaped roof paying tribute to the Vistula River.

Museums as Architectural Icons

As time progressed, further museums followed – outside the city centre – with which Krakow also makes an architectural statement. The German

The Theatre Museum Cricoteka curves over a former small power plant

Uniquely modern in Krakow's Old Town: the narrow Wyspiański Pavilion

office "Pysall.Ruge" is responsible for the unusual design of the new
Polish Aviation Museum, erected on the grounds of the former Rakowice-
Czyzyny airport in 2009. The architects based their plans on the size and
height of the earlier hangars. The shape of the building developed from
a 60 × 60m (197ft × 197ft) baseplate, which they folded and cut a bit like
a paper plane. This created a triangular wing, set in concrete, with nonetheless a very playful and light appearance. Parked behind the large glass
façades are planes from the pioneer times of aviation (al. Jana Pawła II 39;
www.muzeumlotnictwa.pl).

The Italian architect Claudio Nardi changed the former halls of the
Schindler factory in the Podgórze district with its characteristic sawtooth
roof into the home of the **MOCAK Art Museum** (➤ 146), opened in 2011,
and added a modern entrance area. The old industrial architecture
blends well with the light Mediterranean-style new building. The interior
rooms seem light, clear and airy and outshine the dark history of the
former forced labour camp.

The as yet latest new art institution is the **Cricoteka** (➤ 148), also
built in the Podgórze district, at the end of 2014. For the Centre for the
Documentation of the Art of Tadeusz Kantor, architects from the Krakow
office nsMoon and Wizja erected a new table-like building, using corroded
and perforated steel sheet panels, over the existing small listed power plant
on the banks of the Vistula.

Bringing Together the Past and the Future

Opened in 2014, the International Congress Centre **ICE Kraków** (➤ 152)
on the southern bank of the Vistula has become a new emblem of the city.
The offices of Krzysztof Ingarden and Jacek Ewy worked, as they had done
previously for the Manggha Museum, with the Japanese architect Araza
Isozaki. The curved façade of the building that can be used for a variety of

Everything flows: the wave-shaped roof of the Manggha Museum

functions exudes an air of modernity and dynamism and is intended to be a symbol of the new Krakow. At the same time, the history of the city is not forgotten when one looks through the large glass space of the foyer and sees the Old Town and Wawel Hill.

In anticipation of the new congress centre, the futuristic-looking hotel **Park Inn** was erected in 2009. The design of the German architect and artist Jürgen Mayer H. – a dynamic facade, highlighted by light and dark aluminium stripes – has been described by the British magazine *Wallpaper* as a trendsetting architectural icon (ul. Monte Cassino 2; www.parkinn.com).

The "Holy Cow" Old Town

Whilst outside the centre it may seem as if almost anything goes, the Old Town is regarded as sacred by most of the citizens of Krakow. That is why there were heated discussions just a few years ago about a tiny piece of fallow land on Plac Wszystkich Świętych, directly on the Royal Route. The modern **Wyspiański Pavilion** (▶ 104) was built in place of a town house that had already been demolished in 1939 to become the town's information centre. The authorisation procedure dragged on over a number of years. With its clinker facade, the building, which is the work of architects Ingarden & Ewy, references the Gothic churches in the surrounding area. The glass windows integrated into the front facade by Stanisław Wyspiański create a connection to the neighbouring Franciscan church with the famous Art Nouveau works by the same artist, while at the same time the narrow building with its rounded corners and the shutters of vertically positioned bricks add a modern urban accent that even most of its former critics would no longer want to be without.

Finding Your Feet

First Two Hours

Krakow has a modern airport offering connections to most major cities. For those with more time for travelling back and forth, there are also regular bus and train connections. The good road system may also tempt drivers not deterred by long distances.

Travelling by Plane

Kraków Airport: The international airport named after Pope John II (www. krakowairport.pl) is located in Balice, about 12km (7.5mi) west of the city centre. The airport acquired a new terminal not so long ago and a direct train connection into the city centre. The Polish airline LOT offers regular services from the UK.

Airport Transfers

■ **By Taxi:** There is an official taxi service from the airport: smart limousines with multilingual drivers. Fixed prices are charged for the different zones; expect to pay about 70 sloty. It can be a little less expensive in a car from one of the other taxi companies. However, the taxi meter keeps on ticking when the car is sitting in a traffic jam, something that can happen very easily during the rush hour.

■ **By Bus:** Buses nos. 208 (hourly) and 292 (every 20 minutes) as well as a night bus no. 902 (hourly) shuttle between the airport and Krakow's central train station. The trip lasts about 30 to 40 minutes and takes a bit longer during the rush hour. A single ticket costs 4 złoty; anyone needing to continue on a different train, can buy a 90-minute ticket for 6 sloty or a 24-hour ticket for 20 sloty. Tickets are available from vending machines in the main hall or at the bus stop; on bus 292 it is possible to buy tickets on the bus as well.

■ **By Train:** The fastest and most comfortable way into the town centre is by rail. The railway line was recently modernised and extended below the terminal. The Koleje Małopolskie trains run every half an hour during the day from the airport to the main station and on to the salt mine of Wieliczka. The trip between the station and the airport takes about 20 minutes. A single ticket costs 8 złoty, a return 14 złoty (www.malopolskiekoleje.pl).

Travelling by Train

There are good train connections, but it is a long journey and you will have to change trains at least three times. From London, the Eurostar travels either to Paris or Brussels, then it is possible to take a train to Cologne or Berlin and from there to Warsaw and Krakow. See www.seat61.com

Travelling by Bus

There are a number of companies offering direct connections to Krakow from London. As with the train, it is a long trip, but it is not necessary to changes buses and for those on a tight budget it offers an economical alternative. See http://www.europebus.co.uk/.

Travelling by Car

It is a long drive from England across Belgium and Germany to Poland, but the roads are good. In addition to the petrol/diesel costs, there are also tolls on the motorways which can be paid in złoty or euros.

Getting Around

The main tourist attractions centre around the Old Town as well as the districts of Kazimierz and Podgórze. Most of the sightseeing can be comfortably done on foot. There is also a well developed network of trams and buses.

Buses and Trams

- **Trams** run during the day on about a dozen routes, at night three lines are in service (62, 64, 69). The fleet is mainly made up of low-floor trams.
- There is also a comprehensive **bus network**.
- Bus lines that also extend into the Krakow suburbs begin with a 2 or 3, all the others have a route which only covers a area within the city.
- Clear **data screens** in the vehicles facilitate orientation even for foreign visitors. There are also electronic displays at many of the stops as well. These provide information about the arrival time of the next buses or trams.
- **Tickets:** Single tickets for a direct route cost 3.80 złoty, in addition there are tickets that are valid for 20 to 90 minutes (2.80 złoty–6 złoty), which allow you to change as often as you like.
  For longer periods buy one of the inexpensive **fixed-time tickets**.
  This is available for one, two, three or seven days, either for the city or to include the surrounding area and the airport.
  Examples are:
  - 24-hour ticket (24-godzinny), city centre, 15 złoty
  - 48-hour ticket (48-godzinny), city centre, 24 złoty
  - 72-hour ticket (72-godzinny), city centre, 36 złoty
  - 7-day ticket (7-dniowy), city centre, 48 złoty
  - 7-day ticket (7-dniowy), with surrounding area and airport, 62 złoty
  - Weekend card for families (weekendowy rodzinny), valid Sat and Sun with the surrounding area, 16 złoty
  - Another worthwhile option is the **KrakowCard** (➤ 39).
- The tickets can be purchased with cash (coins and notes) or with a bank card at the vending machines. There are also **ticket machines** in the newer trams and buses, but these machines only allow payment with coins. You can buy individual tickets at many kiosks.
- The tickets have to be **stamped before you start** your trip; further information about the lines and prices are available at www.mpk.krakow.pl/en.

Taxis

- There are more than a dozen different taxi companies in Krakow. Unlike other countries in continental Europe, these set their own prices. The basic fare for the first kilometres is eight złoty, and two to four złoty for trips within the city area. It is possible to pay for the fare by car; it usual to receive a receipt (*paragon*).
- You can get taxis by calling the taxi company or at a taxi rank. At the taxi rank you can pick whichever taxi you want.
- Not all companies have modern vehicles and not all of the drivers speak a foreign language. Recommendable are:
  Barbakan Radio-Taxi; tel: 196 61
  Megataxi; tel: 196 25
  MPT Radio Taxi; tel: 196 63

Finding Your Feet

- Since there are quite a few black sheep in Krakow that want to take advantage of tourists, you should always try to take taxis which display:
  - Krakow's municipal coat of arms and taxi number, and where applicable also the logo of the taxi company on the door
  - a sign with the prices in the back window on the passenger side
- Most hotels or restaurants will order a taxi for guests if they ask them.

Driving a Car

Driving a car in Krakow is not actually difficult. However, it is important to know that only cars with special authorisation are allowed to drive in the Old Town. What is more, the vast majority of the city centre is a parking zone where parking is subject to a charge from Mon–Fri from 10am–6pm (first hour 3, second hour 3.50 złoty).

The Most Important Traffic Rules:

- Headlamps have to be on during the day.
- The blood alcohol limit is 0.02%.
- Using mobile phones without a hands-free unit is forbidden.
- The speed limits are 50km/h (30mph) in built-up areas, 90km/h (55mph) on country roads, 140km/h (85mph) on motorways.

Car Rental

There are international and Polish car rental companies at the airport and around the main train station. It is worth comparing prices on the internet, in order to get the best offer. The rental conditions correspond to those in other EU countries.

Cycling

Bike Hire

- **KMK Bike** is the public bike rental system of Krakow. Anyone registered in the system can hire a bike using his/her mobile at any of the bike stations and return it to another one; the first 20 minutes are free, after which the hour cost 3 złoty. However, it is necessary to register first at **www.kmkbike.pl**.
- Private bike hire companies in the town centre, where you can rent bikes for a few hours or days include:
  - **Bike Rental** (also organises guided tours) ul. św. Anny 4; tel: 510 580 055; www.krkbikerental.pl
  - **CoolTour Company** (also organises guided tours and rents out scooters), ul. Grodzka 2; tel: 124 302 034; www.biketrip.pl

Hackney Carriages

Waiting on the Rynek Główny are gleaming white coaches, which are drawn by two stately horses and often steered by a woman. There is space for five people in the carriage. This romantic treat is, at around 400 złoty per hour, not exactly cheap.

Melex Buses

You will see the small Melex buses everywhere in the town: quiet, nimble electric vehicles with space for up to eight people. They transport tourists to the main tourist sights. You can book a series of different themed routes with recorded commentary (multilingual). The prices depend on the duration and number of participants. Expect to pay about 200 złoty for a one-hour tour with up to four people. Since prices and what you get for your money vary tremendously, it is worth comparing the different offers. Organisers include:

- Krakow Guide; tel: 500 820 533; http://guide-krakow.com
- Cracow Tours, ulica Krupnicza 3; tel: 124 300 726; http://cracowtours.pl

Tourist Information

Krakow has a good network of tourist information centres, which can be recognised by the blue sign with **infoKraków** written on it. Information on the Internet is available under www.krakau.travel. The most important offices are:

- Airport (Arrival hall); daily 9am–7pm
- Sukiennice, Rynek Główny 1–3; tel: 123 542 716; daily 9am–7pm, until 5pm in winter
- Pawilon Wyspiański, Pl. Wszystkich Świętych 2; tel: 126 161 886; daily 9am–5pm
- Kazimierz, ul. Józefa 7; tel: 123 542 728; 9am–5pm

KrakowCard

This **Tourist Ticket** allows you to use local public transport, including the airport buses and the buses from the salt mine in Wieliczka. What is more, it also enables you to enter around 40 museums and other sights without having to pay an extra entrance fee. The ticket costs 100 złoty for two days and 120 złoty for three days. It is available at the tourist offices or online at www.krakowcard.com.

Accommodation

Krakow is one of the most popular tourist cities in Central Europe and welcomes around ten million national and international visitors each year. The number of beds available has risen considerably over the last few years and accommodation ranges from cheap hostels with dormitories to luxurious five-star hotels. Since many of the hotels are still very new, the furniture and fittings are generally correspondingly good. Appartments offer a good alternative, especially when on longer trips. Many of them are freshly renovated and very well equipped.

Which part of town?

If you choose a place in the centre of the Old Town or in the Jewish district of Kazimierz, you are where the action is but should not be too sensitive to noise. The nightlife, especially during the summer months and at weekends, continues until dawn. As a result, some of the roads are quite noisy. It is somewhat quieter for instance in the northern district of Kleparz or on the southern side of the Vistula in Podgórze and the surroundings. Depending on the location of the hotel, you can get into the centre very quickly. And there are quite a few quieter roads on the edge of the Old Town.

Finding Your Feet

Book & Reserve

Krakow receives a lot of visitors all year round. In Poland, city trips are particularly popular over bank **holiday weekends**, where with the addition of an extra day it is possible to organise a short holiday. There are a lot of possible "bridge days" (where companies add the Friday or Monday when the **public holiday** is on a Thursday or Tuesday) at the beginning of May. Besides 1 May, 3 May is also a public holiday. Other favourite times are around Corpus Christi (May/June), Assumption Day (15 August) and Poland's National Independence Day (11 November). It is particularly important to reserve rooms early at such times.

Insider Tip   **Reservation portals**, such as Booking.com, Hotel.de and Hrs.de offer numerous hotels, hostels and apartments in Krakow. It is worth comparing the prices with those that the hotels offer on their internet pages. You can occasionally find better offers than those on the booking portal.

Holiday Flats

Krakow offers a very wide range of **private apartments**/flats. Dark rooms crammed full of grandma's old furniture are included in the choice, of course, but so are many chic, spacious designer flats for four or five people. The prices vary accordingly from below 100 to almost 1,000 złoty a night. Apart from checking how the flats are furnished, also take a look at where they are located, since some of them are right in the middle of the nightlife district and others next to very busy roads.

A good tip are the **Designomania-Appartements** (££) in a large new building in the Podgórze district directly by the Vistula – with high-quality fittings and a dream roof terrace. It is only a few steps across the pedestrian bridge to the in-district of Kazimierz (www.designomaina-apartments.com).

The following online rental companies offers a large choice of private flats:
- **Sleeping in Krakow**; www.sleepingkrakow.com
- **Old City Apartments**; www.oldcityapartments.eu
- **Hamilton Suites**; www.krakow-apartments.biz

Hostels

Krakow attracts young backpackers from around the world. There is consequently a rich choice of hostels in which you can find inexpensive accommodation and contact to other backpackers. Most of them are in the Old Town and in Kazimierz – where life really rumbles at night.
- Das **Pink Panther's Hostel** (£, ul. św. Tomasza 8; tel: 124 220 935; www.pinkpanthershostel.com) is located one minute's walk from the market square in the Old Town and offers guests daily events, from soup evenings to vodka tasting.
- The **Mosquito Hostel** (£, Rynek Kleparski 4/6; tel: 124 301 461; www.mosquitohostel.com) is located north of the Old Town. Guests appreciate the generous breakfast as well as the daily events, which range from shisha (hookah) to sangria evenings.
- Das **Moon Hostel** (£, ul. Halicka 11; tel: 124 294 325; www.moonhostel.pl) lends its guests bikes at no cost. It is located on the edge of the Jewish district of Kazimierz.

Hotel Prices
- Anyone who has a flexible timetable will be able to find a double room without breakfast at a five-star hotel for around 400 złoty. Normally, the prices tend to be between 500 and 750 złoty.

Accommodation

- The Old Town and Kazimierz in particular have lots of hostels, in which accommodation in shared rooms only costs about 40 złoty a night. For a slightly higher charge, many hostels offer a double room with a bathroom.
- WLAN is available almost everywhere and is generally free of charge.
- A parking space in the centre of town usually incurs an extra fee. Depending on the type of accommodation, this may vary between 40 and 100 złoty a night. Some hotels in the suburban areas offer parking free of charge.

Accommodation Prices
Expect to pay per double room per night excluding breakfast:
£ under 220 złoty   **££** 220–440 złoty   **£££** 440–650 złoty   **££££** over 650 złoty

---

Andel's by Vienna House Cracow £££

New hotel with young, modern design and spacious rooms directly next to the main station and next to the shopping centre Galeria Krakowska. It offers a good breakfast buffet and an appealing bar for a nightcap.

➕ 195 east F5
✉ Pawia 3
☎ 126 600 100;
www.viennahouse.com

Art & Garden Residence ££

The hotel is in a renovated building in the Kleparz district, less than a mile from the Old Town. It offers light friendly rooms with red-brick walls, wooden floors and modern design. In the restaurant you can enjoy both a good breakfast and a view of the garden.

➕ 195 north D5
✉ Krowoderska 71
☎ 123 542 000;
www.artgardenresidence.pl

Bonerowski Palace ££££

The location is hard to top. This boutique hotel, with 16 rooms, and suites as well as a small wellness area, is housed in a 16th-century town palace directly on the market square. The rooms are furnished with period furniture and have parquet floors. In the lounge bar overlooking the market, guests can listen to the regular classical concerts with music by Frédéric Chopin.

Insider Tip

➕ 195 D3
✉ Rynek Główny 24
☎ 123 741 300;
www.palacbonerowski.com

Ekosamotnia ££

This unusual guesthouse is located in the western suburb of Zwierzyniec, in green surroundings and about six kilometres (3.75mi) from the town centre. The earlier inhabitant and artist Roman Husarski left some of his sculptures in the enchanting park that boasts fruit trees, shrubs and a pond. Guests can enjoy the fruit from the organic garden and eggs from happy hens.

➕ 196 west A5
✉ Żywiczna 10
☎ 124 317 455;
www.ekosamotnia.com

Farmona Hotel Business & SPA ££

The wellness hotel with a large garden is located on the southern border of the town; ideal for guests who want to combine a trip to Krakow with a trip to the Tatra Mountains. The hotel belongs to the natural cosmetics company Farmona, which uses its own products in the hotel's Balinese spa.

Finding Your Feet

📍 197 south D1
✉ Jugowiecka 10 c
☎ 122 527 070; www.hotelfarmona.pl

Grand Hotel £££
The Grand Hotel has been one of the leading buildings in Krakow since 1887. Once the meeting place of the most well-known artists, it fell into a Sleeping Beauty slumber during the Socialist period and now, after extensive renovation, is again providing a tie to the golden years of old. Its restaurant covered in a glass roof in Secessionist style is particularly impressive.

📍 195 E4
✉ Sławkowska 5/7
☎ 124 240 800; www.grand.pl

Hotel Copernicus ££££
A 15th-century town palace that was later rebuilt in Renaissance style is home to Poland's only member of the exclusive Relax & Chateaux hotel association. Prince Charles and the Spanish monarch King Felipe have both spent a night there. The pool in the Gothic vaulted cellar is an absolute dream. No less impressive is the view from the roof terrace over the nearby Vistula.

📍 195 E1
✉ Kanonicza 16
☎ 124 243 421; www.copernicus.hotel.com.pl

Hotel Eden ££
This small middle-class hotel located in the Kazimierz district is very popular with Jewish guests. Besides a sauna, it also has a Mikwe, a ritual Jewish bathhouse.

📍 197 E3
✉ Ciemna 15
☎ 124 306 565; www.hoteleden.pl

Hotel Gródek £££
This boutique hotel is located in a quieter part of the Old Town. The rooms of the medieval town palace all have their own individual style. There is for instance a Renaissance room and a Chinese room. A romantic place for warm summer evenings is the roof terrace of the hotel restaurant Ambasada Pacyfiku.

📍 195 F3
✉ Na Gródku 4
☎ 124 319 030; www.donimirski.com

Hotel Pod Różą £££
Krakow's oldest hotel is in a 17th-century Renaissance palace. The rooms are stylishly furnished. Restaurant with covered winter garden, and gym with a panoramic view of the Old Town.

📍 195 E4
✉ Floriańska 14
☎ 124 243 300; www.podroza.hotel.com.pl

Hotel Pugetów ££
This hotel located in a small city palace between the Old Town and Kazimierz has six individually furnished rooms and suites, named after well-known people, two of whom include Daisy von Pless and Joseph Conrad.

📍 195 F2
✉ Starowiślna 15 a
☎ 124 324 950; www.donimirski.com

Hotel Wentzl £££
Charming boutique hotel with elegant rooms in a 16th-century residence on the south side of the Main Market Square. The history of the gourmet restaurant of the same name stretches back to the late 18th century. Hotel bikes available to guests free of charge.

📍 195 D3
✉ Rynek Główny 19
☎ 124 302 664; www.wentzl.pl

Klezmer-Hois ££
Located at the end of Szeroka Street, in what used to be a Jewish bathhouse, is this small middle-class hotel. Klezmer concerts take place in the restaurant.

Insider Tip

📍 197 F4
✉ Szeroka 6
☎ 124 111 245; www.klezmer.pl

Metropolitan Boutique Hotel £££

The hotel is located in a quiet cul-de-sac on the edge of the Jewish district of Kazimierz, a renovated old building with a modern but refined interior.
The rooms are spacious, the bathrooms light. There is piano music in the restaurant on many evenings in the week.

➕ 197 E4
✉ Berka Joselewicza 19
☎ 124 427 500; www.hotelmetropolitan.pl

Niebieski Art Hotel & SPA £££

The wellness hotel with light modern rooms is on the edge of the city centre, directly by the Vistula, in the green city district of Zwierzyniec. It has spa facilities and a restaurant with organic products.

➕ 196 west A5
✉ Flisacka 3
☎ 122 974 000; www.niebieski.com.pl

PURO Hotel Kraków £££

The hotel is located near the main station and the Old Town. The small Polish hotel chain offers fresh, high-quality design at moderate prices. The rooms are equipped with high-tech and refined lighting fixtures; cappuccino is available for free from the vending machines.

➕ 195 east F5
✉ Ogrodowa 10
☎ 123 142 100; www.purohotel.pl

Queen Boutique Hotel £££

The hotel in a former block of flats between the Old Town and Kazimierz has large, light rooms with broad beds and modern reserved design. You have an excellent view over the Vistula in some of the rooms.

➕ 197 D4
✉ Józefa Dietla 60
☎ 124 333 333; www.queenhotel.pl

Sheraton Kraków Hotel ££££

The modern building is not far from Wawel Hill and directly by the Vistula. The lounge bar on the viewing terrace that overlooks the river is a dream. Under a large glass roof in the atrium, the restaurant serves mainly Mediterranean dishes and a delicious atmosphere to go with it.

➕ 196 west A5
✉ Powiśle 7
☎ 126 621 000; www.sheraton.pl/krakow

Food and Drink

The Poles attach great importance to good food. A soup is as integral a part of the meal as a dessert. Some young cooks take traditional dishes and lighten then up by cleverly combining Old Polish recipes with Mediterranean and Asian ingredients.

International restaurant critics have discovered modern Polish cuisine. In the Michelin Guide *Main Cities of Europe* and in Poland's restaurant guide Gault&Millau the list includes numerous restaurants from Krakow.

Although the majority of Poles still enjoy eating meat several times a week, they have long discovered meals without it. Many restaurants and bars in Krakow now specialise in vegetarian or vegan dishes and in most other restaurants, too, there is more than just a plate of sad-looking vegetables on offer.

In the meantime, many Poles also regard wine as part of a good meal. Thus, the wine menus of the better restaurants offer a choice of mainly

Finding Your Feet

dry wines from various wing-growing areas. Increasingly, you will also see Polish wines on the list, since the country is developing more and more into a wine-growing nation. There are also vineyards in the region of Krakow.

Meal Times

Lunch is generally between noon and 3pm, dinner mostly between 7pm and 10pm. However, in Krakow's main centre, it is not a problem to order a cooked meal at other times during the day.

Prices

A main course (without drinks)

£ under 45 złoty   ££ 45–90 złoty   £££ over 90 złoty

Food-related Tips

- Poles love **soups**. They are available in many different varieties, from light to hearty. The *żurek* is popular, a sour rye soup with sausage, potatoes and boiled eggs that is often served in a large hollowed-out roll. Classics are also the beetroot soup (*barszcz*) and the mushroom soup (*zupa grzybowa*).
- *Pierogi* are the Polish variation of dumplings. They can be sweet or savoury. In Krakow's *Pierogarnias* you can choose between several dozen variations, but there are also *pierogi* as an inexpensive option on the menu of other restaurants with traditional Polish cuisine.
- The *bar mleczny* (**milk bar**) is a relic from Socialist times. In the self-service restaurants, the workers could get a hot meal for a reasonable price. Some of them survived the political turnaround, improved their selection, and now also offer inexpensive and traditional Polish dishes.
- Many Poles enjoy a hearty **breakfast**. Besides cheese, ham and eggs, there are often also cooked or grilled sausages. Fresh fruit on the other hand is also becoming a favourite alternative.
- There are no fixed rules about **tips**, but ten percent is normal.
- Most restaurants accept **credit cards**.
- **Menus** are generally in English. The young people working in most of the restaurants, cafés and bars speak fluent English.
- It is best to make a **reservation** in advance when planning an evening out at one of the more elegant restaurants.

Shopping

You can find souvenirs in the Cloth Hall and around the Main Market Square. Shops in the Old Town, in Kazimierz and Podgórze sell products by young Polish designers and couturiers. The exclusive shopping centre Pasaż 13 is directly on the Rynek Główny, and the shopping centres at the main station and in Kazimierz offer a large choice of products. If you don't find anything there, you will still be able to pick up a souvenir from the large selection of vodka and Polish sweets in the airport shop before you board your flight home.

Typical souvenirs

- The **fire-breathing dragon**, which according to legend once lived under Wawel Castle (►87), is available as a soft toy in various variations; it also adorns t-shirts and cups.
- Inhabitants of the Tatra region sell products made of lambswool, carvings, necklaces with colourful wooden beads and their famous smoked cheese *oscypek*.
- **Handcrafts** from other regions of Poland, such as amber jewellery and Bolesławiec pottery are available in many shops.
- A popular souvenir is Polish **vodka**. One of the most well-known brands is *Zubrówka*, which is flavoured with a tincture of bison grass and has a greenish colour. The crystal-clear *Wyborowa* is also widely available. *Żołądkowa Górzka* presents a more amber look and contains herbs which give it a very zesty aroma.
- The Benedictine monks are well-known for their high-quality crafted products, including cosmetics, liqueurs, jams and honey. You can buy the products directly from the **Benedictine Abbey of Tyniec** (► 171) near Krakow or in a shop in Kazimerz (►137).
- An original souvenir are wines from Krakow. Poland's second-largest vineyard **Srebrna Góra** is near the Camaldolese priory in Bielany (► 181) in the south-western suburbs of Krakow. Riesling, Pinot, Chardonnay, Zweigelt and Regent flourish on the 12 hectare estate. Also available from **Wina.pl** (ul. Krowoderska 46; www.wina.pl; Mon–Fri 11am–7pm, Sat until 3pm).
- **Krakowski Kredens** (www.krakowskiekredens.pl) stands for traditional, handmade foods. On offer in different gift packages are chocolate, marmalade, juices, meat and sausage products. The company not only has a number of sales points in Krakow; it is also represented in many other Polish towns.

Markets

The largest and most original market is located in the centre of Kleparz, just a bit north of the Old Town. Fresh fruit and vegetables, meat, sausage and cheese, as well as household goods (►64) are on offer every day. These days the Rynek Główny (►52) only functions as a market square on special occasions. At its **Christmas and Easter markets**, the many stalls sell regional craft and culinary products.

Department Stores

In both **Galeria Krakowska** by the main station and in **Galeria Kazimierz** (ul. Podgórska 34) you will find over 100 shops under one roof. Besides international chains like H&M, Zara and Mango, there are also Polish fashion brands like Reserved, Eva Minge and Tatuum.

Opening Times

- Most of the shops in Poland open between 9/10 in the morning and close between 6/7, and on Saturday at 2pm.
- In the centre of Krakow, many of the shops are open between 9am and 8pm, some are also open on Sundays.
- Some of the food shops in the centre are open around the clock. The large shopping centres are open every day.

Entertainment

The nights in Krakow are long, there is always something going on in the pubs, bars and clubs until the early hours of the morning. Culture fans appreciate the rich choice of opera and Philharmonic performances as well as the numerous high-quality festivals.

Information

■ Copies of the free monthly magazine *Kraków in Your Pocket* are circulated in many high-end and luxury class hotels. They provide information in English about the places to go and cultural events. Information is also available online at www.inyourpocket.com/krakow.

■ Cultural tips are available in the tourist information offices (➤ 39) as well as online in English at www.krakau.travel.

Opera and Classical Music

■ The around 200 performances that take place each year at the **Opera Krakowska** (➤ 75) are almost always sold out. Tickets cost about 20–150 złoty. You can book from two months before the performance.

■ Concerts in the **Krakow Philharmonic** (➤ 112) usually take place on Fridays and Saturdays. Here, too, the prices at between about 25–50 złoty are very inexpensive. It is best to book early.

Jazz and Klezmer

In the evening around the Main Market Square you can hear music strumming from the jazz clubs in the vaulted cellars below. Among the most well known clubs are **Harris Piano Jazz Bar** (➤ 76), **The Piano Rouge** (➤ 76) and **Piec' Art** (➤ 112). Klezmer concerts regularly take place in restaurants along Szeroka Street in Kazimierz. The most well-known places are **Klezmer-Hois** (➤ 133), **Ariel** (➤ 132) and **Dawno temu na Kazimierzu** (➤ 132).

Festivals

■ The most important music festivals are **Misteria Paschalia** for early music during the Easter period and **Sacrum Profanum** for contemporary music in autumn (www.misteriapaschalia.pl; www.sacrumprofanum.pl).

■ In the second half of August the most beautiful squares and courtyards become the venues for the classical music festival **Muzyka w Starym Krakowie** (Music in Old Krakow; www.mwsk.pl).

■ Each year, one of the largest festivals of Jewish culture in Europe is organised in the Kazimierz district. More than 300 events take place during the ten-day festival. The highlight is the final concert in Szeroka Street (www.jewishfestival.pl).

■ The volume gets turned up a bit at the **Kraków Live Festival** in August on the old airport grounds with rock, pop and hip-hop (www.livefestival.pl).

■ At the **Krakowska Jesień Jazzowa** ("Krakow Jazz Autumn"; www.kjj-festi-wal.pl) international stars from the Free-Jazz-Scene play at the Club **Alchemia** (➤ 134) in Kazimierz.

LGBT Clubs

The **Club Cocon** (➤ 138) on the edge of the Kazimierz district is one of the oldest and most well-known LGBT clubs in Poland. Drag queens regularly take to the stage in the club **Kabaret** (➤ 138). Mainly women, but also some men, meet in the **LaF club** in Kazimierz (➤ 138).

Main Market Square & Northern Old Town

 **Little Treats**

Relaxing Break

Are your feet tired after all the walking? Then pop into **Mariacki SPA** (Plac Mariacki 9/5; www.mariackispa.pl) and enjoy a massage as you stare out at **St Mary's Church** (➤ 56).

Street Food

Learn about Polish specialities during a three-hour culinary tour around the **Main Market Square** (➤ 52; www.viator.com).

Hidden Oases

Enjoy a summer evening in one of the idyllic courtyards, away from the maddening crowds, for instance in the **Budda Bar** (Rynek Główny 6).

Getting Your Bearings

Since 1257, the 200 × 200m (656ft × 656ft) Rynek Główny has been the beating heart of Krakow's historic centre, now a UNESCO World Heritage site. From early morning until late in the night, inhabitants and tourists wander across the grand square lined with palatial residences, enjoy the hustle and bustle from the open-air cafés and listen with rapt attention to the *hejnał*, the famous trumpet call that for centuries has resounded on the hour from the tall tower of St Mary's Church.

Congregated around the square are some of the city's most important sights. The Cloth Hall contains one of the world's oldest markets and an important collection of

Polish paintings, the Underground Museum leads you back to the early days of the town, and at St Mary's Church the main attraction is undoubtedly the world-famous winged altarpiece by Veit Stoß. The memorial to the Polish writer Adam Mickiewicz is a favourite meeting place for young people when they are planning an evening out at the pubs and clubs in the surrounding area.

To the north, the bustling Ulica Floriańska leads to St Florian's Gate and the barbican, the last remains of the medieval city fortifications. Now, instead of the earlier city wall, the Old Town is surrounded by a four kilometre (2.5mi) long green belt, the Planty. Stretching to the north of it is the Kleparz district, in which life proceeds at a more leisurely pace and where for more than 800 years food has been sold at the market on the Rynek Kleparski.

St Mary's Church, The Cloth Hall and the town hall tower present a striking ensemble on the constantly bustling Main Market Square

Getting Your Bearings

TOP 10

⭐ Rynek Główny (Main Market Square) ➤ 52
⭐ Kościół Mariacki (St Mary's Church) ➤ 56
⭐ Podziemia Rynku (Rynek Underground Museum) ➤ 60

Don't Miss

⓫ Brama Floriańska & Barbakan
  (St Florian's Gate & Barbican) ➤ 62
⓬ Rynek Kleparski
  (Kleparz Market Square) ➤ 64

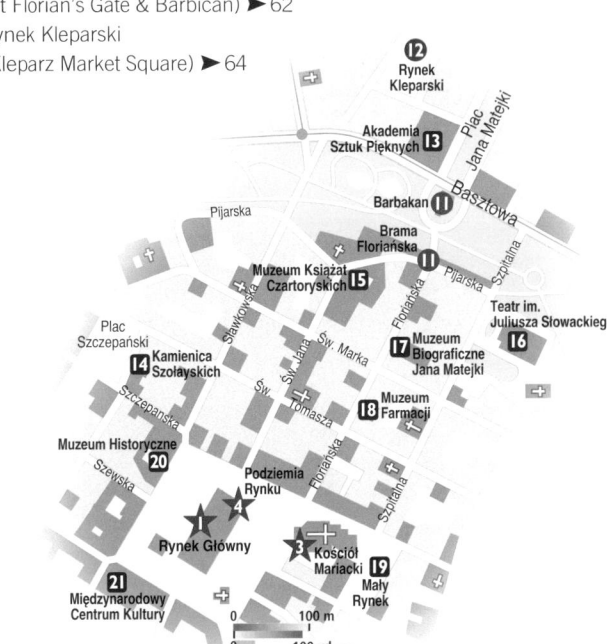

At Your Leisure

⓭ Akademia Sztuk Pięknych w Krakowie
  (Academy of Fine Arts) ➤ 66
⓮ Kamienica Szołayskich (Szołayski House) ➤ 66
⓯ Muzeum Książąt Czartoryskich
  (Czartoryski Museum) ➤ 67
⓰ Teatr im. Juliusza Słowackiego (Słowacki Theatre) ➤ 67
⓱ Muzeum Biograficzne Jana Matejki
  (Jan Matejko Museum) ➤ 68
⓲ Muzeum Farmacji (Museum of Pharmacy) ➤ 68
⓳ Mały Rynek (Small Market Square) ➤ 68
⓴ Muzeum Historyczne (Historical Museum) ➤ 69
㉑ Międzynarodowy Centrum
  Kultury (International Cultural Centre) ➤ 69

Main Market Square & Northern Old Town

The Perfect Day

If you follow our itinerary, you will come to know the heart of Krakow. As you stroll through the town, you visit the most important sights around the Main Market Square and in the north of the Old Town, as well as naturally a couple of places for you to enjoy a little break. And in the evening, the tour continues underground!

🕘 9:00am

Experience how ⭐**Rynek Główny** (▶ 52) comes to life. The street cleaners follow close on the heels of the last night owls. Flower sellers set up their stalls, hackney carriages trot into the square, and waitresses prepare the tables in the coffee houses. When the *hejnał* sounds, shopkeepers open their doors and the square quickly fills up with visitors.

🕙 10:00am

Get to the roots of the town. In the ⭐**Underground Museum** (▶ 60) under the Main Market Square, you can view the foundations of the very first buildings and a multimedia show will enable you to immerse yourself in medieval Krakow.

🕚 11:00am

Time for a coffee, for example in the **Kawiarnia Noworolski** (photo right; ▶ 73), which has had it place in the **Cloth Hall** (▶ 52) since 1910. From the outside terrace you can watch the hustle and bustle on the square.

🕦 11:30am

High time for a visit to ⭐**St Mary's Church** (▶ 56), since at 11:50am the winged panels of the world-famous altarpiece are opened, and this is something that you shouldn't miss.

🕐 12:30pm

Wander through **Pasaż 13** (► 74), the elegant little shopping centre on the main square. Awaiting you there is the **Concept 13** restaurant with its inexpensive lunch menu and a good selection of wines.

🕐 2:00pm

Amble across the bustling Ulica Floriańska (photo bottom left) **⑪ St Florian's Gate** (► 62), where numerous artists exhibit their work. Close by, it is equally

colourful on the traditional **⑫ Kleparz Market Square** (► 64), where you can admire the mountains of fruit and vegetables.

🕐 4:00pm

Meet the leading Polish painters from the early 20th century in **⑭ Szołayski House** (► 66). The museum shows works from the collection of Feliks "Manggha" Jasieński, who introduced the art and crafts of Japan to the people of Krakow (► 152).

🕐 6:00pm

Start the evening off stylishly with an aperitif on the roof terrace of the **Hotel Stary** (ul. Szczepańska 5) overlooking the Main Market Square but pleasantly shielded from the masses.

🕐 7:00pm

Rib Eye, Porterhouse or T-Bone? The most important thing is that the steak is dry aged. If you enjoyed grilled beef, then you will find exactly what you want at **Ed Red** (► 70) just a short distance away from Hotel Stary.

🕐 9:00pm

Fortified, return to the Main Market Square to descend into Krakow's nightlife: those who arrive early are sure of a good place for the live concerts in the vaulted cellar of the **Harris Piano Jazz Bar** (photo above; ► 76).

Rynek Kleparski ⑫
Akademia Sztuk Pięknych ⑬
Brama Floriańska ⑪ Barbakan ⑪
Teatr im. Juliusza Słowackiego ⑯
Muzeum Książąt Czartoryskich ⑮
Muz. Biograficzne Jana Matejki ⑰
Kamienica Szołayskich ⑭
Muzeum Farmacji ⑱
Podziemia Rynku ⑲ Muzeum Historyczne ⑳
Rynek Główny
Kościół Mariacki
Mały Rynek ⑲
Międzynarodowy Centrum Kultury ㉑
0 ___ 100 m
0 ___ 100 yd

★Rynek Główny
(Main Market Square)

After the Tatars had reduced Krakow to ash and rubble in 1241, rebuilding began in 1257. The medieval market square that was laid out then still forms the vibrant core of the Old Town. It has been a while since fabrics were sold in the Sukiennice (Cloth Hall), but the old shops still attract lots of visitors.

Arranged in a square formation, the Rynek Główny measures 200m × 200m (656ft × 656ft) and ranks as the largest medieval market square in Europe. It is surrounded by around 40 aristocratic mansions and palaces with histories that date back to the 16th and 17th centuries. They contain restaurants, shops, banks and cultural institutions. Traditional coffee houses still exude the charm of the Habsburg period. In the corner house on Ulica Sławowska a memorial plate commemorates a visit by **Johann Wolfgang von Goethe** in 1790. On the other side of the square is a branch of the Goethe Institute.

Tidying up in the 19th Century

Over the centuries, building on the Main Market Square developed in a rather haphazard way, with new shops being added all the time. In the second half of the 19th century, the city council decided to introduce some reforms. They put an end to the uncontrolled development, and the buildings of the Great Weigh House and the Small Weigh House were demolished. The old town hall had already been razed in 1820 with the exception of the tower. The large area that resulted focused attention on the **Sukiennice (Cloth Hall)** for the first time. It dominates the square, the Renaissance style exuding a Mediterranean flair that

The attractive shops in the Cloth Hall sell souvenirs and handicrafts

The modern fountain on the Rynek Główny presents a stimulating contrast to the historic town houses around it

together with the Gothic **St Mary's Church** (➤ 56) produces a unique architectural ensemble.

The history of the Cloth Hall stretches back to the 13th century, but its shape changed continuously until the 19th century. In the 14th century a Gothic Hall measuring 108m (354ft) in length was built to give travelling fabric dealers with a royal charter a place in which they could sell their products. After a fire in 1559, the hall was rebuilt by an Italian architect in the Renaissance style. By integrating a barrel-vaulted roof, the hall acquired a second floor. It is topped with a tall classical-style attic bearing a broad arcaded frieze that covers the entire structure. Golden cupolas decorate the tips. **Mascarons** is the name given to the grimacing stone faces that the Renaissance artist Santi Gucci added to the attic. When the Main Market Square was rebuilt in the 19th century, neo-Gothic **arcades** were added to the two long sides of the building.

Place for Trade and Art

Every morning inside the Hall, the wooden doors of the little shops open as they have done for hundreds of years, and inside the shop keepers sell souvenirs, handicrafts, jewellery and regional products.

In 1883, the National Museum moved in on the second floor with the **Galeria Sztuki Polskiej XIX Wieku** (**Gallery of Polish Painting and Sculpture from the 19th Century**). On show in the five departments are 200 artworks covering the time from the Enlightenment to the beginning of Impressionism. The collection includes the monumental painting *Prussian Homage* by **Jan Matejko** from 1882.

Main Market Square & Northern Old Town

Town Hall Tower and Church of St Adalbert

The square town hall tower from the 14th century on the south-west side of the Rynek Główny sports a Baroque spire. The entrance guarded by two lions leads to a branch of the **Historical Museum** with exhibits that focus on the town's history. Also on view are historical photographs of the market square. From the **panoramic terrace**, there is a beautiful view of the Old Town. A favourite photo motif is the enormous head next to the tower. The Polish sculptor Igor Mitoraj (1944–2014) created the bronze figure ⭐ *Eros Bendato* in 2003. Children love exploring its hollow interior.

At the south-east end of the Main Market Square is the small **Kościół św. Wojciecha (Church of St Adalbert)**, which is even older than the market. It is dedicated to the patron saint of Poland, the former Prague Bishop Adalbert. According to legend, he prayed there before he set off on a missionary trip to the heathen Prussians, where he met his death in 997. The single-nave church with a rectangular chancel was built to

replace a place of worship made of wood. Later the church was renovated in the Baroque style and a dome, the sacristy and a chapel were added. With the exception of a Gothic crucifix, the interior also displays the Baroque style.

In 1898 an enormous **memorial** was built to the north of the church to commemorate the 100th birthday of the

The *lajkonik* posing in front of the town hall tower and the Cloth Hall

---

INSIDER INFO

- When the Cloth Hall Museum is open you can visit the **outside terraces** along the longer sides of the hall and enjoy the view of the market square (admission: 2 złoty, free on Sun).

Insider Tip

- The Polish post office has an original branch on the market square. You can buy picture postcards and stamps from the **mail coach** – a nice alternative to the holiday SMS.
- On the east side of the Cloth Hall is a **tourist information office** with everything you need for a visit to Krakow (daily 9am–7pm, until 5pm in winter).
- The Rynek Główny is at its best when it is waking up in the morning. It is not until 9am that it starts filling up, before that you can have it more or less to yourself.

⚑ THE TATAR HORSEMAN

On the market square, jugglers and musicians vie for the attention of passersby. From time to time you will also see the *lajkonik* doing his rounds. He wears colourful attire, a pointed hat and is on a richly bedecked hobby horse. The *lajkonik* is a reminder of the time Tatars came to attack Krakow. In Zwierzyniec, by Krakow, raftsmen espied the enemy forces and overpowered them. As a joke, they dressed up afterwards as Monguls and rode into the city. In recognition of their action, the mayor decreed that from then on every year a *lajkonik*, a raftman dressed as a Tatar, should come to Krakow. On the Thursday after Corpus Christi the large *lajkonik* procession takes place, starting at the Norbertine cloister in the suburb of Zwierzyniec and ending at the Main Market Square. However the foreign rider can occasionally be seen on the market at other times of year and is a favourite photo motif. What is more, anyone hit by his mace is guaranteed a year of good luck.

Poland's national poet **Adam Mickiewicz**. Standing on a high pedestal, the bard is surrounded by four allegorical figures, who symbolise science, courage and the art of poetry. On sunny days, the group receives company as the steps are a popular meeting spot for young people.

No regular markets have been held on the Rynek Główny since the 1950s. These days only flower ladies and souvenir hawkers set up stands there. However, in the run-up to Easter and Christmas, stallholders do descend on the square again. The **Christmas market**, which starts on the first Advent, ranks as one of the largest and most impressive of its kind in Poland. One highlight is the **competition for the most beautiful nativity crib**, which has taken place at the beginning of December every year since 1937. The competitors present their submissions, which have often taken months of work, in front of the Mickiewicz memorial. Afterwards, the prize-winning cribs are exhibited in the Historical Museum (▶69).

TAKING A BREAK

After a visit to the National Museum, enjoy a delicious coffee in the small **Café Szał** on the first floor of the Cloth Hall – ideally on the terrace outside with a dream view of St Mary's Church (daily 10am–11pm)

➕ 195 D/E3
🚊 Tram 1, 3, 6, 6pm, 20, 69, 73 (Pl. Wszystkich Świętych)

Galeria Sztuki Polskiej XIX Wieku
(Gallery of Polish Painting and Sculpture from the 19th Century)
✉ Rynek Główny 3 ☎ 124 335 400; http://mnk.pl
🕐 Tue, Wed, Fri, Sat 10am–6pm, Thu until 8pm, Sun until 4pm
🎟 16 złoty (free on Sun)

Wieża ratuszowa (Town Hall Tower)
✉ Rynek Główny 1 ☎ 124 264 334; www.mhk.pl
🕐 Daily 10:30am–6pm (summer), noon–6pm (winter)
🎟 9 złoty (free on Mon)

⭐ Kościół Mariacki
(St Mary's Church)

The two unequal towers of St Mary's Church are the landmark of Krakow. From the top the traditional *hejnał* rings out on the hour. The main altarpiece carved out of wood by Nuremberg's master sculptor Veit Stoß ranks as one of Poland's most valuable art treasures. Every day at noon, the wings are opened with great ceremony.

The Gothic church received its present form in the 15th century, but building was actually started on it in 1290, and the church interior was continually changed until the end of the 19th century.

The taller tower measures 82m (269ft) and has a Gothic cupola. The spire in the middle is adorned with a golden crown of the Madonna; it is surrounded by eight smaller spires. Every hour from its tower room the trumpeter plays the traditional ***hejnał*** tune from the north, south, east and west windows of the tower (▶ 20). The second tower is 69m (226ft) high and has a pinnacle in late Renaissance style and contains five medieval bells.

Daily Ritual

An exhilarating moment awaits the visitor every day at 11:50am. After a short prayer, a nun open the two enormous wing panels of the main altarpiece with a long rod to reveal its full splendour. At 6pm the doors are closed again – a procedure that has not changed in hundreds of years.

The Krakow city council commissioned the Nuremberg sculptor **Veit Stoß** (around 1447–1533) to build a new altarpiece after mishap destroyed the old one. It became his most important work. In 1477 Stoß moved to Krakow and worked on the new wooden altarpiece in his atelier for twelve years. His fee corresponded to the town's budget for an entire year. Stoß remained in Krakow for several years after finishing his masterpiece and completed among other things a tomb for King Kazimierz (Casimir) IV. Famous and rich, he returned to Nuremberg in 1496, where he was less lucky in the following years. He frittered away money in speculative business, was branded on

St Mary's Church bathed in the rays of the evening sun

FRATRICIDE

The reason for the unequal towers of St Mary's Church has become the stuff of legend: two brothers are said to have been commissioned with the building of the church. After one of the brothers had completed his tower, he killed the other to avoid his tower becoming any taller. As a result, the second tower was not continued and topped with a cupola. However, the murder's conscience plagued him to such an extent that on the day of the inauguration he threw himself off "his" tower.

both cheeks for document fraud and prohibited from leaving Nuremberg without permission. It was a number of years before he was pardoned by Emperor Maximilian I and could continue working normally.

His work for St Mary's Church that measures 13m (42.5ft) by 11m (36ft) ranks as the world's largest late Gothic carved altarpiece. Veit Stoß used the oak from trees that were about 500 years old for the construction. The approximately 200 larger than life figures that adorn the altarpiece are carved of softer lime wood, painted and gilded. The altarpiece has two fixed panels on the exterior sides as well as two movable panels in the middle, which bear relief sculptures on both sides. Thus it is possible by opening and closing the panels to change between two different depictions. Closed, the altarpiece shows twelve scenes from the life of Mary and Jesus. When opened, the altarpiece displays its full splendour. In the centre, you can see how Mary surrounded by the twelve apostles passes away and is escorted by angels up into Heaven. On the two side wings, Mary's joy is depicted in six scenes. In the culmination over the large altar picture, the Virgin Mary receives her crown in the presence of St Adalbert and St Stanislaus, Poland's two patron saints.

Odyssey of the Altarpiece

Shortly before the outbreak of World War II, the altarpiece was removed from St Mary's Church in order to conceal it from the Germans. However, somebody betrayed its hiding place and the altarpiece was taken to Nuremberg as booty. After the end of the war it was given back to Poland, underwent lengthy restoration and was then exhibited in Wawel for seven years before returning to the church in 1957.

Coloured light from three narrow stained glass windows at the end of the choir room falls onto the high altarpiece.

The magnificent church interior of St Mary's Church with Veit Stoß's famous carved altarpiece

The main shrine of the opened high altarpiece shows the dying Mary surrounded by the Apostles

The windows date back to the 14th century and in 120 pictures present scenes from the Old and New Testaments. The roof of the choir room is adorned with a stellar vault that was decorated with a blue starlit sky during the renovation work in the period from 1887 to 1892. Responsible for the rearrangement of the church interior was the history painter **Jan Matejko**, who produced a series of murals for the place of worship. Quite a few of his students were involved in this work, some of whom later became important artists in their own right, such as **Józef Mehoffer** and **Stanisław Wyspiański**. The two artists also created the large stained glass window on the west side of the main nave, which depicts scenes from the life of Mary, and from the Old Testament. In the church, you will see the tomb slabs of rich Krakow families who financed much of the church interior in past centuries and received their last resting place there.

TAKING A BREAK

The small restaurant **Bianca** (Plac Mariacki 2, ➤ 70), right next to St Mary's Church, is ideal for a lunchtime snack. Tasty pasta dishes are prepared in the open kitchen.

195 E3 Pl. Mariacki 5
124 220 521; www.mariacki.com
Mon–Sat 11:30am–6pm, Sun 2pm–6pm
Tram 1, 3, 6, 18, 20, 69, 73 (Pl. Wszystkich Świętych)
10 złoty

INSIDER INFO

- The main entrance leading out onto the Rynek Główny is reserved for people attending a church service. You will find the **entrance for tourists** on the south side on Plac Mariacki. *Insider Tip*

- If you wish to be present to see the **opening of the winged altarpiece**, make sure you get a ticket in good time because especially during the summer months demand can be high. *Insider Tip*

- Don't miss the opportunity to climb the tower and **watch the trumpeter at work**. The view makes up for the 273 steps (April–Oct daily 9:10am–11:10am, 1:10pm–5:40pm every half an hour; admission: 15 złoty).

⭐4 Muzeum Podziemia Rynku
(Rynek Underground Museum)

Those wishing to get to the roots of Krakow need to go underground. The museum under the Main Market Square not only leads to the oldest foundations in this part of the town, it also brings the Middle Ages back to life with its films and installations.

The archaeological excavations under the Rynek Główny in 2005 were only originally intended to last six months. They proved so successful, however, that the timeline was extended. The scientists were rewarded with an impressive haul of more than 10,000 objects. This unusual subterranean museum, which covers an area of around 4,000m² (43,000ft²), was set up in 2009 to show off the results and whisk you back to the Middle Ages.

A "Growing" Market Square

In the early days of the town, rubbish was not removed but simply covered with sand. Old buildings were destroyed during military conflicts or natural catastrophes, and new buildings were set up on their ruins. Thus over the centuries, the level of the ground has slowly raised. That is why you can still find sealed roads from past eras five metres (16ft) under the paving stones of the main market.

During excavation work, the archaeologists came across the foundations of earlier houses and shops. Maintained and conserved for posterity are remains of the walls of for instance the **Kramy Boleslawowe Stalls**, in which people traded the luxury articles of that period, as well as the Great and Small Weigh Houses. Also uncovered were the graves of an early medieval cemetery from the 10th/11th century which contained some precious burial objects. Another discovery were the

INSIDER INFO

Insider Tip

- The **capacity of the museum is very limited**, a maximum of 30 people are allowed in every 15 minutes; the last visitors are allowed in 90 minutes before the end of the opening time.
- **Reserving online** is very recommendable; on the website you can see how many places are available and at which times.
- You should **plan at least an hour** for the tour.
- **Audio guides** in English are available, the descriptions of the exhibits are also multilingual.

so-called "vampire burials", in which deceased people had been buried in an embryonic position or with their hands tied together. The bones of the dead were laid in the crypt of St Mary's Church and replaced by copies in the museum.

Vivid Historical Narrative

Numerous finds like old coins, clay figures, tools and jewellery are on view in the Underground Museum. Pictures show how the town looked before the Tatars

attacked in 1241. Exhibits also show the very varied trade connections which Krakow had with other European towns and the role of the town in the Hanse Group. Other displays offer visitors an opportunity to dip a little deeper into the history.

Medieval Krakow comes to life in the films and 3-D presentations. Sound installations complement the visual impressions. You can hear the creaking of wagons, the calls of the market hawkers and the sounds of the craftsmen at work and thus experience the hustle and bustle of a medieval market as if you were there. Equally vivid is the experience of watching a virtual display of two wooden houses going up in flames.

Concealed beneath the Rynek Główny are the oldest traces of the town

This unusual museum has always been met with great interest both by the people of Krakow and tourists. Since the capacity is limited and although there are long opening times, a visit is only possible if you register in good time. Kids also find the 👪 **adventurous trip** though Krakow's Underground Museum and its history interesting; the inter-active exhibition gets them really involved.

TAKING A BREAK

There is an enormous choice of coffee houses around the Main Market Square. If you are looking for a bit more peace and quiet, walk on a bit further to, for example, **Café Camelot** at no. 17 Ulica św. Tomasza (➤73), where you can enjoy your coffee and cake on the secluded forecourt.

Insider Tip

➕ 195 E3 ✉ Rynek Główny 3 (entrance in the Cloth Hall)
☎ 124 265 060; www.podziemiarynku.com
🕐 April–Oct Mon 10am–8pm, Tue 10am–4pm, Wed–Sun 10am–10pm;
Nov–March daily 10am–8pm (Tue until 4pm only)
🚊 Tram 1, 3, 6, 18, 20, 69, 73 (Pl. Wszystkich Świętych)
💰 19 złoty (free on Tue)

Ⓟ Brama Floriańska & Barbakan
(Florian's Gate & Barbican)

Krakow learned its lesson from the devastating attack by the Tatars in 1240/41: from the end of the 13th century new fortifications were built of which the imposing barbican, the magnificent Florian's Gate, the arsenal and a small section of the city walls remain.

A 3km (1.85mi) long double wall with 47 bastions and eight gates surrounded Krakow's Old Town from the Middle Ages until the end of the 18th century. However, as over the years, the wall fell into disrepair and lost it military significance, it was decided to remove it at the beginning of the 19th century and create a green belt around the Old Town, the **Planty**.

The square tower of Florian's Gate was built of natural stone at the be-ginning of the 14th cen-tury and a red-brick section was added in the 15th century with a protruding ledge for the marksmen. In 1697, the Baroque pinnacle was added during the renovation work after the Swedish Wars. The gate took its name from the nearby **Kościół św. Floriana (St Florian's Church)** in the Kleparz district in which the relics of St Florian are preserved. A bas-relief of the saint adorns the gate on the Old Town side.

The former city wall by Florian's Gate in its new role as an open-air gallery

Florian's Gate was the main gate through which the Polish kings entered into the town. It also provided entrance to the merchants who wanted to do business in Krakow. A tram traversed the narrow entrance right up to 1953 and had to fold in the current collectors just before it passed through. Today, the 34m (111ft) tall St Florian's Gate is a popular tourist meeting point.

BULWARK AGAINST ILLNESS
At the beginning of the 19th century, the Krakow senator Feliks Radwański came up with an original reason for why the barbican, arsenal and part of the city wall should be maintained: the walls would hold back the north winds, which would otherwise bring illness to the town and lift women's skirts. His plea was accepted.

The preserved remains of the city wall on both sides of the entrance turn into an open-air gallery during the day. Naive artworks, copies of famous paintings and first work by young art students wait there for buyers.

Europe's largest barbican

The entrance to Florian's Gate leads to the barbican, an imposing round defensive brick edifice, which was erected at the end of the 15th century owing to the fear of Turkish attacks at the time. It used to be connected to Florian's Gate by a walled bridge that led over the moat, but this so-called neck was demolished in 1825. It was also planned to pull down the barbican and the city wall, but strong opposition from Feliks Radwański (► box) stopped this and the edifice was preserved and remains the largest of its kind in Europe.

It was hoped that the up to three-metre (10ft) thick walls would provide protection from attacks with modern firearms. From the seven slender turrets it was possible to detect the enemy before he reached the city and then use the 130 embrasures to keep him at bay. In addition, there were machicolations at the top, floor openings through which boiling water or pitch could be dropped on attackers to dispel them. The barbican, which was mainly intended to protect the arsenal behind it was never taken. Today, the defensive structure, now part of the Historical Museum (►69), is open to visitors. In the summer, medieval pageants and jousting contests take place in the central courtyard.

Late Medieval stronghold: Krakow's imposing barbican

With the ticket for the barbican, you can also visit what is left of the **city wall** confined between two bastions. There is a beautiful view of the bustling Ulica Floriańska, which leads to the Main Market Square. The sandstone **arsenal** built in 1566 was once used to store guns and powder; now it is part of the Czartoryski Museum (►66).

TAKING A BREAK
You can buy delicious chocolate and coffee specialities at **Karmello** in Ulica Floriańska (40).

➕ 195 F4/5
✉ Pijarska
☎ 124 211 361; www.mhk.pl
🕐 April–Oct daily 10:30am–6pm (closed every 2nd Mon)
🚋 Tram 2, 7, 8, 14, 18, 24, 69, 73 (Stary Kleparz)
💵 8 złoty (Barbican and city wall)

⑫ Rynek Kleparski
(Kleparz Market Square)

Traders have been selling their wares on Kleparz Market Square for over 600 years. Every day the stall-owners set up their stands offering fresh fruit and vegetables, cheese and hams. It is a colourful spectacle that you should try not to miss.

Unlike the Old Town with its beautiful architecture or Kazimierz with its bars and cafés, Kleparz remains a quiet district, seemingly resistant to current trends. Despite its central location, there has been no large investment boom here, no new in-pubs have opened, and life tends to proceed at a quiet pace. If you would like to experience normal city life outside the tourist spots take a stroll through this district north of the Old Town.

Kleparz was once an independent town located just outside Krakow's city gates. King Kazimierz Wielki (Casimir III the Great) awarded the settlement town status in 1366; it was not until 1791 that it merged with Krakow. Since Kleparz was often the victim of pillage and destruction over the centuries, it has few medieval buildings of any significance. The majority of the buildings were erected in the 19th and 20th centuries. One of the few exceptions is **Kościół św. Floriana** (**St Florian's Church**) in Ulica Warszawska (no. 1), in which Karol Wojtyła, later to become John Paul II, held his first rectorate from 1949 to 1951. The church has existed since the 12th century and was renovated in Baroque style after the destruction by the Swedes at the end of the 17th century.

Tasty regional produce and exotic delicacies from all over the world: the Kleparz market offers a rich choice

A Shrunken Market Square

Until well into the 19th century, the Kleparz market square was almost as big as the Main Market Square. Today it is not even a quarter of its original size. New rows of houses were built, followed by the **Jan Matejko Academy of Fine Arts** in the south-east section by 1879 (➤ 66), and it was also separated from the elongated **Plac Jana Matejki** to the east. The focal point of the square is the impressive Grunwald Monument commemorating the **Battle of Tannenberg**, at which the joint Polish-Lithuanian troops defeated the Knights of the Teutonic Order in 1410.

St Florian's Church rises up behind the Memorial to the Battle of Tannenberg on the small Matejko Square

The market tradition is continued on the smaller Rynek Kleparski. Even during the time of martial law in the 1980s, the products sold there were still slightly better than at many places in the country. These days, the Stary Kleparz Market sells exotic fruits next to stands selling local smoked sheep cheese, tomatoes in all shapes and colours, in spring asparagus and in the autumn fresh mushrooms. Even city inhabitants who live on the other side of Krakow come to the market because the choice is staggering. Fresh fruit and vegetables tower like pyramids as far as the eye can see. Milk and butter, cheese and ham, fish and meat, honey and jams, as well as all kinds of household goods can be found here; and there are more than one or two chefs who fetch the ingredients they need from the more than 70 stalls. Stall-holders take time to chat to many of the customers that are old acquaintances in the meantime. Tourists, too, are among the crowds of visitors wandering through the long aisles with covered stands and past the permanent stalls.

TAKING A BREAK

The name says it all: **Wyszukane Desery Braci Szewczenko** – "Sophisticated desserts by the Szewcenko brothers". The two confectioners serve their handmade delights in a small café on Rynek Kleparski 14 (Mon–Fri 9am–8pm, Sat, Sun 10am–5pm), from the classic *crème brûlée* to more unusual creations.

✚ 195 F5 ✉ Rynek Kleparski

☎ 126 341 532; www.starykleparz.com

🕐 Market times: Mon–Fri 6am–6pm, Sat 6am–4pm, Sun 8am–3pm

🚋 Tram 2, 7, 8, 14, 18, 24, 69, 73 (Stary Kleparz)

At Your Leisure

⓭ Akademia Sztuk Pięknych w Krakowie

Poland's oldest art school, the **Jan Matejko Academy of Fine Arts**, is named after the Polish history painter Jan Matejko, who was its dean from 1873. After his death, he was followed by the well-known Krakow landscape painter Julian Fałat. Under Fałat's management, the academy became the centre of Poland's art world, and leading painters, such as Stanisław Wyspiański, Jacek Malczewski and Józef Mehoffer taught there.

To this day, the academy is one of the most important art universities in Poland. Besides teaching painting and sculpture, it also has faculties for design and restoration. Located in the main building is the **Gallery of the Art Faculty**, which shows contemporary work by Polish and European artists.

A further gallery of the academy is located on the corner in Ulica Basztowa 18 (Mon–Fri 10am–6pm, Sat from noon).

➕ 195 F5
✉ Pl. Jana Matejki 13
☎ 122 992 000; www.asp.krakow.pl
🕐 Galeria Wydziału Malarstwo: Mon–Fri 11am–3pm, 4pm–6pm
🚊 Tram 2, 7, 8, 14, 18, 24, 69, 73 (Stary Kleparz)
🎟 Free

⓮ Kamienica Szołayskich (Szołayski House)

In 1904 the Szołayskis, an aristocratic family, bequeathed their three-floor house to the Krakow National Museum, which from 1934 exhibited pieces from the 15,000 works that had been collected by **Feliks Jasieński** (1861–1929). Later the building was occupied by the Nazis and after World War II it became home to a collection of medieval art. It

The Czartoryski Museum has a unique collection of Roman antiquities

was not until after its renovation in 2012 that Jasieńskis's treasures – which has also been bequeathed to the museum – returned. The collection mainly includes works by contemporaries of the collector, such as Jacek Malczewski, Leon Wycółkowski, Stanisław Witkiewicz and Józef Mehoffer. On the ground floor there is also an additional small exhibition entitled **"Szymborska's Drawer"** with personal items from the home of the Nobel prize-winner for Literature Wisława Szymborska (1923–2012).

➕ 195 D4 ✉ Pl. Szczepański 9
☎ 124 445 450; www.mnk.pl
🕐 Tue–Sat 10am–6pm, Sun 10am–4pm
🚋 Tram 2, 8, 14, 6pm, 24, 69, 73
(Teatr Bagatela)
🎫 12 złoty (free on Sun)

➕ 195 E4
✉ Pijarska 8 (Gallery of Antiquities)
☎ 123 705 460; www.mnk.pl
🕐 Tue–Sun 10am–4pm   🚋 Tram 2, 7, 8, 14,
18, 24, 69, 73 (Stary Kleparz)
🎫 9 złoty (free on Sun)

🄑 Muzeum Książąt Czartoryskich (Czartoryski Museum)

Since 1876 the valuable artworks of the princely Czartoryski family have been on show in Krakow. The exhibition is distributed between the town palace of the family in Ulica św. Jana (no. 19), an annexed cloister building in Ulica

🄖 Teatr im. Juliusza Słowackiego (Słowacki Theatre)

Based on the model of the Paris Opera, this theatre was built (1891–1893) on Plac św. Ducha, and later named after the poet and playwright Juliusz Słowacki. Its richly adorned facade in historicist style has earned it a place as one of the architectural jewels of the city. Stanisław Wyspiańskis's key play *Wesele* (The Wedding) was premiered there in 1901. It was also here that the performance of a piece by Polish avant-garde artist Witkacy caused a small scandal in the theatre world 20 years later. Misused for Nazi propaganda during World War II,

Paris architecture in Krakow's Old Town: the Słowacki Theatre

Pijarska as well as in the former city arsenal located opposite. The museum has been undergoing restoration since 2010, and the date for the reopening has been postponed several times, but it is now planned for 2018. In the meantime, the collection's most famous painting, *The Lady with the Ermine* by Leonardo da Vinci, has found a temporary home at Wawel Castle (▶84). The Czartoryski Museum's **Gallery of Antiquities** is on view at the arsenal, and it includes, among other things, two Egyptian mummies.

the theatre, which can sit 530 spectators, rose again after 1945 to become one of Poland's most important stages.

Life is a bit quieter at the small market than at the bustling nearby Main Market Square

In the town's oldest electric plant next door, the Small Stage was set up in 1976. Since 2000 there has also been an open-air theatre on the square, on which song recitals and jazz concerts take place.

🞤 195 F4 ✉ Pl. św. Ducha 1
☎ 124 244 526; www.slowacki.krakow.pl
🕐 Ticket Office: Mon 10am–6pm, Tue–Sat 9am–7pm (Pause 2pm–2:30pm)
🚊 Tram 2, 3, 7, 14, 20, 24, 52, 62, 69, 70, 73 (Dworzec Główny)
✋ 15–80 złoty

🔟 Muzeum Biograficzne Jana Matejki (Jan Matejko Museum)

The most famous history painter Jan Matejko (1838–1893) is commemorated in the house in which he was born and lived. His large works, in which he glorified Polish history served at the time of the Polish Partition as a way to maintain national identity. Very soon after his death, Krakow's citizens set about turning his house into a museum. You can visit the artist's house and studio and see numerous works and documents pertaining to his life.

🞤 195 F4 ✉ Floriańska 41
☎ 124 335 960; www.mnk.pl
✉ Tue–Sat 10am–6pm, Sun 10am–4pm
✉ Tram 2, 7, 8, 14, 18, 24, 69, 73 (Stary Kleparz)
✋ 9 złoty (free on Sun)

🔟 Muzeum Farmacji (Museum of Pharmacy)

The exhibition of the Museum of Pharmacy stretches over five floors, from the cellar to the roof of a medieval town house. Old wooden barrels in the cellar are a reminder that even during the Middle Ages wine was used to treat various illnesses. On the other floors are pharmacy fittings and pharmaceutical devices from various centuries. One room is dedicated to the pharmacist **Ignacy Łukasiewicz** who studied in Krakow, ranks as the inventor of the petroleum lamp and who developed the world's first oil field in Subcarpathia.

🞤 195 E4 ✉ Floriańska 25
☎ 124 219 279; www.muzeumfarmacji.pl
✉ Tue noon–6:30pm, Wed–Sun 10am–2:30pm
✉ Tram 2, 7, 8, 14, 18, 24, 69, 73 (Stary Kleparz)
✋ 9 złoty

🔟 Mały Rynek (Small Market Square)

In the shade of St Mary's Church is the Small Market Square, where Krakow's butchers used to sell their meat until the beginning of the 19th century. Even today **Insider Tip** market stands are set up on special occasions such as the "Festival of Pirogi" in August.

Since cars were banned a few years ago, the rectangular square has gained in leisure value. A broad

terrace connects the eight buildings on the eastern side, which is full of beer tables in the summer. The *Merkuriusz Polski* was printed in the Mały Rynek House no. 6 in 1661, the first newspaper to appear regularly in Poland.

Headquartered in the **Lamelli House** in Ulica Mikołajska 2, on the north side of the square, is the cultural centre. It contains two galleries presenting contemporary art (Tue–Fri 11am–5pm). Standing out on the west side is the semi-circular rear of the **Kosciół św. Barbary** (**St Barbara's Church**).

The former cemetery chapel was erected at about the same time as St Mary's Church and was later extended.

✚ 195 E3 🚊 Tram 1, 3, 6, 18, 20, 69, 73
(Pl. Wszystkich Świętych)

THE MARKET PIGEONS

Life is good for Krakow's pigeons on the Rynek Główny. Many passersby feed them. Perhaps the sympathetic attitude of the locals towards the pigeons has something to do with the legend that claims pigeons are actually bewitched knights. A witch is said to have helped Duke Henryk IV Probus (the Righteous) in the 13th century when he was in financial difficulties by turning his knights into pigeons. They then flew up to St Mary's Church, pecked stones out of it, which then turned into gold coins before they hit the ground. The duke wanted to use the money to travel to Rome and ensure the pope's support for his claim to the throne. However, the king spent all the money on the way and never returned to Krakow, so his bewitched men are still waiting for him.

⓴ Muzeum Historyczne (Historical Museum)

Since 1965 the Historical Museum has had its headquarters in the **Krzysztofory Palace**, which takes its name from a statue of St Christopher formerly on the façade. In the 1960s and 1970s its Baroque cellar was the venue of the Teatr Cricot of Tadeusz Kantor (➤ 148).

The building has been undergoing renovation for many years, and when the work is finished it will house a permanent exhibition entitled "Krakow from the beginning without an end". Presenting a first impression of it is the digital exhibition "**cyberteka**", at which you can stroll through the history of Krakow. Every year from the beginning of December and until February the museum exhibits the best nativity cribs from the Christmas competition (➤ 55). *Insider Tip*

✚ 195 D3/4 ✉ Rynek Główny 35
☎ 126 192 335; www.mhk.pl
🕐 Tue–Sun 10am–5:30pm
🚊 Tram 1, 3, 6, 18, 20, 69, 73
(Pl. Wszystkich Świętych)
✋ 12 złoty (free on Tue)

㉑ Międzynarodowy Centrum Kultury (International Cultural Centre)

The **Pod Kruki** (The Ravens) House on the Main Market Square, in which the NS headquarters for the General Government was located during World War II, has been the home of the International Cultural Centre since 1991. It provides the venue for educational events and international conferences, contains a comprehensive scientific library as well as a gallery in which temporary exhibitions of modern art are held. Tip: at "Happy Hour" (Tue, Wed 10am–11am) the entrance fee is only one instead of 10 złoty. *Insider Tip*

✚ 195 D3 ✉ Rynek Główny 25
☎ 124 242 800; www.mck.krakow.pl
🕐 Gallery: Tue–Sun 10am–6pm
🚊 Tram 1, 3, 6, 18, 20, 69, 73
(Pl. Wszystkich Świętych) ✋ 10 złoty

Where to...
Eat and Drink

Prices
A main course (without drinks)
£ under 45 złoty   ££ 45–90 złoty   £££ over 90 złoty

RESTAURANTS

Amarone ££
Fine Italian cuisine is served at the restaurant of the Hotel Pod Różą (►42). Most of the ingredients come directly from Italy, and the handmade pasta tastes delicious. Don't miss out on the unbeatably reasonable 5-course lunch menu for 50 złoty.

195 E4 ☒ Floriańska 14
☎ 124 243 381; www.likushoteleirestauracje.pl
🕐 Daily 11am–11pm

Bianca ££
White is the dominant colour in this small Italian restaurant on the edge of the market square. The menu comprises simple, but hearty seasonal food made without the use of convenience products and flavour enhancers. Many of the ingredients come directly from Italy.

195 E3 ☒ Pl. Mariacki 2 ☎ 124 221 871; www.biancoristorante.pl 🕐 Daily noon–10pm

Cyrano de Bergerac £££
The restaurant in the medieval cellar vault serves French food that will win you over in no time. Connoisseurs of *foie gras* or oysters can also eat outside in the lovely garden in summer and enjoy their cooled Champagne there. Be prudent when you are choosing your starter and main course so that you have enough space left for the delicious desserts, such as the chocolate soufflé with rum sauce.

195 E4 ☒ Sławkowska 26
☎ 124 117 288; www.cyranodebergerac.pl
🕐 Daily noon–11pm

Ed Red ££
Here more or less everything revolves around steak. Regardless of whether rib eye, T-Bone or Porterhouse, the main thing is that it should be dry aged, in other words hung up to dry. In the open kitchen, the meat is then grilled to perfection. To accompany it, there is a wide selection of wines to choose from.

195 E4 ☒ Sławkowska 3
☎ 690 900 555; www.edred.pl 🕐 Mon–Thu noon–11pm, Fri–Sat noon–midnight

Jarema £
One of the few good restaurants in the Kleparz district that transports guests back to the time of the Polish aristocratic republic. In matching ensemble, Old Polish dishes as well as traditional food from the areas of what used to be East Poland are served. The specialities include venison, or duck in a honey and cinnamon sauce with baked apples

195 F5 ☒ Pl. Matejko 5
☎ 124 293 669; www.jarema.pl
🕐 Daily from noon

Kogel Mogel ££
Everyone in Poland knows the *kogel mogel*, a dessert comprising of egg yolks and sugar beaten together to form a creamy texture. In the restaurant of the same name, the dish is served in a slightly refined form. Interpreting traditional Polish and Galician dishes in a modern way is the idea behind the restaurant, which has several dining rooms and a beautiful summer garden.

Insider Tip

✚ 195 E3 ✉ Sienna 12
☎ 124 264 968; www.kogel-mogel.pl
🕐 Daily noon–11pm

Milkbar Tomasza £

An Irishman had the idea for this modern variation of the Polish milk bar. Its large windows and modern furnishing are intriguing. Inexpensive, good quality soups, salads, *pierogi* and pancakes as well as panini are on the menu. The milk bar is also a good address for breakfast. **Insider Tip**
✚ 195 F3 ✉ św. Tomasza 24 ☎ 124 221 706
🕐 Mon–Sat 8am–10pm, Sun 9am–10pm

Pierogowy Raj £

In the paradise for *pierogi*, they serve 50 different sorts of Poland's delicious and inexpensive national pies. It is available with or without meat, hearty or sweet. Choose your own combination and enjoy the great selection. **Insider Tip**
✚ 195 E4 ✉ Sławkowska 25
☎ 122 658 927; www.pierogowyray.pl
🕐 Daily 11am–9pm

Scandale Royal ££

Don't worry if you think the name sounds a little dodgy. The glamour factor is high and with its mix of café, lounge and bistro, this elegant restaurant appeals to a chic, generally younger clientele. The menu is Polish-Mediterranean, and after 10pm night owls can buy snacks to accompany the beer, wine or cocktails and a hearty breakfast the following morning.
✚ 195 D4 ✉ Pl. Szczepański 2
☎ 124 221 333; www.scandale.pl 🕐 Sun–Thu 7:30am–midnight, Fri–Sat 7:30am–2am

Sukiennice £

The restaurant in the Cloth Hall attracts bargain-hunters. **Insider Tip** On Mondays, the beer costs less than 8 złoty, on Tuesdays you can buy a large pork cutlet for 17 złoty and on Wednesdays when you buy one portion of scampi you get an extra one free. The quality is good as well, which is why there are always a lot of guests in the spacious rooms.
✚ 195 E3 ✉ Rynek Główny 6 ☎ 124 210 909; www.sukiennice-kompaniakuflowa.pl
🕐 Daily noon–midnight

Szara ££

Despite its prominent position on the Main Market Square with its view of the Cloth Hall, this restaurant is not a tourist trap, but one of the top restaurants, elegant but not overly formal. The imaginative menu brings together dishes from many parts of Europe. Try the *plankstek* served on an oak board with duchess potatoes, beans wrapped in bacon and Béarnaise sauce.
✚ 195 E3 ✉ Rynek Główny 6 ☎ 124 216 669; www.szara.pl 🕐 Daily 8am–11pm

Trufla ££

The little Italian restaurant looks rather unspectacular from the outside but has a large quiet garden in the courtyard. It is an ideal place for hot summer evenings. The menu is not particularly adventurous, but everything that leaves the open-plan kitchen is of convincing quality.
✚ 195 D4 ✉ św. Tomasza 2
☎ 124 221 641; www.truflakrakow.pl
🕐 Mon–Fri 9am–11pm, Sat–Sun 10am–11pm

Trzy Rybki £££

For years, the restaurant belonging to the luxury hotel Stary has had a top place on the Michelin list for Kraków. In keeping with the style of the hotel, the restaurant combines tradition and modern, and presents a fine European cuisine. As the name denotes ("three fish") there are always several fish dishes to choose from.
✚ 195 D4 ✉ Szepańska 5 ☎ 123 840 801; www.likushoteleirestauracje.pl 🕐 noon–11pm

Wesele ££

It can feel like being at a traditional Polish wedding (*wesele*) on this two-floor restaurant, because it is generally very full and the atmosphere is good. Traditional meals are served in the Old Polish surroundings; the goose breast is highly recommended.

➕ 195 E3 ✉ Rynek Główny 10
☎ 124 227 460; www.weselerestauracja.pl
🕐 Daily noon–11pm

Wentzl £££

The elegant restaurant in the historical, richly decorated, premises belongs to the emporium of Magda Gessler, one of the most dazzling personalities in the Polish restaurant scene. Her speciality is traditional Polish recipes interpreted in a contemporary way.

➕ 195 D3 ✉ Rynek Główny 19
☎ 124 295 299; www.restauracjawenttzl.pl
🕐 Daily noon–11pm

Wierzynek £££

The history of the restaurant goes back to the year 1364. Besides crowned heads of state, visitors have also included celebrities like topmodel Kate Moss and actor Robert de Niro. Old Polish recipes have been freshened up a bit, and all the meals are cooked using regional products. There is a choice between dining with a historic backdrop or surrounded by surrealist paintings. Enjoy like the kings of old the five-course traditional menu that is served for 15 people each day (from approx. 250 złoty per person).

➕ 195 E3 ✉ Rynek Główny 16
☎ 124 249 600; www.wierzynek.pl
🕐 Daily 1pm–11pm

PUBS AND BARS

Baroque

These flamboyantly arranged rooms and the large summer garden are mainly full at the weekend. The Baroque is a combination of bar, restaurant and club, prized for its good cocktails and its selection of different vodkas.

➕ 195 E4 ✉ św. Jana 16
☎ 124 220 106; www.baroque.com.pl
🕐 Sun–Thu noon–midnight, Fri, Sat noon–4am

Hard Rock Café

The Krakow offshoot of the Hard Rock Cafés is located in one of the most beautiful buildings on the Main Market Square, right next to St Mary's Church. The concept is the same as it is everywhere: on the walls are mementoes of well-known rock stars, a small shop, good burgers, loud music. What makes this one unique is the view from the upper floors over the square.

Insider Tip

➕ 195 E3 ✉ Rynek Główny/Pl. Mariacki 9
☎ 124 291 155; www.hardrock.com/krakow
🕐 Daily 10am–2am

House of Beer

The name says it all. Guests can choose from more than 150 kinds of beer; a good dozen of them are draft beers. You can try numerous kinds, from small Polish breweries to beers from the Czech Republic, Belgium and the Ukraine.

➕ 195 F3 ✉ św. Tomasza 35
☎ 794 222 136; www.houseofbeerkrakow.com
🕐 Daily 2pm–1am

Klub Kulturalny

This cellar bar has been a favourite meeting point for Krakow students for many years. The beer is inexpensive, elegant outfits are not necessary. Most Tuesdays, there is live music.

➕ 195 D4 ✉ Szewska 25
☎ 124 221 673 🕐 Daily noon–4am

Pijalnia Wódki i Piwa

Many Krakow students start their night on the town here. Beer, vodka and fortifying snacks are available for just a few złoty. Since the bar is mostly crowded, you will soon find yourself chatting to your neighbour.

➕ 195 E4 ✉ św. Jana 3–5
☎ 124 228 075 🕐 Daily 9am–6:30am

Restauracja Browarna Browar Lubicz

In 2001 the renowned Götz brewery was shut, and 14 years later the local brewery Lubicz opened in vthe historical malt house. Its non-pasteurised and unfiltered beer has already won quite a few awards.

✚ 195 east F4 ✉ Lubicz 17
☎ 123 539 884; www.browar-lubicz.com.pl
🕐 Mon–Thu noon–midnight, Fri noon–1am, Sat 1pm–1am, Sun 1pm–11pm

Viva la Pinta

One of the first and most success-ful Craft Beer breweries in Poland opened a beer-pub directly on the Royal Route in 2014. The summer garden is very popular. You can choose from 14 kinds of freshly tapped "barley juices" from bottle beers that come from Poland. Beers from competitors are also on offer.

✚ 195 E4 ✉ Floriańska 13
☎ 124 210 590; www.browarpinta.pl
🕐 Mon–Sat 4pm–midnight, Sun 2pm–midnight

CAFÉS

Camelot

The interior of the artist café is decorated with folk art, including numerous works by the naïve artist Nikifor. At the old tables with lace table cloths, you can enjoy coffee specialities, cakes and simple dishes and forget the time. In high summer, the shady forecourt offers a welcome place to cool down.

✚ 195 E4 ✉ św. Tomasza 17
☎ 124 210 123
🕐 Daily 9am–midnight

Charlotte

The home backed baguettes and croissants can pass the comparison with their French counterparts. Located over several floors, the café and bistro is never empty at any time of the day. People meet there in the morning for breakfast, midday for a light lunch and in the evening for a glass of French wine.

✚ 195 D4 ✉ Pl. Szczepański 2
☎ 600 807 880; www.bistrocharlotte.com
🕐 Mon–Thu 7am–midnight, Fri 7am–1am, Sat 9am–1am, Sun 9am–10pm

Jama Michalika

In 1895 Jan Michalik opened a patisserie and since his café only consisted of a single room without a window, it soon received the nickname "Michalik's cave". Since his cakes were delicious and students from the nearby art academy could pay for their food there with their paintings, he was soon very popular especially in the art circles. With its Art Nouveau interior and the many artworks on the walls, this dark café remains a popular meeting place to this day.

✚ 195 F4 ✉ Floriańska 45
☎ 124 221 561; www.jamamichalika.pl
✉ Mon–Thu 9am–10pm, Fri–Sat 9am–11pm

Noworolski

For more than 100 years, this café in Viennese style has had its firm place in the Cloth Hall. The elegant Art Nouveau interior looks as though it has been carefully looked after over the centuries, and even the cellars seem to be from another time. Nationalized during the Socialist period, the coffee house has been in the possession of the founding family again since 1992. A generally older generation of guests dig into the generous slices of cake while they look out at the Main Market Square.

✚ 195 E3 ✉ Rynek Główny 1
☎ 124 224 771; www.noworolski.com.pl
🕐 Daily 8am–10pm (later in summer)

Pijalnia Czekolady E. Wedel

The Warsaw chocolate and sweet manufacturer has a shop on Krakow's Main Market Square. There, in coffee-house ambience or in the covered courtyard, you can enjoy superb cakes with a hot chocolate in which the spoon seems to stand upright for a moment.

✚ 195 E3 ✉ Rynek Główny 46
☎ 124 294 085; www.wedelpijalnie.pl
🕐 Mon–Thu 9am–10pm, Fri–Sun 9am–midnight

Where to...
Shop

Around the Main Market Square you will find everything from souvenir shops and small boutiques to luxury stores. Next to the main station, a shopping "city" has evolved, Galeria Krakowska, with more than 200 shops. A few paces away on Rynek Kleparski, you can buy little souvenirs as well as fresh food at the oldest weekly market.

RYNEK GŁÓWNY

Are you looking for a souvenir from Krakow for someone? Then go to the **Cloth Hall**. At 9am the wooden shops open to reveal their treasures. Amber jewellery, not altogether typical for Krakow but at least for Poland, the Wawel dragon (►86/87) in various shapes and sizes, traditional necklaces with large colourful wooden beads or carved pieces from the Tatra – there is plenty of choice (daily 9am–8pm).

In one of the most beautiful town houses on the Main Market Square, right next to St Mary's Church, the Spanish fashion chain **Zara** offers shopping on five floors (Rynek Główny 5; Mon–Sat 10am–10pm).

The fashion of the Polish label **Tatuum** is young, modern and inexpensive (Rynek Główny 36, Mon–Sat 9am–8pm, Sun until 7pm).

Sweet memories are available at **Wawel**, Krakow's traditional chocolate company. Besides the different kinds of chocolate bars, you will also find chocolate-covered plums (*śliwka*), the popular "cow sweets" (*krówki*) and various sorts of truffle (Rynek Główny 33; daily 10am–7pm; also a branch in the castle on the Wawel; www.wawel.com.pl).

If you are searching for something very special, then go to **Galeria Niuans**, where you will find Chinese porcelain, exclusive crystal glass, silver tableware and table linen (Rynek Główny 39; Mon–Fri 9am–7pm, Sat until 5pm; www.galerianiuans.pl).

You would like something luxurious? Then go to the elegant **Pasaż 13 store**. The historical walls of the old town house are stylishly highlighted with steel, glass and a refined lighting concept. On three floors, small galleries present the fashion, shoes and accessories of well-known brands like Alexander McQueen, Gucci and Kenzo as well as some of the leading Polish designers and couturiers. A delicatessen shop and the very well-stocked wine shop rounds off the offer (Rynek Główny 13; www.pasaz-13.pl; Mon–Sat 11am–9pm, Sun until 5pm).

IN THE SURROUNDING AREA

Andrzej Mleczko is one of the most well-known Polish caricaturists, often taking a dig at politicians and the Catholic church. Some of his best works adorn posters and postcards, cups and t-shirts and can be purchased from the gallery in Ulica św. Jana. Even if you don't speak any Polish, you will understand a lot of his work (ul. św. Jana 14; www.sklep.mleczko.pl; daily 10am–6pm).

You can find Polish folk art at **Krakuska Sztuka Ludowa**, including national costumes, historical games, Bunzlauer pottery and embroidery from the Tatra region (ul. Szewska 9; Mon–Fri 10am–8pm, Sat 11am–6pm, Sun 11am–4pm).

Earthenware from Bunzlau and Silesian porcelain as well as Polish glassware is also available from **Mila** (ul. Sławkowska 14;

Mon–Fri 10am–7pm, Sat until 5pm).

Pass through an enchanting courtyard to the Concept Store **LuLu Living**. Go up the stairs and immerse yourself in a wonderful world of home accessories: fabrics, cushions, lamps, glasses and mirror, all designed in a very individual vintage style (ul. św. Tomasza 17; www.lulu living.pl; Mon–Sun 11am–7pm).

Joanna Hawrot's small shop sells stylish designer clothing. The couturier combines art and design, blending Far-Eastern shapes with European style, taking for example inspiration from the traditional kimono to create her elegant dresses that can be worn every day (ul. św. Marka 16; www. joannahawrot.com).

Galeria Krakowska at the main station is ideal on rainy days. More than 200 shops as well as numerous cafés and restaurants are congregated under one roof. In addition to international chains from Benetton to Zara, you will also find numerous Polish fashion, shoe and jewellery shops (ul. Pawia 5; Mon–Sat 9am–10pm, Sun 10am–9pm; www.galeria krakowska.pl).

Krakow's oldest market on **Rynek Kleparski** (►64) makes a nice change from the pragmatic shopping centres.

Where to...
Go Out

Every once in a while you can enjoy a concert free of charge on the Rynek Główny, in the evenings jazz music is everywhere, opera fans like the area near the main station, while the younger crowd turns night into day at the clubs.

OPERA AND THEATRE

Opera Krakowska
The Krakow opera, founded in 1954, did not receive its own building until the end of 2008, the first new opera house to be built in Poland since World War II. It was erected on Ulica Lubicz, where a riding hall had been used since the 1960s as the venue for operettas. The modern concert hall sits 760. For the around 200 events a year, 98 per cent of these seats are fully booked. Depending on the performance, tickets cost between 15 and 140 złoty and can be booked online on the website. A highlight is the summer festival with performances in the opera house and in the courtyard of Wawel Castle.
✚ 195 east F4 ✉ Lubicz 48
☎ 122 966 200; www.opera.krakow.pl

Narodowy Teatr Stary
In earlier days, the National Theatre was associated with the names of well-known artists such as Jerzy Grotowski, Tadeusz Kantor and Andrzej Wajda. Despite a history that stretches back over 200 years, the theatre has stayed young, often addressing and getting involved in current topics.
✚ 195 D4 ✉ Jagiellońska 5
☎ 124 224 040; www.stary.pl

MUSIC

At 7pm every evening in the Renaissance room of **Bonerowski Palace** on the Main Market Square, you can listen to the piano music of Fryderyk Chopin. The normal entrance ticket includes a glass of wine, the premium ticket a three-course meal.

Insider Tip

Piano music by Poland's most famous composer is also on offer in the **Concert House** in Ulica Sławkowska (no. 14). The proarts concert agency also organises tickets for the daily concerts of the Krakow Royal Chamber Ochestra in **Kościół św. Wojciecha (St Adalbert Church)** on the Main Market Square and in Ulica Sławkowska (14). Programmes, information and booking options at www.cracow concerts.pl

Harris Piano Jazz Bar

There is live music in the vaulted cellar every evening. Beside jazz bands, blues singers and rock musicians also perform here too. The seats are in great demand at the weekend – and although the temperature inside is subtropical at times, hardly anyone leaves their seat early. That is why it makes sense to arrive early or reserve a seat.

✚ 195 D3
✉ Rynek Główny 28
☎ 124 215 741; www.harris.krakow.pl
🕐 Mon–Fri from 11am, Sat, Sun from 10am till the last guest

The Piano Rouge

Surrounded by red light as well as a generous amount of velvet and chenille, guests invariably feel as though they have been transported to Montmartre. Yet it is not leg-kicking Can-Can that awaits you in the vaulted cellar but foot-tapping jazz music, mainly in a piano music and song combination. You can enjoy a Polish or international dish as you listen to them.

✚ 195 E3 ✉ Rynek Główny 46
☎ 124 310 333; www.thepianorouge.pl
🕐 Daily from 10am till the last guest

Piwnica Pod Baranami

This legendary cellar club at the main station celebrated its 60th anniversary in 2016. The literary cabaret founded then now only performs on a Saturday. Of more interest to guests from other countries are the tango evenings on Wednesday and the jazz con-

certs on Thursdays. People also just meet there for a coffee or a beer.

✚ 195 D3 ✉ Rynek Główny 27
☎ 124 220 177; www.piwnicapodbaranami.pl
🕐 Daily 11am–2am

NIGHTLIFE

Coco Music Club

At three bars in four lounges and on two dance floors you meet the young and elegant crowd. Well-known DJs from Poland and abroad are guests here. Female guests are lured to some of the events with bargain drinks and free admission before midnight.

✚ 195 F4 ✉ Szpitalna 38
☎ 124 296 983; www.clubcoco.pl
🕐 Wed–Sat 10pm–6am

Forty Kleparz

The former Bastion III, part of the city fortifications that the Habsburgs had built, has been home to a popular music club for some years. Dance parties and concerts with stars from the Polish rock scene take place in red-brick vaulted rooms. Since there is plenty of space, you can choose between Latin and hip hop music on some evenings.

✚ 195 north E5 ✉ Kamienna 2–4
☎ 606 388 313; www.fortykleparz.pl
🕐 Fri–Sat 8pm–4am

Pod Jaszczurami

The student club founded in 1960 weathered the political turnaround extraordinarily well, maintaining its character and still remaining popular with the young people of Krakow and tourists alike. People meet here at the weekend for the retro disco parties and during the week for karaoke evenings or live concerts with jazz and rock bands.

✚ 195 E3 ✉ Rynek Główny 8
☎ 124 294 538; www.podjaszczurami.pl
🕐 Daily from 10am

Southern Old Town & Wawel

 **Little Treats**

Gondola Tour on the Vistula

Experience the **Wawel** (▶ 82) from the water: small gondolas transport you to the **Benedictine Abbey of Tyniec** (▶ 171) just outside Krakow.

Full of Energy

Can you feel the spiritual energy at the Wawel wall (▶ 83)? Some people believe that one of the seven **chakra stones** the Hindu god Shiva threw down to earth landed here...

Fashion of Past Times

You can admire the latest trends of the 19th century in the eclectic fashion exhibition in the Gallery for Decorative Arts at the **National Museum** (▶ 103).

Getting Your Bearings

"Every piece of stone here is Poland." That is how the Polish artist Stanisław Wyspiański once described the significance of Wawel Castle. Poland's kings ruled their country for 500 years from this stronghold. Many leading Polish figures have found their last resting place in Wawel Cathedral. It is not only the royal chambers and the crown jewels that appeal to visitors. Krakow's most famous painting, the *Lady with the Ermine* by Leonardo da Vinci has also found a temporary home here. In summer, concerts in the castle courtyard pull people in, as does the fantastic view of the Vistula all year round. According to legend a fearful dragon once lived in a cave under the castle – making dragon souvenirs a favourite with tourists, too.

From Wawel, the picturesque Ulica Kanonicza ("Street of the Canons") leads towards the Main Market Square. Many regard this cobbled street with its medieval palaces as Krakow's most beautiful boulevard. Karol Wojtyła, who later became Pope John Paul II, once lived in what is now the Museum of the Archdiocese, during the time that he was the Bishop of Krakow. Running parallel to Ulica Kanonicza is the bustling shopping street Ulica Grodzka with its numerous little shops.

The university district stretches out towards the south-west of the Old Town. Founded in 1364, the Uniwersytet Jagielloński (Jagiellonian University) is the second oldest university in Central Europe. Today it has almost 50,000 students. The Collegium Mais with its cloisters in the interior courtyard dates back to the very beginning and is now home to the university museum. Numerous institutes and the administration of the university have their headquarters in the Old Town. The Kościół akademicki św. Anny, Collegiate Church of St Anne, ranks as one of the most beautiful churches in the town.

TOP 10

- ⭐ Wzgórze Wawelskie (Wawel Hill) ➤ 82
- ⭐ Ulica Kanonicza ➤ 90
- ⭐ Collegium Maius ➤ 93

Don't Miss

- ㉒ Kościół akademicki św. Anny (Collegiate Church of St Anne) ➤ 96
- ㉓ Kościół Franciszkanów (Church of St Francis of Assisi) ➤ 98
- ㉔ Muzeum Archeologiczne (Archaeological Museum) ➤ 101

Getting Your Bearings

At Your Leisure

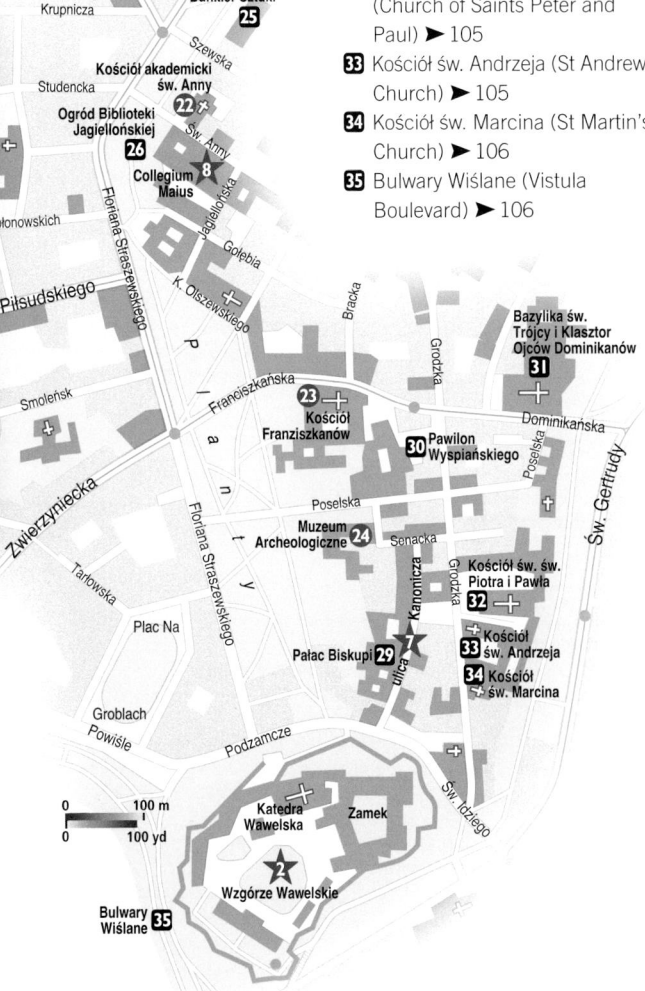

The Perfect Day

On this tour for which you should reserve at least a day, you will discover the most important sights of the Southern Old Town and on the banks of the Vistula. After the sightseeing, enjoy a walk to the banks of the Vistula and treat yourself to something very special to finish off the day.

🕘 9:00am
While the students stream into their lecture halls, you can enjoy the tranquillity of the beautiful courtyard at ☆ **Collegium Maius** (photo left; ➤ 93) and dip into the history of this historic university.

🕙 10:00am
Walk on to the **22** **Collegiate Church of St Anne** (➤ 96), resplendent with colourful frescoes; it is one of Poland's most important Baroque buildings.

🕚 11:00am
A small detour leads you west to the **Muzeum Narodowe**, the **27** **National Museum** (➤ 103). Enjoy some refreshment in the elegant museum café before going up to the second floor to familiarise yourself with 20th-century Polish art as you wander around the extensive collection.

🕐 1:00pm
Take a look at the **23** **Franciscan Church** (➤ 98) that boasts exceptional Art Nouveau stained glass windows by the Polish artist Stanisław Wyspiański. You will find more of his work in the nearby modern **30** **Wyspiański Pavilion** (➤ 104).

🕑 2:00pm
It is time for a light lunch. Don't be put off by the crumbling facade of the **Nowa Prowincja** (➤ 110). It is really comfortable inside and you can order for example delicious salads or freshly made hummus.

🕒 3:00pm
After you have fortified yourself, wander down Krakow's most beautiful road, the medieval ☆ **Ulica Kanonicza** (➤ 90), to the ☆ **Wawel** (➤ 82).

🕓 4:00pm
On **Wawel Hill** it is best to focus on a few highlights. The view of the **Arcade Court of the Palace** is free of charge, as is a tour of the **Cathedral**. You need a ticket to see the royal chambers, the crown jewels, the museum, the crypt and the Dragon's Den. Don't miss a visit to see the *Lady with the Ermine*, Leonardo da Vinci's masterpiece.

🕕 6:00pm

After looking down on the Vistula (photo above) take a little walk along the **35** **waterside promenade** (▶ 106). Look out for the fire-breathing dragon in front of his cave and watch the gondolas travelling along the river. Enjoy the evening atmosphere on the sundeck of the **Batory Restaurant Boat** (▶ 107).

🕗 8:00pm

After a drink it is back to ⭐**Ulica Kanonicza**. There you can treat yourself to something special for dinner: test the Chef Menu from Marcin Filipkiewicz in the much-awarded restaurant at the **Copernicus** hotel (▶ 108). The five to twelve courses are really worth the money.

★ 2 Wzgórze Wawelskie (Wawel Hill)

Polish kings ruled the country from Wawel Castle for more than 500 years, and when they passed away were buried in Wawel Cathedral. No other place is more closely associated with the eventful history of Poland. The former royal residence and Krakow's Old Town have been on the UNESCO World Heritage list since 1978.

After King Kazimierz (Casimir) I transferred the capital of his kingdom from Gniezno to Krakow in 1038, Wawel Hill developed into Poland's power centre. It was not until Krakow had slipped to the periphery of the huge kingdom after Poland grew through its alliance with Lithuania that King **Zygmunt III Wasa** (Sigismund III Vasa) moved the royal residence to Warsaw in 1596. He, himself, did not leave Krakow for good until 1609. Yet Poland's kings continued to be crowned and interred in Wawel Cathedral until 1734.

During the time of the Polish Secession, the Habsburgs used the castle as a barracks. When the soldiers moved

out in 1905, donations from the population made it possible to preserve the crumbling buildings. **Stanisław Wyspiański** (➤ 17) designed a plan intended to turn the Wawel into Poland's "acropolis", with the seat of the government, the National Museum, the Curia and Polish Academy. However, his plans were never implemented.

Anyone entering through the **Coat of Arms Gate** in the north or the **Bernardine Gate** in the south is amazed by the size of the complex. It is surrounded by a **momentous wall** with many gates and bastions. The Habsburgs had part of the dense construction removed in the 19th century to make room for a parade ground. On the lawn of the interior courtyard you can see the foundation walls of St George's Chapel and St Michael's Chapel, as well as of the house of the canon Stanisław Borek.

Restaurant ships moored along the banks of the Vistula set against the imposing backdrop of the Wawel in the evening light

Zamek Królewski (Royal Castle)

A mighty Gothic fortress developed from the first royal residence (Zamek Królewski), some of the substructure of which has been maintained. It was, with the exception of the foundation walls, torn down after a fire in 1499 to make room for a new castle. Italian architects, including Francesco Fiorentino and Bartolomeo Berrecci, played

Southern Old Town & Wawel

a part in creating one of the most spectacular Renaissance structures north of the Alps. The heart of the edifice is the arcaded inner courtyard. It is now home to the **State Art Collections**.

The main exhibition encompasses the royal chambers, which are furnished with period furniture and artworks.

She has found temporary "exile" in the Royal Castle: Leonardo da Vinci's *Lady with the Ermine*

The tour of the castle starts in the former residential and work areas on the ground floor and leads to the reception rooms in the east and north wings on the second floor in which envoys used to be received, meetings held and festivities took place. The Flemish tapestries from Arras adorning the walls in several rooms are real treasures. In the 16th century, King Zygmunt II August (Sigismund II Augustus) purchased in total 360 of these large *arrazi* woven with silk, gold and silver thread that, among other things, depict biblical scenes and landscapes. After Poland's defeat in the war against tsarist Russia, the valuable Gobelins were looted and carried off to St Petersburg. Only 136 of them were returned in 1921, others were destroyed or were never found. During the German occupation, the then chief conservator Adolf Szyszko-Bohusz managed to save the valuable collection. After an extensive odyssey it was returned to Poland in 1961.

INSIDER INFO

Insider Tip

- You can visit **Wawel Hill** free of charge every day from 6am till dusk. The cathedral is also accessible during opening times.
- For the royal tombs, the Sigismund Bell and the **Cathedral Museum** you need a ticket (12 złoty). The museum containing the cathedral's art treasures and objects from the coronation ceremony is closed on Sundays.
- There is no cumulative ticket for all the sights at the **castle, just single tickets** (10 to 25 złoty) for the individual **exhibitions**.

Insider Tip

- In order to avoid overcrowding, there is a limit to the number of visitors allowed to enter the castle at any one time; tickets are for a specific admission time. Most of the exhibitions at the castles are open from Tue–Fri 9:30am–5pm, Sat, Sun from 10am (until 4pm in winter). It is worth reserving in advance.
- It is only possible to visit the **Royal Private Apartments** as part of a guided tour (included in the ticket price); this stipulation does not apply for any of the other exhibitions (admission free Mon 9am–1pm in summer, Sun 10am–4pm in winter).

A second tour takes you through the royal private chambers on the first floor, in which in addition to period furniture, Meissen porcelain and works by Italian Renaissance artists, you can also admire some of the valuable tapestries. The crown jewels and armoury in the north-eastern section of the ground floor offer an alternative route. The most valuable exhibit here is the 13th-century *Szczerbiec* (coronation sword). Objects lost during earlier conversions and then rediscovered during the archaeological work can be viewed in an exhibition entitled "The Lost Wawel" in the cellar of the former castle kitchen. A lapidarium exhibits finds from the castle and cathedral dating from various periods, a multimedia room provides simulations of the Roman buildings that once stood on Wawel Hill. Also on view are the remains of the pre-Romanesque rotunda dedicated to Saints Felix and Adauctus, which dates back to around the 10th/11th century.

In temporary "exile" in Wawel Castle is the *Lady with the Ermine* (1489/90). **Leonardo da Vinci's** masterpiece belongs to the collection at the Krakow Czartoryski Museum (►67) and has been moved to Wawel while the museum is being renovated. It is on show in an apartment once resided in by the Italian-born Queen **Bona Sforza**.

Insider Tip

Crowned with a golden dome, Sigimund's Chapel provides the mausoleum for the two last kings of the Jagiellon dynasty

Katedra Wawelska (Wawel Cathedral)

The majority of Poland's monarchs were crowned in the Royal Archcathedral Basilica of Saints Stanislaus and Wenceslaus, and many of them are buried there as well. Also more simply known as Katedra Wawelska, the cathedral in which **Karol Wojtyła** was Archbishop before being elected Pope, it is the most important church in Poland. The oldest sections date back to 1090, the majority of this tripled-naved Gothic building with its three

towers was built using brick and white limestone in the 14th century. Over the next century, a total of 19 chapels were added, the architectural styles ranging from Gothic to Renaissance and Baroque. The furnishings inside today are mainly from the Baroque period, but valuable objects from earlier periods have been preserved. Leading artists, such as Veit Stoß, Santi Gucci and Giovanni Battista Trevano, created works for Wawel Cathedral.

The mighty doors of the main entrance, which bear the royal monogram of King **Kazimierz III Wielki (Casimir III the Great)**, lead the way into the interior of the church.

Centrally placed between the main nave and the presbytery is the sarcophagus of St Stanisław, which is the work of Giovanni Trevano. Standing under a gilt-plated dome, supported by four angels is the silver sarcophagus bearing the relics of the martyr killed in 1079. Located in the main nave and the aisles are the sarcophagi and sculptures of seven Polish kings, including Kazimierz Wielki (Casimir III the Great) and Władysław II Jagiełło.

Heralded as one of the masterpieces of Renaissance architecture is the **Sigismund Chapel**, with its golden dome, which was finished in 1533. It contains the tombs of the last two kings of the Jagiellon dynasty, Zygmunt I Stary and Zygmunt II August. The tomb designed by the Nuremberg sculptor Veit Stoß for King Kazimierz (Casimir) IV in 1492 with a marble sculpture of the king is in the **Chapel of the Holy Cross**.

Steps lead from the chapel of the Czartoryski down to the **crypt** with it numerous burial chambers. Apart from numerous kings and queens, other prominent Polish figures, such as national hero Tadeusz Kościuszko and

Nobody is afraid of the fire-breathing dragon any more…

INSIDER INFO

Look out for the fossilized bones of a mammoth, a whale and a woolly rhino at the entrance to the cathedral. It is said that the church will remain in existence as long as the bones hang in their place.

The Wawel bell-ringers only sound the Sigismund Bell on public holidays

authoritarian "First Marshal of Poland" Józef Piłsudski who played an important role between the World Wars. After heated discussions, President Lech Kaczyński was also interred there with his wife Maria in 2010 after dying in a plane crash in Smolensk. An individual entrance to the chapel of the Lipski family provides access to the crypt of the national poet and the sarcophagi of Adam Mickiewicz and Juliusz Słowacki.

One of Poland's national symbols is the **Sigismund Bell**, which hangs in the tower of the same name and can be reached from the sacristy. It was cast in 1520 by Hans Behem from Nuremberg; it weighs around 12 tons and is about 2.5m (8.2ft) across. It is only rung on public holidays and to celebrate special events.

TAKING A BREAK

The traditional Krakow chocolatier **Wawel** (➤ 74) operates a branch on its namesake. Enjoy a sweet break in the **Słódki Wawel**, in summer on the beautiful terrace. For those with a healthy appetite, try the **Trattoria Wawel** (daily 9am–6pm).

✚ 196 B4/5

Visitor Centre of the State Museums
☎ 124 221 697; www.wawel.krakow.pl ◷ April, Sep daily 9am–7pm, May–Aug 9am–8pm; Oct, Dec–March 9am–6pm; Nov 9am–5pm

Information Centre of Wawel Cathedral
☎ 124 299 516; www.katedra-wawelska.pl ◷ April–Oct Mon–Sat 9am–5pm, Sun 12:30pm–5pm; Nov–March Mon–Sat 9am–4pm, Sun 12:30pm–4pm

⚅ SMOCZA JAMA (THE DRAGON'S DEN)
According to legend, a dragon living in the cave under Wawel Hill presented a constant threat to the citizens of Krakow. King Krak promised his beautiful daughter's hand to the man that liberated the town from the dragon. Many failed until a cobbler's apprentice used a clever ploy to overcome the dragon. He filled a dead sheep with sulphur; the dragon ate it and then became dreadfully thirsty. He drank and drank from the Vistula River until he burst. As a result, the cobbler's apprentice was allowed to marry the princess. During the summer months it is possible to visit the cave (admission: 3 złoty); the entrance is via a staircase in a brick tower (a former well) by the Thieves' Tower, the exit is on the Vistula Boulevard, where the metal sculpture of the fire-breathing dragon by Bronisław Chromy has stood since 1972.

Insider Tip

Shrine and National Symbol

The Royal Archcathedral Basilica of Saints Stanislaus and Wenceslaus was with a few exceptions the coronation church and burial place of Poland's kings. Since national heroes and famous Polish artists are also buried here, the cathedral is regarded as a shrine and national symbol.

❶ Sigismund Tower
The tower was built in the late 14th century as part of the city's fortifications. Poland's most famous bell hangs here: the 12-ton Sigismund Bell, which only rings on public holidays.

❷ Main Entrance
Hanging on the walls of the entrance area are the walls of a mammoth, woolly rhinoceros and a whale, put there to protect the cathedral. According to legend, as long as the bones hang there, the cathedral will continue to exist.

❸ Chapel of the Holy Cross
The last resting place of Casimir IV Jagiellon, and his wife Elisabeth von Habsburg (Elżbieta Rakuszanka), also called "Mother of Queens". Veit Stoß sculpted the tomb of Casimir IV from red marble.

❹ Shrine of St Stanislaus
In the centre of the church stands the silver sarcophagus of the Krakow bishop and patron saint of Poland, St Stanislaus of Szczepanów (around 1030–1079). The cathedral is dedicated to him.

❺ Main Altar
This is where the royal heads of Poland were crowned. At the foot of the altar is the bronze tombstone of Cardinal Fryderyk Jagiellończyk (Frederick Jagiellon, 1468–1503), a son of King Casimir IV Jagiellon. As the primate of Poland and Lithuania, he was the highest dignitary of the Roman-Catholic church in Poland and thus had the right to crown Polish kings.

❻ Sigismund Chapel
It is in this chapel with the golden roof that the two last Jagiellon kings, Sigismund I und his son Sigismund II Augustus, found their last resting place.

★ Ulica Kanonicza

Ulica Kanonicza, "Street of the Canons", curves gently from the foot of Wawel Hill towards the Main Market Square. It forms the last section of the Royal Route that kings used to take towards the castle. Once upon a time the canons of Wawel Cathedral lived in the picturesque road, and even today many of the buildings on Ulica Kanonicza belong to the church.

Medieval palaces and small Renaissance and Baroque town houses line both sides of this cobbled street which looks like something from another time. The history of quite a number of the houses here stretches back to the 14th century. Unlike Ulica Grodzka, a road that runs parallel to Ulica Kannonicza and has many shops, life here is much quieter. Passersby switch down a gear almost automatically in order to be able to soak up the atmosphere.

The Chronicler's House

During a town fire in 1455 almost all of the buildings in the street were destroyed and had to be rebuilt. Only house no. 25 at the south-west end was spared from the fire. It belonged to **Jan Długosz** (1415–1480), the most important Polish chronicler of the Middle Ages. Długosz, who had studied in Krakow, was a canon and later a trusted aide of the Polish king **Kazimierz** (**Casimir**) **IV**. Among other things, he acted as a mediator at the Second Peace of Thorn between the king and the Teutonic Knights. His Annals or Chronicles of the Famous Kingdom of Poland rank as an important source for information about the geography and history of the country. Today, the two-storey building is part of the pontifical university named after **John Paul II**, which

Art students use Ulica Kanonicza as an atelier

**Stroll through
"Street of
the Canons";
during the
1950s house
no. 19, now the
Archdiocesan
Museum, was
the home of
the later pope
John Paul II**

also uses other buildings in the road. Above the entrance is a Latin inscription that says: *Nil est in homine bona mente melius* (There is nothing better in man than a just mind).

Reminders of Karol Wojtyła

House number 19, a city palace built originally in the Renaissance style and then later modified according to the Classical style, was the home of Karol Wojtyła while he worked as a priest from 1953 to 1958. Afterwards, he lived in the neighbouring dean's house at no. 21, the traditional residence of Krakow's bishops. The building with its Sgraffiti facade and a beautiful arcade court was designed by Santi Gucci an Italian architect of the Renaissance.

Since 1994, the two connected houses form the base of the **Muzeum Archidiecezjalne (Archdiocesan Museum)**. Its rich collection used to be shared between various buildings. On show is religious art from the 13th to 20th century, including a number of valuable Gothic wooden sculptures. Also on view is the room in which Karol Wojtyła worked as a priest, complete with the original furnishings and personal possessions.

Medieval religious art is also exhibited at no. 17. The **Pałac Biskupa Erazma Ciołka** was built at the beginning of the 16th century for Erazm Ciołek (1474–1522), the king's close aide and Bishop of Płock, and displays the architectural transition from the Gothic to Renaissance style. Inside, murals from the period of the early Renaissance have been preserved. During the time of the Habsburgs, it was a police station and prison. Now a **Department of the National Museum** organises exhibitions on Polish art from the 12th to 18th centuries, as well as orthodox art from Old Poland. One of the rooms is dedicated to the art of the Nuremberg sculptor **Veit Stoß**, who carved the altarpiece in St Mary's Church (➤ 56).

Southern Old Town & Wawel

One of the most impressive buildings on the east side of the street, also formerly the property of a canon, is the city palace **Pod Motylem** which has a red-brick façade and an interior in Renaissance style. In the 16th century, it was the home of Krakow's canon and later Warmian Prince-Bishop Martin Cromer (1512 to 1589), one of the most important representatives of the Counter-Reformation in Poland. Nicolaus Copernicus, as the representative of the Warmian cathedral chapter is said to have stayed in the house during his visits to Krakow. The luxury hotel now located in the palace pays tribute to him with its

Insider Tip name (**Copernicus** ➤ 42). There is a lovely view over the Konicza street to Wawel from the roof terrace.

Not something you see every day: the pool in the vaulted cellar of Hotel Copernicus

TAKING A BREAK

Enjoy a coffee or a snack in the cosy **Bona Książka i Kawa** (➤ 110) in Ulica Kanonicza. When something a little more extravagant is desired, then try the Italian regional cuisine in the garden of the Trattoria **La Campana** just a few steps further along the street (➤ 108).

➕ 196 B/C5
🚊 Tram 1, 3, 6, 18, 8pm, 69, 73 (Pl. Wszystkich Świętych)

Muzeum Archidiecezjalne (Archdiocesan Museum)
✉ ul. Kanonicza 19–21 ☎ 124 218 963; www.muzeumkra.diecezja.pl
🕐 Tue–Fri 10am–4pm, Sat, Sun 10am–3pm ✋ 5 złoty

Pałac Biskupa Erazma Ciołka
✉ ul. Kanonicza 17 ☎ 124 335 920; http://mnk.pl
🕐 Tue–Sat 10am–6pm, Sun 10am–4pm ✋ 9 złoty

INSIDER INFO

Insider Tip

- There is a wonderful atmosphere in Ulica Kanonicza at dusk when the fading light of day blends with the light of the street lamps.
- In the vaulted cellar of no. 18, the **Centrum Jana Pawła II (John Paul II Centre)** has a beautiful photo exhibition dedicated to the time of Karol Wojtyła in Krakow (daily 9am–4pm; admission free).

★8 Collegium Maius

The Uniwersytet Jagielloński (Jagiellonian University), founded in 1364 is Poland's oldest seat of learning and Collegium Maius the oldest university building. The Collegium continues to be used for festive events and is home to the university museum.

King **Kazimierz III Wielki (Casimir III the Great)** founded Central Europe's second university in 1364 in Krakow, although teaching ground to a halt after his death in 1370. It did not really take off again until 1400 when King **Władysław II Jagiełło** promoted Collegium Maius to a fully-fledged university. Over the following centuries it attracted scientists and students from many parts of Europe. Nicolaus Copernicus attended the lectures in astronomy and mathematics. Now almost 50,000 young people study at the 15 faculties of the university that ranks as one of the largest and most renowned in Poland.

University visitors in the arcaded courtyard of the Collegium Maius

Southern Old Town & Wawel

Foundation of Queen Jadwiga

For some years, the so-called third campus has been growing in the south of Krakow offering modern teaching and research facilities. Yet the heart of the university beats in the southern section of the Old Town where, with the Collegium Maius, the oldest university complex is located. Its building was made possible by a foundation provided by **Jadwiga**, the wife of King Władysław II Jagieło. By the end of the 15th century a monastic-like complex had developed. In late-Gothic style, and with a square inner courtyard, the basic shape of the university has changed very little over the years.

The courtyard is surrounded by arcades with crystalline vaulting. The square is broken by the "Professors' staircase" leading up to the first floor. Located on the ground floor of the building were the lecture rooms. On the upper floor was the **Stuba Communis**, in which the professors ate their meals, the **treasury** and the **library** as well as the lecture hall of the theological faculty later used as an assembly room. Also located on the second floor were the residences of the professors.

University Museum

Since 1964, the historic rooms have provided a fitting setting for the museum of the renowned university. The library has a ribbed ceiling decorated with the portraits of scientists and graduates of the university as well as replicas of instruments once used by **Nicolaus Copernicus**. This splendid room now provides the venue for the meetings of the Academic Senate. In the heavy oak surroundings of the **Stuba Communis**, there is a valuable 14th-century statue of King **Kazimierz III Wielki** that immediately catches the eye. Kept in the treasury are not only the insignia of earlier rectors – sceptre, gold chains and rings – but also prestigious awards made to people connected with the university, including the Oscar presented to film director **Andrzej Wajda** and the Nobel Prize medal awarded to the poet **Wisława Szymborska**. Doctoral and postdoctoral graduates still receive their titles in the medieval assembly hall full of paintings.

The tour through the museum leads to the professor's rooms, a room in honour of **Nicolaus Copernicus** as well as to a chapel dedicated to **St John Cantius** (➤ 96). Paintings by Jan Matejko and Eugène Delacroix decorate the Green Salon as well as memorabilia of Frédéric Chopin, including a piano on which he played on a visit to Scotland in 1847.

Whilst the piano is only a (silent) exhibit, visitors can listen to the musical clock in the courtyard every two hours

> **COLLEGIUM NOVUM**
>
> The neo-Gothic **Collegium Novum** (photo ➤ 14) was set up as the headquarters of the university at the end of the 19th century in Ulica Gołębia (no. 24). On 6 November 1939, the Nazis arrested 183 professors and research assistants in the building as part of their "Special Krakow Campaign" and dragged them off to prison and concentration camps. Some of them were murdered or died as a result of the imprisonment. The campaign was directed against the Polish intelligentsia.

A blue sky with fluffy white clouds curves over the former university library

between 9am and 5pm. The **glockenspiel** is followed by the melody of the well-known student song "Gaudeamus igitur" (So let us rejoice), and the clock figures are set in motion. They depict well-known figures connected with the university, including King Władysław II Jagiełło and his wife Jadwiga. The clock is actually already the fourth in the history of the Collegium. The first dates back to 1465 whilst the youngest started ticking in 2000.

TAKING A BREAK

A fitting way to finish a visit to the Collegium Maius is in the vaulted cellars under the oldest section of the building. There in the **Kawiarnia U Pęcharza** you can enjoy your coffee and cake in medieval surroundings (Mon–Fri 8am–5pm, Sat 9am–5pm, Sun 10am–5pm).

✚ 195 D3 ✉ Jagiellońska 15
☎ 126 631 307; www.maius.uj.edu.pl
🕐 Mon, Wed, Fri 10am–2:20pm, Tue, Thu 10am–5:20pm
(until 3:20/2:20pm in winter), Sat 10am–2:40pm
🚋 Tram 2, 8, 14, 18, 24, 69, 73 (Teatr Bagatela)
💷 12 złoty

INSIDER INFO

- The **inner courtyard** of the Collegium Maius is open to visitors during the day free of charge; the glockenspiel is at 9am, 11am, 1pm, 3pm and 5pm.
- It is only possible to visit the exhibition at the **museum** as part of a guided tour; tours start every 20 min. and last about 30 min. (it is necessary to reserve in advance).

㉒ Kościół Akademicki św. Anny
(Collegiate Church of St Anne)

The beginning of the new university year is celebrated with a holy mass in the Collegiate Church of St Anne, one of Poland's most beautiful Baroque churches.

The Dutch architect Tilman van Gameren, who is responsible for many of the Baroque edifices in Poland, designed the new church for the Jagiellonian University, and it was built from 1689 to 1703 in the university district not far from Collegium Maius (▶93). Its Gothic predecessor donated by the Polish king Władysław II Jagiełło had proved to be too small.

The three-nave church was modelled on Sant' Andrea della Valle in Rome, using the floor plan of a cross. Both towers are adorned with late-Baroque spires. A painting by Jerzy Siemiginowski-Eleuter, the court painter of the Polish King Jan (John) III Sobieski adorns the main altar. It depicts St Anne, the church's namesake with the Virgin Mary and Jesus. Italian sculptor Baldassare Fontana created the lavish Baroque interior with its fine stucco decoration. The brothers Carlo and Innocenti Monti, also from Italy, contributed to the murals as did the Swedish painter Karl Dankwart. The dome pendentives depict the four cardinal virtues: wisdom, justice, courage and temperance.

In Memory of St John Cantius
The church also venerates Jan Kanty (John of Kanty), **St John Cantius** (1390–1437), the patron saint of

The Collegiate Church of St Anne has an elaborate Baroque interior

Heaven bound: the façade of the Collegiate Church of St Anne

Jagiellonian University. As a priest and university professor, he was famous for his compassion and is very respected in Krakow. His tomb in the right section of the transept is borne by four figures, which symbolise the theological, legal, medical and philosophical faculty of the university. Every year in October, there is a large procession in his honour.

The church crypt has become the last resting place for many university professors. Portraits of well-known university professors adorn the interior of the church. There is a sculpture of a famous student in the left aisle; it is of the astronomer Nicolaus Copernicus. The bust was donated in 1823, when his work was still on the Catholic church's List of Prohibited Works.

TAKING A BREAK

Many students also spend their lunch break in the green courtyard of the **Chimera** restaurant (św. Anny 3; ► 107). At the self-service counter, you will find fresh salads, juices and delicious vegetable dishes at reasonable prices.

Insider Tip

✚ 194 C3 ✉ św. Anny 11
☎ 124 225 318; www.kolegiata-anna.pl
🕐 Open daily to visitors (when mass is not taking place)
🚊 Tram 2, 8, 14, 18, 24, 69, 73 (Teatr Bagatela)

㉓ Kościół Franciszkanów
(Church of St Francis of Assisi)

The stained glass window above the entrance to the Gothic Church of St Francis of Assisi depicts the "Creation of the World" and is regarded as one of the most important works by Art Nouveau artist Stanisław Wyspiańsk.

In the mid-13 century, Duke Boleslaw the Chaste founded this church for the Franciscan monks who had come from Prague to Krakow in 1237. Over the years, the church experienced several calamitous fires and now presents a colourful mix of different architectural styles. What has survived the centuries is the early Gothic façade of the transept with its red-brick arched moulding, which can be seen from the Ulica Franziskańska.

In 1850 a city fire caused the worst damage the church had ever suffered. Rebuilding work dragged on until 1912. During this work, the interior was redesigned in neo-Gothic style.

Besides the large window over the west entrance, **Stanisław Wyspiański** (1869–1907) created seven other stained glass windows with floral motifs and figurative compositions for the choir and the transept, which bathe the interior in an enchanting light of various colours. Even the author Alfred Döblin enthusiastically noted in the mid-1920s after visiting the church: "A dark-green floral window. And on the right the most blazing of all colours that I have ever seen, a bright yellow, a satanic russet brown, a colour more searing than a fiery red, conceived as the vibrant light of descending sun rays coupled with the slumbering cast colours."

Stanisław Wyspiański's glass artwork *Let there be Light!*

The Church of St Francis of Assisi was repainted in vibrant colours at the beginning of the 20th century

Colourful Wall Paintings

The wall paintings in the choir and transept are also by Wyspiański, and they too display his favourite floral motifs: pansies and nasturtium. The other sections were painted by the Polish artist **Tadeusz Popiel** in 1904/15 whose work includes four scenes from the life of St Francis. The wall paintings dedicated to Christ's Passion are well worth seeing as well. Between 1933 and 1946 Józef Mehoffer created a cycle of 14 paintings depicting the stations of the Cross.

Adjoining the church building is the **Franciscan monastery**, which received its present architectural form in the 15th century. A gallery of Krakow bishops decorates the walls of the cloisters. It includes frescoes with 15th-century portraits but also portraits painted on canvas, most of which were done after the death of the respective bishop. One of the paintings shows the late Pope John Paul II who was particularly fond of this Franciscan church.

TAKING A BREAK

Do you want something sweet? At **Karmello** (➤ 111) on Plac Wszystkich Świętych/corner Ulica Grodzka enjoy some tasty cake, sweets or truffles with your cup of tea or coffee.

✚ 195 D2 ✉ ul. Franciszkańska 2
☎ 124 225 376; http://franciszkanska.pl
🕐 Mon–Sat 10am–4pm, Sun 1:15pm–4pm
🚊 Tram 1, 3, 6, 18, 20, 69, 73 (Pl. Wszystkich Świętych)

㉔ Muzeum Archeologiczne
(Archaeological Museum)

The Archaeological Museum is housed in a building with a very chequered history. Once a monastery, the Habsburgs turned it into a prison that was subsequently used by various political regimes until 1956.

In the 17th century, a monastery was set up not far from Wawel Hill for Discalced Carmelite nuns. The nuns lived behind thick walls in tiny cells with small windows. After the Polish Secession, Krakow was turned over to the Habsburgs and the nuns were forced to leave the building. It took little effort to then transform the building into a prison, which was used mainly for political opponents. The Piłsudski regime continued this ignoble tradition from 1926. During the German occupation political prisoners were also incarcerated and murdered there.

After the end of World War II, the opponents of Stalin's system caught up with one another in the cells. It was not until 1956 that the prison was closed and the building was handed over to the Archaeological Museum.

Extensive Collection
Poland's oldest archaeological museum, founded back in 1850, moved into its new premises in 1965 and exhibits, among other things, objects from Poland, Ancient Egypt

The former cloister garden at the museum has been transformed into a sculpture park

Slavic sun god Svetovid

and Eastern Europe. The collection comprises around half a million exhibits.

Its most important piece is an around 2.5m (8.2ft) tall limestone column that was found on the river bed of the Zbruch River in what is now Ukraine in 1848. Researchers see in it the only preserved depiction of the Slavic deity **Svetovid**. This slim rectangular totem-like column dates back to the 9th or 10th century. Beneath a shared head covering, two male and two female faces each look out in separate directions. Svetovid was regarded as a god of the sun, war, fire and fertility. However, some scientists believe the statue could originally be from other cultural circles and only later came into the possession of the Slavs.

The statue is part of the permanent exhibition on the Małopolska region covering the prehistoric period to the early Middle Ages, in which on the basis of finds and replicas earlier times are brought to life. In the second permanent exhibition about "Deities in Ancient Egypt", the exhibits include four sarcophagi discovered by the first Polish Egyptologist, Tadeusz Smoleński, in El-Gamhud at the beginning of the 20th century.

TAKING A BREAK

Enjoy some refreshment at the **Krak-Rest** milk bar in Ulica Grodzka 43. There you can try some traditional and very reasonably priced dishes such as *bigos* and *pierogi* (tel: 124 220 874; www.bar-mleczny.com.pl; daily 9am–8pm).

➕ 195 D2 ✉ Senacka 3 (entrance ul. Poselskiej 3)
☎ 124 227 100; www.ma.krakow.pl
🕐 Mon, Wed, Thu, Fri 9am–3pm, Tue 9am–6pm, Sun 11am–4pm;
July, Aug Mon–Fri 10am–5pm, Sun 10am–3pm
🚋 Tram 6, 8, 18, 70, 73 (Wawel)
💵 9 złoty (free on Sun)

INSIDER INFO

Don't miss the museum's former **cloister garden** (admission: 1 złoty), which is one of the largest and most beautiful gardens in the city centre. During the establishment of the museum, it was restored in Renaissance style and is the perfect setting for sculptures by Krakow artists. It occasionally provides the venue for concerts as well.

Insider Tip

At Your Leisure

25 Bunkier Sztuki

It looks a little out of place between all the historical buildings. Only small, narrow window slits penetrate the dark concrete facade of the "**Art Bunker**", which was opened in 1965 and remains to this day one of the most important exhibition centres for contemporary art in Poland. Until the political turnaround in 1989, it remained the only modern building in the Old Town. Six rooms are available for exhibitions, including a beautiful vaulted cellar, which was once a dance café. The art centre assigns great importance to direct exchange between the artists and gallery visitors; for some years a project has been running that helps children and young adults to appreciate contemporary art.

✚ 195 D4
✉ Pl. Szczepański 3a
☎ 124 221 052; www.bunkier.art.pl
⊙ Tue–Sun 11am–7pm
🚋 Tram 2, 8, 14, 18, 24, 69, 73 (Teatr Bagatela)
💵 12 złoty

26 🏫 Ogród Biblioteki Jagiellońskiej (University Library Garden)

In the 15th century there was a garden next to the Collegium Maius in which fruit and vegetables were grown for the professors. It is still called the **"Professors' Garden"** to this day. At the end of the 19th century it was newly planned by the university's Botanic Department, but just a few years later sections of the garden had to make way for the new Collegium Witkowski. The last redesign took place in 2010 and since then the little garden has become an oasis of calm. At five info stations, visitors can read about the development of the Jagiellonian University. Each period is represented by a model of a scientific experiment that is comprehensible to young and old alike. For instance, the time of the Enlightenment is symbolised by Otto von Guerickes's Magdeburg hemispheres.

✚ 194 C3
⊙ 22. April–Oct daily 10am–4pm

Statues of former scholars and scientific models decorate the "Professors' Garden"

(Entrance: ul. Jagiellońskiej, between
Collegium Maius and Collegium Witkowski)
🚋 Tram 2, 8, 14, 18, 24, 69, 73 (Teatr
Bagatela) 🖐 Free

27 Muzeum Narodowe (National Museum)

Few people in English-speaking
countries know much about the
great Polish painters and sculptors.
That is a mistake as a tour of the
National Museum, founded in
1879, will show you. The museum's
main building was started in 1934
but not finished until 1990.

A large room in the extensive
permanent exhibition about Polish
art in the 20th century is dedicated
to the "**Young Poland**" movement
that took place before World War I
and marked a departure from
earlier ideas. Artists moved away
from History Painting, refocused on
Romanticism, and took inspiration
from Surrealism and Art Nouveau.
The group included artists like Julian
Fałat, Jacek Malczewski, Józef
Mehoffer and Stanisław Wyspiański.

INSIDER INFO

If when you visit the National
Museum you wish to see both `Insider Tip`
the extensive arts and crafts collection
as well as the exhibition of weapons
and uniforms, then you should plan at
least half a day. You can fortify yourself in-between rounds at the museum café on the ground floor.

In labyrinth-like passageways,
you pass through the various decades, meeting remarkable artists
such as the Expressionist painter
and author Stanisław Ignacy
Witkacy, the Constructivist sculptor
Katarzyna Kobro and Edward
Dwurnik, who depicts the political
reality of the 1970s in his large-
scale paintings, and end up in an
original installation with mirrors
and columns by Leon Tarasewicz
completed in 2005.

➕ 194 A3 ✉ al. 3 Maja 1
☎ 124 335 500; www.mnk.pl
🕐 Tue–Sat 10am–6pm, Sun 10am–4pm
🚋 Tram 20, 24, Bus 109, 124, 134, 144, 152,
164, 169, 173, 179, 194 (Cracovia)
🖐 permanent exhibitions 11 złoty
(18 złoty including temporary exhibitions)

28 29 Pracownia i Muzeum Witrażu (Workshop and Museum for Stained Glass)

Krakow is the city of stained glass.
Hundreds of artistic stained glass
windows adorn churches and
private houses. The most well-
known examples are works by
Stanisław Wyspiański, which can
be found for example in the Church
of St Francis of Assisi (► 98).
Numerous windows come from this
workshop founded in 1902, located
on Aleja Krasińskiego, and it is also
where Józef Mehoffer produced
his work. Today, the workshop is a `Insider Tip`
vibrant museum, in which visitors
can learn how stained glass is
made using traditional techniques.

In the museum shop there are
pretty Art Nouveau motifs available
in stained glass as well as views of
the Wawel, or you can take part in
a workshop (minimum two people)
and make your own colourful
stained glass souvenir.

➕ 194 A2 ✉ al. Krasińskiego 23
☎ 512 937 979; www.stainedglass.pl
🕐 Tue–Sat noon–6pm; Guided tours on
the hour in English
🚋 Tram 20, 24, Bus 109, 124, 134, 144, 152,
164, 169, 173, 179, 194 (Cracovia)
🖐 32 złoty

Southern Old Town & Wawel

29 Pałac Biskupi (Bishop's Palace)

Krakow's Archbishop, **Karol Wojtyła** lived in the Bishop's Palace in Ulica Franziskańska from 1963 until he was appointed pope in 1978. He also stayed there when he visited Krakow as Pope John Paul II and spoke from the window to the Christians congregated outside. The bishop's see was moved here from Wawel Hill back in the 14th century. In the following centuries the palace was extended and renovated on many occasions. It assumed its present form, in the style of a Romantic residence, at the beginning of the 19th century. A memorial by Jole Sensi Croci in the courtyard commemorates the Polish pope.

✚ 195 D2 ✉ ul. Franziskańska 3 🚋 Tram 1, 3, 6, 18, 20, 69, 73 (Pl. Wszystkich Świętych)

30 Pawilon Wyspiańskiego (Wyspiański Pavilion)

This slim, elongated new building is a real eye-catcher. Opened in 2007, the Wyspiański Pavilion's clear lines make it stand out from the historical buildings around it, while at the same time the red brick creates a link with the Gothic churches. Special bricks were made that are mounted vertically on steel rods and act as moving blinds. Inserted into the facade are three large-format glass windows, created by the Krakow artist **Stanisław Wyspiański** at the beginning of the 20th century. They depict St Stanisław, Henry II the Pious and King Kazimierz Wielki (Casimir III the Great) and were originally intended for a conversion of Wawel Cathedral.

The pavilion is the headquarters of the city's festival office and a **tourist information centre**; exhibitions take place here from time to time.

✚ 195 E2 ✉ Pl. Wszystkich Świętych 2 🕐 Daily 9am–7pm (summer), 9am–5pm (winter) 🚋 Tram 1, 3, 6, 18, 20, 69, 73 (Pl. Wszystkich Świętych)

The "Pope's Window" above the entrance of the Bishop's Palace

The Wyspiański Pavilion is the only modern building in the Old Town

31 Bazylika św. Trójcy i Klasztor Ojców Dominikanów (Basilica of the Holy Trinity and Dominican Monastery)

The first Dominican monks came to Krakow in 1222, and their monastery became the order's stronghold in Poland. St Hyacinth led the expansion of the order from there. Around 100 monks still live on the large premises today, many of whom are students of theology. One of the two inner courtyards is surrounded by a beautiful cloister; particularly worth seeing is the chapter house and the

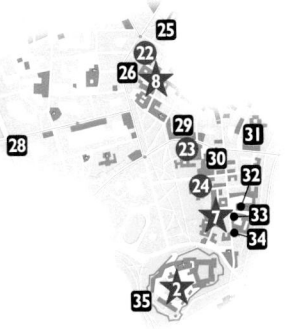

refectory, both of which date back to the 13th century. Adjoining the monastery is the Gothic Basilica of the Holy Trinity. After the great fire of 1850, the interior was rebuilt in neo-Gothic style. Funded by respected Krakow families in the 16th and 17th centuries, the richly decorated side chapels have survived the ages well. Relics of St Hyacinth are preserved in the chapel bearing his name.

🕂 195 E2/3 ✉ Stolarska 12
☎ 124 231 613; www.krakow.dominikanie.pl
✉ Tram 1, 3, 6, 18, 20, 69, 73
(Pl. Wszystkich Świętych)

32 Kościół św. św. Piotra i Pawła (Church of Saints Peter and Paul)

King Zygmunt III Wasa (Sigismund III Vasa) funded the church for the Jesuit order. Based on the Roman church Il Gesù, it was finished in 1619 and ranks as the first Baroque building in Krakow. A row of sculptures depicting the 12 apostles separates the church forecourt from Ulica Grodzka, and saints from the Jesuit order adorn the magnificent facade. In the choir room are scenes from the life of Saints Peter and Paul, while the imposing dome is decorated with gilded figures of the four Evangelists.

In the extensively branched **crypt** a **pantheon** is planned for famous artists and scientists. Already entombed there since his death in 2013 is the playwright Sławomir Mrożek.

🕂 195 E1 ✉ Grodzka 52
☎ 124 226 573; www.panteonnarodowy.org
🕐 Tue–Sat 9am–5pm, Sun 1:30pm–5:30pm (summer); Tue–Sat 11am–3pm, Sun 1:30pm–5:30pm (winter)
✉ Tram 1, 3, 6, 18, 20, 69, 73
(Pl. Wszystkich Świętych)

33 Kościół św. Andrzeja (St Andrew's Church)

Built as a fortified church at the end of the 11th century, it survived the attack of the Mongols in the mid 13th century. The Romanesque church is one of the oldest houses of worship in Krakow. The church is distinguished by its thick walls, the high position of the narrow windows and the two towers with Baroque spires. In the 18th century, the interior was also renovated in the Baroque style.

The stucco decoration is the work of the Italian sculptor Baldassare Fontana, the murals ascribed to Karl Dankwart, the court painter of King Jan III Sobieski. Also of interest is the pulpit, which is in the shape of a boat.

🕂 195 E1 ✉ Grodzka 54
☎ 124 221 612; www.klaryski.pl
🕐 Daily 8am–6pm (apart from during services)
✉ Tram 1, 3, 6, 18, 20, 69, 73
(Pl. Wszystkich Świętych)

Southern Old Town & Wawel

34 Kościół św. Marcina (St Martin's Church)

The church completed in 1640 is the work of Italian architect Giovanni Trevano. The early Baroque building was built on the foundations of an earlier Romanesque church for the order of Discalced Carmelite nuns. This community broke up in 1787, and it took almost 30 years before the Senate handed the church over to the Protestant community in 1816. The small church is still being used by the Evangelical Church of the Augsburg Confession, which has about 500 members in Krakow. In the rather austere interior, the eye-catcher is the 1882 altarpiece of *Christ Silencing a Storm* by the Polish-Ukrainian artist Henryk Siemiradzki.

🕀 195 E1 ✉ Grodkzka 58
☎ 124 222 583; http://krakow.luteranie.pl
🕐 Services: Sun, hol. 10am and noon
🚊 Tram 1, 3, 6, 18, 20, 69, 73
(Pl. Wszystkich Świętych)

35 Bulwar Wiślane (Vistula Boulevard)

At the foot of the Wawel Hill, the northern section of the Vistula Boulevard is called **Bulwar Czerwieński**. Pedestrians and cyclists are out and about here

A pleasant stroll along the Vistula at the foot of the Wawel

in summer, enjoying the sun from the park, the harbour wall or the deck of the restaurant boat "Batory" (➤ 107).

Guarding the exit of the 🔝 **Dragon's Den** (➤ 87) is a seven-headed dragon made of steel, which blows fire every five minutes to the delight of young and older visitors alike. Stars in the asphalt commemorate musicians like Céline Dion and Michael Jackson as well as stars in the film world ranging from Volker Schlöndorf to Andrzej Wajda.

It gets crowded on Bulwar Czerwieński each year on 23 June when the town celebrates the ancient Slavonic **Wianki Festival**. Young women float braided wreaths made of flowers and herbs bearing a burning candle on the Vistula. If a girl's wreath is fished out by a young man, it tells her that she will marry soon. This ritual takes place at the same time as the Fete de la musique, when music of all types is performed on the banks of the Vistula as well as many other stages in the town.

🕀 196 A5–B3 🚊 Tram 6, 8, 18, 70, 73 (Wawel)

Where to…
Eat and Drink

Prices
A main course (without drinks)
£ under 45 złoty   **££** 45–90 złoty   **£££** over 90 złoty

RESTAURANTS

Amarylis ££
The minimalistically appointed restaurant in the vaulted cellar of Queen, a boutique hotel, offers seasonal dishes for which its team of chefs seek inspiration from all over the world. Specialities include fish and meat dishes meticulously prepared according to the sous-vide method. If you have time, try the seven-course meal served in the evening with corresponding wines.
✚ 197 D4
✉ Józefa Dietla 60
☎ 124 333 306; www.queenhotel.pl
🕐 Mon–Wed 1pm–10pm, Thu–Sun 1pm–11pm

Aqua e vino ££
For more than ten years, the two Italian owners have been captivating guests in their vaulted cellar restaurant with meals and wines from their home in Veneto. There is a select choice of dishes, and from Thu to Sun fish and fruits de mer dishes supplement the standard menu.
✚ 195 D3
✉ Wiślna 5/10
☎ 124 212 567; www.aquaevino.pl
🕐 Daily noon–11pm

Bar Grodzki £
Locals also enjoy the hearty Polish fare served under the vaulted ceilings of the Grodzki bar.
✚ 195 E2
✉ ul Grodzka 47
☎ 124 226 807; www.grodzkibar.zaprasza.net
🕐 Mon–Sat 9am–7pm, Sun 10am–7pm

Boscaiola £
In Boscaiola, you can either sit looking out on the street on the ground floor or surrounded by wine bottles in the medieval cellar vault. Pasta and pizza dominate the choice on the menu, both of a good quality and reasonable price. There is a good choice of Italian wines to accompany them, but wines from Poland and other countries are also available.
✚ 195 D4 ✉ Szewska 10
☎ 124 264 127; www.boscaiola.eu
🕐 Daily 11am–11pm

C.C. Stefan Batory £
The 19th-century Dutch barge on the banks of the Vistula is an ideal venue for mild summer evenings. From the deck you can look out at the illuminated Wawel, people strolling along the lively promenade and the gondolas gliding on the river. When the weather is bad an elegant dining room awaits you below deck. You can choose between Polish and Italian dishes.

Insider Tip

✚ 196 A4 ✉ Bulwar Czerwiński
☎ 664 929 016; www.stefanbatory.com
🕐 Mon–Thu 11am–10pm, Fri–Sun 11am–11pm

Chimera £–££
The enchanting courtyard, which is covered, full of green plants and offers cosy nooks, is very popular with the students of the surrounding institutes. At the salad bar you will find that you are also able to serve yourself to cooked dishes with vegetables and meat. You can select six small delicacies for the large plate; at 17 złoty, the

price is unbeatable. It is slightly more expensive in the cellar restaurant of the same name, which mainly serves traditional Polish dishes.

➕ 195 D3
✉ św. Anny 3
☎ 122 921 212; www.chimera.com.pl
🕐 Daily 9am–10pm (salad bar), noon–11pm (Restaurant)

Copernicus £££

In the medieval atmosphere of the small hotel restaurant, the young head chef presents food that deserves a star or two. To accompany his menu that changes every month and offers five, seven or twelve courses, he is happy to recommend the corresponding wines. Filipkiewicz reinterprets traditional Polish recipes taking his inspiration from other parts of the world. There is also a comparatively inexpensive lunch menu for testing purposes.

➕ 195 E1
✉ Kanonicza 16
☎ 124 243 421; www.copernicus.hotel.com.pl
🕐 Daily noon–11pm

Corleone ££

Awaiting you at the door of this restaurant which takes its name from a Sicilian town are two elderly gentlemen. They are actually mannequins, but still manage to exude Italian flair, an impression which is compounded by the interior with its pastel colours and slight patina and in the secluded garden. It is an ideal place to go in the evening and enjoy grilled vegetables, fresh pasta and *ossobuco*.

➕ 195 E2
✉ Poselka 19
☎ 124 295 126; www.corleone.krakow.pl
🕐 Daily noon–midnight

Corse ££

This restaurant with Corsican cuisine must be fairly unique in Poland. The owner discovered his love for this Mediterranean island and its cuisine very early on. On the menu you will find specialities such as chestnut soup *bajana* and naturally a rich selection of fresh fish and seafood. To accompany the food is beer and wine from Corsica in maritime-elegant surrounding.

➕ 195 E2
✉ Poselka 24
☎ 124 216 273; www.corserestaurant.pl
🕐 Daily 1pm–11pm

La Campana ££

Traditional country cuisine from Italy is served in the medieval cellar rooms and beautiful garden of the inner courtyard. From *carpaccio* or *bresaola* as a starter to various pasta dishes, fish and meat as the main course and *tiramisu* and *panna cotta* as a dessert, everything shows experience and the presentation is very appealing; to top it off, the service is both friendly and discreet.

➕ 195 E1
✉ Kanonicza 7
☎ 124 302 232; www.lacampana.pl
🕐 Daily noon–11pm

Marmolada ££

The team in the kitchen combines the best of traditional Polish cuisine with the aromas and herbs of the south. A particular speciality are the dishes from the large stone oven, for example goose breast marinated with oranges, red wine and cloves, and served in a red wine sauce with Amarone cherries. On Fridays and Saturdays the meal is accompanied by classical or film music played live.

➕ 195 E2
✉ Grodzka 5
☎ 124 220 233; www.marmoladarestauracja.pl
🕐 Daily noon–11pm

Miód Malina ££

Honey (*miód*) and raspberry (*malina*) symbolise the wish for good, genuine flavour. The menu that changes to reflect the seasons offers traditional Polish dishes as well as Italian classics. Great importance is assigned to using fresh regional products.

➕ 195 E2
✉ Grodzka 40
☎ 124 300 411; www.miodmalina.pl
🕐 Daily noon–11pm

Pod Aniołami ££

The medieval vaulted cellar on the Royal Route offers a fitting setting for a traditional meal of the kind once served to the Polish aristocracy. Some of the specialities, such as haunch of venison Old Polish style have to be ordered in advance, but the menu leaves little to desire even for spontaneous guests. In summer, you can sit in the beautiful "Under the Angels" restaurant on the patio.

➕ 195 E2
✉ Grodzka 35
☎ 124 213 999; www.podaniolami.pl
🕐 Daily 1pm–midnight

Pod Norenami ££

Located between the old university district and the new campus is this restaurant furnished in Oriental style. Cuisine chef Paweł Albrzykowski even learned Chinese to help him to understand some of the secrets of the Far Eastern cuisine and has collected inspiration for his fine vegetarian and vegan dishes from various regions of Asia. The intensive flavour of his creations even wins over carnivores.

➕ 194 C4
✉ Krupnicza 6
☎ 661 219 289; www.podnorenami.pl
🕐 Sun–Thu 10am–10pm, Fri–Sat 10am–11pm

Pod Nosem £££

Gourmets can begin their meal with the finest 5-star caviar accompanying it as they wish with either Champagne or an exclusive Polish vodka. Those who do without the caviar can still lap up the elegant surroundings and enjoy the modern, high-quality Polish-International cuisine without getting a nasty shock when the bill arrives.

➕ 195 D1
✉ Kanonicza 22
☎ 123 760 014; www.kanonicza22.com
🕐 Daily 10am–10pm

Pod Wawelem £

Large portions, specials that change every day and a very reasonably priced beer are what make Pow Wawelem so successful. The quality is reliable and has ensured that larger and smaller groups have been coming to this traditional restaurant at the foot of Wawel Hill for more than 25 years.

➕ 196 C4
✉ św. Gertrudy 26–29
☎ 124 212 336; www.podwawelem.eu
🕐 Mon–Sat noon–midnight, Sun noon–11pm

PUBS AND BARS

Ambasada Śledzia

Cushioned between the consulates and embassies of Germany, Great Britain and the USA is "Herring embassy", a popular pub with Krakow's young crowd. Besides herring snacks, there are other Polish tapas to choose from as well as beer and vodka at reasonable prices. Stolarska street actually has two Ambasadas.

➕ 195 E2
✉ Stolarska 5 and Stolarska 8/10
☎ 662 569 460
🕐 Daily 10am–6am and 8am–midnight

Enoteka Pergamin

The house on the Royal Route in which the Nuremberg woodcarver lived offers good cocktails and open wines from around the world. The selection of wines from Poland is very comprehensive. You can choose between various degustation menus in the restaurant or enjoy a ham or cheese platter in the bistro. A visit to the Cigar Room is a nice way to finish off the evening; A large choice of cigars and digestifs are on offer.

➕ 195 E2
✉ Grodzka 39
☎ 797 705 515; www.enotekapergamin.pl
🕐 Daily 11am–11pm

Pierwszy Lokal

This pub probably has the longest name in the world: its full name is "Pierwszy Lokal Na Stolarskiej Po Lewej Stronie Idąc Od Małego Rynku" – which actually only describes its location in Ulica Stolarska. You will find many students in this cosy pub, either sitting in the leather chairs or at a candlelit table drinking a beer and eating snacks.

➕ 195 E3
✉ Stolarska 6/1
☎ 124 312 441
🕐 Mon–Fri 7:30am–3am, Sat, Sun 9am–3am

Qube Vodka Bar & Café

The elegant bar in the Sheraton Hotel has a tempting selection of more than 200 different sorts of vodka from Poland and the world. It also offers a tremendous variety of cocktails. A good alternative to the bar in the atrium of the hotel is the summery lounge-bar on the roof, which has a fantastic view of the Vistula.

Insider Tip

➕ 196 west. A5
✉ Powiśle 7
☎ 126 621 674; www.sheraton.pl
🕐 Daily 8am–1am

CAFÉS

Bona Książka i Kawa

Sit back in the comfortable chairs between rows full of books and enjoy your coffee and a choice of cakes that changes every day. In the book café you can also order light meals such as salmon tartar, various vegetable tarts, panini or salads.

➕ 195 E1
✉ Kanonicza 11
☎ 124 305 222; www.bonamedia.pl
🕐 Daily 9am–7pm

Bunkier Café

In summer, the visitors sit outside directly next to the green Planty park, in cooler months, they can follow what is going on outside in the protected winter garden. Krakow students as well as many tourists sit here in front of the art bunker to sip coffee specialities and enjoy homemade cake.

➕ 195 D4 ✉ Pl. Szczepański 3 a
☎ 124 310 585; www.bunkiercafe.pl
🕐 Daily 9am–1am

Café Botanica

As the name suggests, you sit here surrounded by plants on the upper floor in a pretty Orangerie with a glass roof. Many students meet here for breakfast or in the evening for a drink. During the day, small lunch dishes, homemade cakes and tarts are available.

➕ 195 D3 ✉ Bracka 9 ☎ 530 717 438; www.
cafebotanica.pl 🕐 Mon–Wed 8:30am–11pm,
Thu–Sat 8:30am–midnight, Sun 9am–11pm

De Revolutionibus

The title of Copernicus's main work provided the name for this bookshop with a café. While the Copernicus Centre occupies itself with questions relating to philosophy, theology and mathematics, and sells the corresponding books, you can enjoy a good cup of coffee and cake baked according to old Krakow recipes.

➕ 195 D2 ✉ Bracka 14
☎ 530 769 530; www.derevolutionibus.com.pl
🕐 Mon–Fri 8:30am–9pm, Sat, Sun 9am–6pm

Nowa Prowincja

Don't be put off by the grey facade and crumbling plaster, inside is a cosy little candlelit café on two levels where you can can sit until late in the evening. Besides good homemade cakes there are fresh salads and other light meals. Try the hot chocolate, one of the best in Krakow

Insider Tip

➕ 195 D3 ✉ Bracka 3–5 ☎ 124 305 959
🕐 Mon–Wed 8am–midnight, Thu–Sat
8am–2am, Sun 9am–midnight

Where to...
Shop

In the small shops on the Ulica Grodzka, the road that connects the market square with the Vistula, you can find interesting souvenirs, ranging from culinary products to jewellery and designer fashion.

JEWELLERY AND CLOTHING

In **Boruni** gallery, Ulica Grodzka 60, you will find a large selection of amber jewellery, classic and modern in design (tel: 124 285 086; www.boruni.pl; daily 9am–8pm).

Galeria Ambra Stile specialises in jewellery made of silver, precious stones and amber (no. 45; tel: 124 211 129; www.ambrastile.krakow.pl, Mon–Sat 11am–8pm).

The rings, bracelets and necklaces of the Danish company **Pandora** are on sale at no. 38 (tel: 123 572 202, Mon–Sat 11am–7pm, Sun until 4pm).

Red Rubin Elegant jewellery from small manufacturers from various parts of the world including numerous engagement and marriage rings (no. 25; tel: 124 211 134; www.redrubin.pl; Mon–Sat 10am–8pm, Sun until 6pm).

Timeless beautiful and high quality woman's fashion made of linen, wool and silk from Polish designers is available at **Lniane Marzenie** ("linen dream") (no. 59; tel: 790 466 103; www.lnianemarzenie.pl, Mon–Fri 11am–6pm, Sat until 3pm).

Elegant shoes for men and women by the Polish company **Conhpol** are on offer at the company shop in Ulica Grodzka 30 (tel: 124 229 047; www.conhpolelite.pl; daily 9:30am–8:30pm).

FOLKLORE

The artistically crafted glass balls are exported to many countries in the world as Christmas decorations. You can find a selection in the new company shop in Ulica Grodzka 4 (tel: 124 217 760; www.calik.pl). Traditional Polish ceramic predominantly from Bunzlau is available at **Kobalt pottery & more** in Ulica Grodzka 62, not far from Wawel Hill (tel: 798 380 431; Mon–Sun 10am–8pm).

SWEET AND HEARTY

Particularly popular with kids is **Fabryka Cukierków CiuCiu**. Every day on the hour, between 11am and 6pm, you can enter the tiny sweet manufacturer in Ulica Grodzka 38 free of charge and find out how the colourful sweets are made – and naturally also buy them in small triangular bags. If requested, the company also manufactures sweets to order, for instance with names or initial (tel: 698 521 542; www.ciuciukrakow.pl; daily 10am–8pm).

Insider Tip

At the **Karmello** chocolatier you can buy fanciful chocolate creations, sweets and truffles to take away, or sit and have them served at the pretty café on Plac Wszystkich Świętych, on the corner of Ulica Grodzka (Mon 6am–10pm, Tue–Sun until 11pm; (second branch: ul. Floriańska 40; www.karmello.pl).

Krakowski Kredens stands for high-quality food, free as far as possible of additives, and produced using traditional recipes and methods. The product range includes cold meats, jams, honey, juices as well as a comprehensive selection of chocolate and is available among other places at Ulica Grodzka 7 (tel: 696 490 012; www.krakowskikredens.pl, Mon–Fri 10am–7pm, Sat 11am–7pm, Sun 11am–6pm).

Where to...
Go Out

You can experience live jazz in Krakow every evening, a quaint sailor's tavern always hosts Shanties on Thursdays, and on Fridays and Saturdays there are concerts in the Philharmonic Hall.

MUSIC

Centrum Kultury Rotunda
The student cultural centre has been an important event location for more than three decades. Many well-known Polish musicians have made their first stage appearance here. It is the venue for film and theatre festivals as well as international contests for young jazz bands. Concerts by well-known bands and newcomers take place here many times each month.
✚ 194 west A3 ✉ Oleandry 1 ☎ 122 926 516; www.rotunda.pl ⏰ Daily 11am–11pm

Filharmonia Krakowska
The history of the internationally renowned Krakow symphony orchestra stretches back to 1909. International orchestras often perform at the Philharmonic; its large auditorium sits 700 people. Star violinist Nigel Kennedy who has made Krakow his home has stood here on the stage many times. Concerts usually take place on Fridays and Saturdays. Occasionally there are 👫 matinees for children.
✚ 194 C2 ✉ Zwierzyniecka 1 ☎ 126 198 733; www.filharmonia.krakow.pl 🎟 40–50 złoty

Kościół św. św. Piotra i Pawła
On several evenings during the week the church of Saints Peter and Paul (► 105) provides the beautiful setting for concerts of classical and film music, played by Orkiestra Miasta Krakowa. Infos about the programme and tickets (60 złoty) are available on location at www.newculture.pl.

Piec'Art
In the vaulted cellar, internationally renowned jazz musicians share the stage with Polish bands. Around 50 kinds of whisky are served at the long bar on the ground floor.
✚ 195 D4 ✉ Szewska 12 ☎ 124 291 602; www.piecart.pl ⏰ Daily noon–2am

Stary Port
It may be a long way to the sea, yet a large Shanty festival still takes place in Krakow every year in February. The rest of the year seafarers and landlubbers who enjoy drinking and singing meet up in this tavern, which is furnished in a style reminiscent of an old sailboat. Thursdays is the day for sea shanties, Friday and Saturdays for Blues, Rock and jazz.
✚ 194 C3 ✉ Straszewskiego 27 ☎ 124 300 962; www.staryport.com.pl ⏰ Sun–Wed noon–1am, Thu–Sat noon–3am

NIGHTLIFE

Baccarat Music Club
On large leather sofas, the young, beautiful and rich enjoy the evening sipping on cold drinks listening to house and disco music. It is possible to choose between ten differently furnished rooms; anyone wishing to have a private get-together rents the VIP lounge.
✚ 195 E3 ✉ Stolarska 13 ☎ 124 211 541; www.baccaratclub.pl ⏰ Thu–Sat 9pm–4am

Klub 30
The name says it all. Whilst most of the clubs draw in the young crowd, Klub 30 is for the 30+ generation, although the doorman has been known to allow the odd 28-year-old in. Covering an area of more than 1,000m² (11,000ft²), this venue offers three dance floors; occasionally live concerts take place here.
✚ 194 B1 ✉ Kościuszki 3 ☎ 725 700 215; www.klub30.pl ⏰ Fri, Sat 9pm–4am

Kazimierz

 **Little Treats**

Beer depot Stara Zajezdnia
Traffic no longer flows at the **depot** (▶135),
but in the huge halls and in the beer garden
the beer certainly does.

Milongas in Kazimierz
The people of Krakow love tango, and there
are dance evenings organised every day. Take
to the dance floor yourself, for example on
Wednesdays or Sundays in **Stajnia** (▶135).

Be the Beauty Queen's Guest
Enjoy the luxurious atmosphere at the
Cristal Suites Chez Helena (▶127) in the
house in which cosmetics icon Helena
Rubinstein was born.

Getting Your Bearings

At the end of the 15th century, a royal order decreed that Krakow's Jewish citizens had to move to the eastern part of Kazimierz. Before World War II, up to 70,000 Jews lived in Kazimierz. Today, there are only a few hundred, but the Jewish traditions live on – in the seven synagogues, the Klezmer restaurants around Szeroka Street and at the Jewish Culture Festival that takes place every year in summer and brings in crowds of visitors. These days the many bars in Kazimierz make it one of the city's most popular nightlife areas. Many young people stop off on Plac Nowy for *Zapiekanki*, a toasted baguette sandwich, before hitting the town.

Until just a few years ago, Kazimierz was regarded as a problem district, and many of the city's citizens avoided it. However, the run-down houses offered niches for young people who opened studios, shops and pubs there. Kazimierz quickly developed into a new in-district. Even now, when an increasing number of the run-down houses have been renovated, resulting in a growing number of expensive apartments, elegant restaurants and cafés, the district has managed to maintain its original charm. That is why so many people still prefer to meet in dimly lit restaurants like the Alchemia or Singer, where the candles burn on old tables and you order the beer from the bar.

Technology fans of all ages like visiting the Muzeum Inżynierii miejskiej, the Museum of Municipal Engineering, located on the land that used to belong to the former tram depot. There you can view vintage trams, cars and motorbikes, early household appliances and office machines, as well as carry out exciting experiments in all areas to do with the wheel.

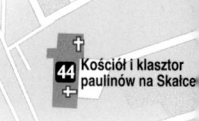

Kościół i klasztor paulinów na Skałce

At Your Leisure

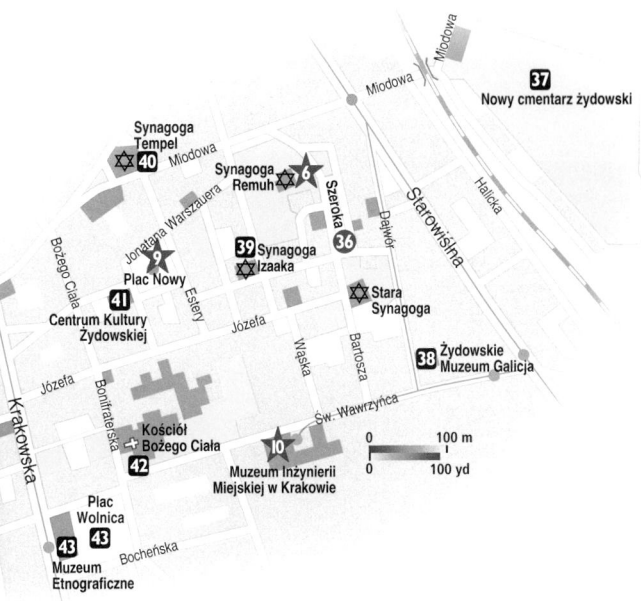

The Old Synagogue in Ulica Szeroka, the oldest remaining Jewish place of worship in Poland, is now a museum of Jewish history and culture

The Perfect Day

Spend a whole day in the old Jewish district of Kazimierz, visit 15th and 16th-century synagogues, marvel at vintage vehicles and go on a little shopping trip. If you follow our itinerary for the day, you will not only cover the most important sights but also experience the special atmosphere of this district.

⊕ 10:00am

Start the day with a cup of coffee in one of the numerous restaurants around **9 Plac Nowy** (➤ 121).

⊕ 10:30am

Visit the 16th-century ⭐**Remuh Synagogue** (photo on the right; ➤ 118), which is still used by the city's small Jewish community to this day. It takes its name from the famous Rabbi Moses Isserles, whose gravestone you will find in the adjoining Jewish Cemetery.

⊕ 11:30am

Continue your walk through Krakow's Jewish district with a visit to the **Stara Synagoga** in **36 Ulica Szeroka** (➤ 126). The Old Synagogue was built at the end of the 15th century and is now home to a collection of Jewish cult objects as well as an exhibition about the Jewish suffering during World War II.

⊕ 12:30pm

Time for a snack in the original restaurant **Dawno Temu na Kazimierzu** (➤ 132), which not only reminds you of the old times in Kazimierz with its name but also with the furnishing. Besides traditional Jewish meals, there are also Polish meals. How about a choice of delicious *pierogi*?

Synagoga Tempel **40**
Synagoga Remuh
37 Nowy cmentarz żydowski
Synagoga Izaaka
Plac Nowy
9
Centrum Kultury Żydowskiej **41**
39 **36**
ul. Szeroka
0   200 m
0   200 yd
Kościół Bożego Ciała **42**
38 Żydowskie Muzeum Galicja
10
Muzeum Inżynierii Miejskiej w Krakowie
Kościół i klasztor paulinów na Skałce **44**
43 Plac Wolnica & Muzeum Etnograficzne

🕐 2:00pm

Stroll afterwards along the **Ulica Józefa**, in which you will find lots of small shops with designer products and original fashion (➤ 136).

🕐 3:00pm

Have a quick look inside the **42 Corpus Christi Basilica** (➤ 129), which soars up over Ulica Józefa. The basilica was funded by King Kazimierz and is one of the city's largest churches; the imposing Baroque choir stall is particularly worth seeing.

🕐 4:00pm

Just a few paces further on is the **Museum of Municipal Engineering** (➤ 123) that offers enjoyment to visitors of all ages because here technology is not just presented as something to look at but also offers plenty of hands-on activities. Among other things, you can admire an impressive number of vintage vehicles in the former tram depot.

🕐 6:00pm

Start off the evening with a glass of wine. At **BARaWINO** (➤ 134) opposite **43 Plac Wolnica** (➤ 130), you can buy wines from all over the world and try one or other of the wines and bubblies beforehand.

🕐 7:00pm

Enjoy the evening in the **restaurant boat Barka** (➤ 132), which is anchored, not far from the BARaWINO, by the Bernatka pedestrian bridge. Below deck, the converted barge offers a cosy interior, but on summer evenings eating al fresco on deck is even nicer.

🕐 9:00pm

After dinner return to **Plac Nowy** (photo below; ➤ 121), where the night owls are beginning to congregate. Finish off the day with a leisurely drink in one of the many bars lining the square.

Kazimierz

⭐ Synagoga Remuh
(Remuh Synagogue)

Krakow's small Jewish community meets in Remuh Synagogue to worship. The Stary cmentarz żydowskiej (Old Jewish Cemetery) directly behind it is the goal of Jewish pilgrims from all over the world who go there to visit the grave of Rabbi Moses Isserles, better known as Remuh.

"The New Synagogue of the blessed memory Remuh" is inscribed in Hebrew on the tympanum above the entrance to the house of worship on Ulica Szeroka. The synagogue behind it is only new in comparison with the Old Synagogue (▶ 126) in the same street, but is otherwise the second oldest of its kind in Kazimierz. Members of the small Jewish community, which now only numbers about 200 souls, meet in the synagogue to worship on the Sabbath and other important days in the Jewish calendar. It is also the goal of visitors from all over the world.

Misused as a Storeroom

Israel Isserles Auerbach, a Jewish trader, founded the little synagogue in 1533. Just four years later, the first wooden building caught fire and was rebuilt in stone in 1553. The synagogue was initially only used by the close friends and family of the benefactor. The original Late Renaissance style was lost to a large extent during the conversion and extension work in 1829. During World War II, the Nazis ravaged the synagogue. The furnishings disappeared and the rooms were used as a storeroom for fire brigade equipment and body bags.

The "New Synagogue" is about 500 years old

By 1968 the synagogue had been repaired and could be again used for religious services. Among the few original pieces that were preserved from the interior are the offertory box and the entrance to the men's section, which is inscribed with "gold, silver, copper", which was intended to encourage visitors to make a donation. Also preserved is the Torah shrine decorated with four pilasters. The rectangular bema in the centre of the prayer room, from which the Torah roll is read, was rebuilt based on the historical model and surrounded by high wrought-iron railings. Colourful bas-reliefs decorate the wooden double door that leads into the sanctuary.

Israel Isserles Auerbach had the synagogue built in memory of his deceased wife and gave it to his son, Moses Isserles (1525–1572), who at the time was the chief rabbi of the Jewish community. **Moses Isserles**, known as **Remuh**, having completed his degree, founded a Talmud school in Krakow and wrote numerous religious and philosophical texts that were distributed widely among the Ashkenazic Jews in Central and Eastern Europe. To this day, Jews from all over the world pilgrim to his tomb in the Old Jewish Cemetery adjoining the synagogue.

Old Jewish Cemetery

Even before the construction of the synagogue, the cemetery was laid out on an area covering about a hectare. Anyone who sees the rows of graves today will not immediately realise that the necropolis was almost completely eradicated and unrecognisable during the occupation of Poland by the Nazis who misused it as a rubbish tip. One of the few graves that survived the war years is that of Moses Isserles. Devout Jews see this as evidence of the rabbi's miraculous powers and, according to legend, the first worker who tried to demolish the grave was hit by lightening and died.

Tombstones destroyed by the Nazis have been put on the cemetery's surrounding wall

When the restoration of the cemetery began in the 1950s, the builders discovered hundreds of gravestones were concealed just below the surface under a thin layer of soil. More than 700 were salvaged and repaired. However, many of the tombs no longer stand in their original place. The fragments of destroyed tombstones have found a new home on the interior side of the cemetery wall.

Kazimierz

Many devout Jews make a pilgrimage to the grave of Rabbi Remuh in the Old Jewish Cemetery

In the cemetery, which was closed in 1800, you will find some of Poland's oldest Jewish funeral monuments. Many scholars and other important personalities from the Jewish community found their last resting place there. Simple gravestones stand next to richly ornamented tombs. Many are now overgrown with ivy. Jewish visitors often leave little stones on the graves, as is their tradition.

Moses Isserles's last resting place is located by the west wall of the synagogue. The scholar lies surrounded by his relatives, including his father, two siblings and his first wife. A fence surrounds the entire family tomb. Written on a gravestone in Hebrew is the inscription: "From Moses to Moses there was no other such worthy Moses." Many pilgrims place notes with intercessory prayers on the tomb.

TAKING A BREAK

Right next to the entrance to the synagogue is the restaurant and café **Szara Kazimierz** (► 135), where you can sit and relax in the garden outside in summer.

➕ 197 E4 ✉ Szeroka 40
☎ 124 295 735
🕐 May–Oct Sun–Fri 9am–6pm; Nov–April Sun–Fri 9am–4pm
🚊 Tram 3, 19, 24, 69 (Miodowa)
💰 5 złoty

INSIDER INFO

- Men must wear a hat when visiting the synagogue and cemetery. You can borrow paper kippas at the entrance of the synagogue.
- Look out for the panel to the right of the torah shrine. It commemorates the fact that Remuh used to pray there. One of the chairs by the wall is reserved for him.

★ 6 Plac Nowy (New Square)

Plac Nowy is to Kazimierz, what the Main Market Square is to Krakow's Old Town – the meeting place per se for locals and tourists alike – bustling with life from early in the morning to late at night. Yet when you look at the two squares, they actually have nothing in common.

Even today, the people of Krakow still refer to the square that is laid out in the shape of a convex rectangle as Plac Żydowski (Jewish Square). The area around it was added to the Jewish district of Kazimierz in 1608. At the end of the 19th century, in an aim to attain some kind of order among the maze of stalls, the municipal authorities decided to redesign the square and have a permanent market hall built. The flat round brick building (Okrąglak hall) completed in 1900 remains the focal point of the square. It comprises of two sections: a round core and an exterior ring. Initially used to house market stalls, the Jewish community used the building from 1927 as a kosher poultry abattoir. Today various grocers and butchers sell their products inside the round building.

As evening approaches, the first stop is Alchemia

Nightlife Centre

For just a few zloty, you can buy the famous *zapiekanki*, the open baguette sandwiches toasted with cheese at the windows of the market hall. Despite the number of vendors, long queues build up, especially in the evenings and at night, because Plac Nowy is now also the centre of Kazimierz's nightlife. The former shops and workshops in the surrounding houses have gradually disappeared and pubs, bars and restaurants have moved into the empty

Insider Tip

Kazimierz

facilities. Among the first were alternative student pubs like **Alchemia** (▶ 134) full of patina, old furniture and candles that produce a dim light. They have been followed by increasingly refined restaurants, popular particularly with the young crowd. Groups of tourists meet Krakow's young crowd there and, at the weekends in particular, turn night into day.

Clothes, Pigeons and Jumble

Plac Nowy has remained one of the most popular market squares in Krakow. Every day, the rather wind-slanted stalls sell regional fruit and vegetables, flowers, bread and cheese. Besides that, you can also find jewellery, hand-crafts and practical household products. On Tuesdays and Fridays, pigeon breeders meet from 6–9 in the morning to buy new birds and pigeon-related products.

On Saturdays, the **flea market** attracts lots of visitors looking for old books and CDs, coins and stamps, table-ware, lamps and clocks. From 7am–3pm valuable antiques are also on sale. Then on Sundays, you can buy elegant second-hand clothes and every kind of accessory to go with them.

For years, people have been talking about redesigning the square. An old design submitted as part of a competition, for instance, proposed raising the square optically from the surrounding streets with steps. The aim was to produce a stage-like gallery next to the market hall. Yet many visitors like the square precisely because things are not perfect or totally stylish, and they actually have quite a soft spot for the potholed streets.

TAKING A BREAK

You are spoilt for choice with the selection of products on Plac Nowy: over coffee and a snack in Café **Les Couleurs** (▶ 135), you admire it from a French perspective.

At the flea market, the main rule is: seek and you will find...

✚ 197 E3
🕐 Food stands: Mon–Sat 6am–8pm; restaurants in the market hall: Mon–Sat 6am–2am
🚋 Tram 6, 8, 12, 18, 22, 52, 62, 70, 73 (Stradom)

⭐10 Muzeum Inżynierii miejskiej w Krakowie (Museum of Municipal Engineering)

Technology enthusiasts tend to hope that it will rain at least one day during their visit. That provides them with a good opportunity to visit the treasures exhibited at the former tram depot of Kazimierz. With everything from vintage vehicles to early televisions and classic household appliances, the Museum of Municipal Engineering is guaranteed to please hobby inventors of all ages.

Once a depot for trams, now a museum

It was when the first horse-drawn tram made its way through Krakow in 1882 that the depot on the Ulica św. Wawrzyńca in Kazimierz came into being. As time went by, the network grew, electric power replaced "horse power" and the depot expanded even further. In the 1920s garages and ateliers were added for the city buses, and it was not until the 1960s that a new depot went into operation and the old one gradually dwindled into insignificance.

Museum for Local Public Transport

The original idea for a museum was conceived in 1975, during the celebrations for the 100th anniversary of local public transport in Krakow.

INSIDER INFO

Take a 🎫 **sightseeing tour in a vintage tram**. During the summer months, some of the museum trains operate on two lines through the town (schedule at www.muzealna. org). Some of the vintage town buses are also used for special excursions from time to time.

Insider Tip

However, It took until 1994, before the historical fleet of public transport vehicles could be presented in the former hall for narrow-gauge trams. Over the following two decades additional sections of the historical buildings were renovated and the exhibition area grew.

Yet, although the collection has been extended, the focus of the museum remains on the history of local public transport. Old tickets, ticket machines and uniforms illustrate the development since 1882.

One of the halls contains eleven **vintage trams**, all carefully refurbished, most of them in their traditional blue and white colours. The oldest one is from 1912 and, like the others, is still roadworthy.

Not only children enjoy experimenting "all around the wheel"

Vintage Car Collection

In a further hall are burnished two-, three- and four-wheelers, mainly vintage models produced in Poland. You can also see a fleet of *Polski Fiat 126p* – in the People's Republic of Poland, these tiny cars called *Małutki* were what the Trabi was for the former East Germany: small, practical and very popular; beside them is the *Polski Fiat 508*, a luxury limousine from 1936.

Two prototypes are particularly eye-catching: in order to get into the *Smyk*, a rather unshapely compact car from 1957, it was necessary to raise the entire front including the windscreen, something that did not catch on in the end. In contrast, the 1983 *Beskid*, a very modern, low-fuel compact car was well ahead of its time, but for political and economic reasons was never built. It remains nonetheless reminiscent of quite a few cars from the West, which did not appear until many years later. The fact that the vehicles are now in the museum is thanks to the engineers that ignored official directives to destroy the seven prototypes.

Muzeum Inżynierii miejskiej w Krakowie

Household Appliances, Office Machines and More

A battery-run radio from 1929 belongs to the treasures of the department for **consumer electronics**, where you can see old record players, tape recorders, cameras and televisions from the early days of the People's Republic. In another department the exhibits include household appliances from the time between the World Wars and the time after World War II. In the department for office technology, the collection ranges from a 19th-century typewriter to the first portable computer. There is also a department dedicated to urban electricity, gas and water, and another one shows various measuring instruments.

As a university town, Krakow was the cradle of the printing craft in Poland. Jagiellonian University has the oldest preserved example of Polish print work, a calendar from 1474. In the former hall of the horse-drawn tram, an extensive exhibition recounts the history of **printing** in Krakow from the 15th to 20th century. Exhibits include old printing machines and also different printing procedures and book binding.

It is not only children and adolescents who particularly enjoy spending a bit longer in the 🏃 **Around the Wheel** department. There are 27 hands-on stands in the department, at which they can learn the rules of physics through entertaining experiments and, for example, lift a weight of more than 100 kg with very little effort.

TAKING A BREAK

Parts of the old tram depot were transformed into Krakow's largest local brewery. Continue your visit of the historical site in the **Stara Zajezdnia** (➤ 135) and enjoy a freshly tapped lager.

➕ 197 E3
✉ św. Wawrzyńca 15
☎ 124 211 242; www.mimk.com.pl
🕐 Tue–Sun 10am–4pm, (June–Sep Tue, Thu, Sun until 6pm)
🚋 Tram 3, 19, 24, 69 (św. Wawrzyńca)
🎫 10 złoty (free on Tue)

INSIDER INFO

If you fancy doing some experiments yourself, take a trip to the east of town. There the Muzeum Inżynierii miejskiej w Krakowie has opened an external department the **Ogród Doświadczeń**, which takes its name from the science fiction author Stanisław Lem's 🏃 **Garden of Experiments**. On a 6 ha area, you can find different experiments to do on the topic of mechanics, acoustics, optics, magnetism and water. There is also a maze, a geological garden as well as a scented garden (al. Pokoju 68; tel: 123 461 285; www.ogroddoswiadczen.pl/en, April–Aug Mon–Fri 8:30am–7pm, Sat, Sun from 10am (June, July until 8pm); Sep Mon–Fri 8:30am–5pm, Sat, Sun 10am–7pm; Oct 8:30am–3pm, Sat, Sun 10am–5pm; admission 10 złoty).

Insider Tip

㊱ Ulica Szeroka

In the evenings, you will hear Klezmer music playing in the restaurants on Szeroka Street again. And at the south end of the street, the exhibition in the Stara Synagogue, the Old Synagogue, takes visitors back to the Jewish Kazimierz of pre-war days.

Szeroka means wide and Szeroka Street really is the widest street in Krakow and used to form the centre of the Jewish district. Before the turnaround in 1989, it presented a bleak sight. Many of the houses were empty, the grey façades crumbling. Yet gradually, they have been completely renovated and now the Ulica Szeroka is the centre of Krakow's Jewish culture, in which you will find not only the most important synagogues but also a good number of cafés and restaurants serving Jewish food. At the Jewish Culture Festival, the largest of its kind in Central Europe, thousands of people crowd the street during the final concert at the beginning of July.

Centre of Jewish Life
Apart from the Remuh Synagogue (► 118) – still used by the Jewish community today – and the Old Synagogue, also located on this street directly next to the Ariel restaurant (► 132) is the little **Popper Synagogue**, which was founded by the Jewish banker Wolf Popper in 1620. All of the interior furnishings were destroyed during World War II; today the building is used by the Youth Community Centre. At the north end of the street is the former Jewish Mikwe Bath, which now houses the hotel and restaurant Klezmer-Hois (► 42 and 133).

Museum for Jewish History and Culture
The **Stara Synagogue**, the **Old Synagogue**, ranks as the oldest synagogue building still standing, not only in Krakow but in all of Poland. It is thought to have been built around 1407 in the Late Gothic style and after a fire in 1557 rebuilt in Renaissance style by the Italian architect Matteo Gucci; since then an attic crowns the exterior walls. The synagogue used to be the most important synagogue in Krakow. It was here that the Polish national hero **Tadeusz Kościuszko** rallied the Jewish citizens in 1794 to support the uprising against the division of the country by Austria, Prussia and Russia.

INSIDER INFO

- If you wish to learn more about Jewish traditions during your visit to the Stara Synagogue, then hire an audio guide, which is also available in English (10 złoty).
- Since the Old Synagogue no long functions as a place of worship, men do not need to cover their heads.

At the Ariel restaurant live Klezmer music accompanies the delicious food

After the beginning of World War II, the German occupiers destroyed the interior of the synagogue and used it as storage space. A memorial in front of the synagogue commemorates 30 Polish citizens that were shot there in 1943.

After the restoration, the former synagogue became the home for the Historical Museum's department for **Jewish History and Culture**. Whilst in the earlier prayer room the focus is on Jewish men and the cultural objects pertaining to the most important Jewish holidays, the exhibition in the smaller prayer room focuses on the women and Jewish tradition in the family from the birth to the grave.

TAKING A BREAK

You can't really miss the Café-Restaurant **Ariel** (ul. Szeroka 18; tel: 124 217 920; http://ariel-krakow.pl).

✛ 197 F3/4

Stara Synagoga
✉ ul. Szeroka 24
☎ 124 220 962; www.mhk.pl
🕐 Mon 10am–2pm, Tue–Sun 9am–5pm (earlier in winter)
🚋 Tram 3, 19, 24, 69 (Miodowa)
🎫 10 złoty (free on Mon)

THE BEAUTY QUEEN FROM KRAKOW

Helena Rubinstein was born in 1870 in Ulica Szeroka (no. 14) the child of a Jewish merchant's family, and the oldest of eight children. It was from here that she started her international career. When she emigrated to Australia in 1888, she took twelve jars containing creams belonging to her mother, some of which she passed on to the farmers' wives in her neighbourhood. She discovered a market opportunity, soon opened the first beauty salons in Australia and thus laid the foundation stone for her empire. Her birth house in Kazimierz now accommodates the luxurious **Cristal Suites Chez Helena** (www.crystalsuites.info). Don't look for a memorial to one of Kazimierz's most famous citizens, there isn't one.

At Your Leisure

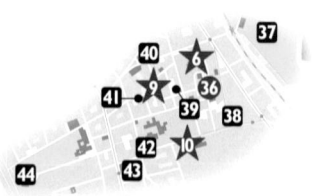

37 Nowy cmentarz żydowski (New Jewish Cemetery)

The New Jewish Cemetery, which is separated from the residential areas of Kazimierz by a railway embankment was set out in 1800 and covers an area of 19ha (47 acres). After the establishment of the Jewish ghettos (➤ 150), the cemetery was closed and the street in the Płaszów Concentration Camp (➤ 155) was partly paved with the gravestones. From 1957, the badly damaged necropolis was rebuilt. Pieces of the destroyed gravestones can be found in the cemetery wall and in a memorial to the Jews killed by Nazis that is next to the entrance. Many of the around 10,000 graves are overgrown and the inscriptions are no longer really legible. New graves can also be seen, because the cemetery is still being used by the Jewish community.

Remember that men visiting the cemetery much cover their heads.

➕ 198 A5 ✉ ul. Miodowa 55
🕐 Sun–Fri 9am–5pm
🚊 Tram 3, 19, 24, 69 (Miodowa)

38 Żydowskie Muzeum Galicja (Galicia Jewish Museum)

For the book *Traces of Memory: The Ruins of Jewish Civilization in Polish Galicia*, British photographer Chris Schwarz set off on an investigative journey through the former Galicia. On more than 1,000 photos, he shows the ruins of former Jewish sites, evidence of Jewish culture that has been preserved, but also the sites of massacre and destruction. He wanted to give the photographs a permanent place in their own museum. In 2004, he found an empty warehouse and created on his own initiative an impressive place of remembrance. Schwarz died quite unexpectedly just three years later, but the work is being continued according to his wishes. Tens of thousands of people visit his **photo exhibition** as well as temporary exhibitions about Jewish life in Galicia each year. The museum has a mediathek as well as a well-stocked bookshop with Judaica. Cakes, snacks and kosher wine are served in the museum café.

➕ 197 F3 ✉ Dajwór 18
☎ 124 216 842; www.galiciajewishmuseum.org
🕐 Daily 10am–6pm
🚊 Tram 3, 19, 24, 69 (św. Wawrzyńca)
💰 15 złoty

39 Synagoga Izaaka (Izaak Synagogue)

This early Baroque synagogue founded by the business man **Izaak Jakubowski** in 1644 once ranked as the largest in Kazimierz. A magnificent barrel vault covers the large men's section below and the women's gallery above reached by an external staircase. In December 1939, Maksymilian Redlich, a member of staff of the Jewish community was shot dead by SS men because he refused to set fire to the synagogue. Later, the synagogue was raided and its treasures stolen. Among other things, the magnificent bima disappeared of which today only the bordered space where it once stood can be seen. The building remained empty for a long time and was not properly renovated until the 1990s. The wall paintings with liturgical texts that were discovered during the process were partially reconstructed. Today the synagogue is used by Chabad Lubavitch Jews and is open to visitors. In the entrance hall is a small shop selling kosher food.

🚹 197 F3 ◻ ul. Kupa 16/ul. Jakuba 25
🕐 Sun–Thu 9am–8pm, Fri 9am–2:30pm
🚋 Tram 6, 8, 12, 18, 22, 52, 62, 70, 73 (Stradom)
💵 7 złoty

40 Synagoga Tempel (Tempel Synagogue)

Completed in 1862 and then later improved on numerous occasions, the Tempel Synagogue was a meeting place for progressive Krakow Jews. That is why it is still referred to as the progressive synagogue. Services were held there by turns in Polish and German, the sequence similar to a church service. Women were also allowed to sing.

The interior is designed in the Moorish style. With its wall paintings, elaborate stucco, wooden galleries and colourful glass windows, the synagogue is one of the most beautiful of its kind.

Services are no longer held there very often, but the synagogue provides the venue for concerts from time to time. Among other events, it is here that the Jewish Culture Festival is opened each summer.

🚹 197 E4 ◻ Miodowa 24
🕐 Sun–Fri 10am–5pm (until 4pm in winter)
🚋 Tram 3, 19, 24, 69 (Miodowa)
💵 10 złoty

41 Centrum Kultury Żydowskiej (Center for Jewish Culture)

After substantial renovation of the B'nei Emun synagogue, originally built in 1886, it became the home of the Center for Jewish Culture in 1993, an institution run by the **Judaica Foundation**. It is an important point of contact for Polish and foreign visitors interested in Jewish life and Jewish history. The centre organises talks and

Concerts often take place in the Moorish Revival interior of the Tempel Synagogue

conferences on Jewish topics. Film presentations, concerts and exhibitions take place in the rooms.

In the Café Sara, you can enjoy coffee and cake away from the hustle and bustle on Plac Nowy.

🚹 197 E3 ◻ Meiselsa 17
📞 124 306 449; www.judaica.pl
🕐 Mon–Fri 10am–8pm, Sat, Sun 10am–2pm
🚋 Tram 6, 8, 12, 18, 22, 52, 62, 70, 73 (Stradom)

42 Kościół Bożego Ciała (Corpus Christi Basilica)

In terms of size, the Corpus Christi Basilica founded by King Kazimierz (Casimir) III in 1340 is almost on a par with St Mary's Church on the Main Market Square. The imposing tower, crowned with a Late Renaissance cupola that was added in the mid 17th century, is visible for miles around. In 1655, the Swedish king Karl (Charles) X

Kazimierz

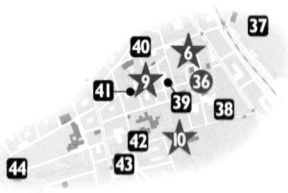

✚ 197 E3 ✉ Bożego Ciała 26
☎ 124 305 995; www.bozecialo.net
🚌 Tram 6, 8, 70, 73 (Pl. Wolnica)

Gustav took up residence here and controlled the siege of Krakow. His soldiers plundered the three-nave Gothic church, which during repairs later received an even more elaborate Baroque interior.

The design of the wooden pulpit is very original; it is shaped like a sailboat and carried by two sirens and dolphins. Light enters through the lovely 15th-century glass window and shines directly on the choir room with its medieval choir stalls. A row of columns connects the church with the cloister of Canons Regular of the Lateran. The order has been resident here since 1405 and is responsible for the church.

43 Plac Wolnica & Muzeum Etnograficzne (Wolnica Square & Ethnographic Museum)

The market square of Kazimierz, located on the salt street from Krakow to Wieliczka and Bochnia, used to be an important trading area. Covering an area of 195m × 195m (640ft × 640ft), it was not much smaller than Krakow's Main Market Square. Today's Plac Wolnica now only covers about a quarter of the space of the old market, but has remained a lively centre of the district and, like Plac Nowy (► 121) another nightlife hotspot in Kazimierz.

The fountain with the sculpture *Three Musicians* in the south-east section of the square is a work by Krakow sculptor **Bronisław Chromy** (b. 1925), whose other work also includes the Wawel Dragon (► 86/87). After some of the Wolnica Square was taken

Festivities are often celebrated around the "Musicians' Fountain" on Plac Wolnica (against the backdrop of the Corpus Christi Basilica)

After visiting the Pauline monastery it's time for an excursion on the Vistula

44 Kościół i klasztor paulinów na Skałce (Pauline Church and Monastery "on the rock")

The two white towers of the late Baroque church rise up over the banks of the Vistula. Together with the monastery next to it, it forms an architectural entity. There was a Romanesque place of worship here even in the 11th century. A sweeping double staircase leads into the richly ornamented interior. In the vaulted cellars decorated with Art Nouveau paintings a "**national pantheon**" gradually evolved as distinguished artists and scientists found their last resting place there. Among them are the sarcophagi of the painter Stanisław Wyspiański (➤ 17), the composer Karol Szymanowski (1882–1937) and the literature Nobel Prize Winner Czesław Miłosz (1911–2004).

The church is linked with the legend surrounding the Krakow bishop Stanisław Szczepanowski (Stanislaus of Szczepanów), who on the order of the then king Boleslaw the Bold was tortured to death. Every year, in memory of the martyr, there is a procession from Wawel Cathedral to the church on the rock.

A relic, a tree stump on which the blood of the martyr is said to have dripped, is kept in a side chapel. The church pond is adorned with a statue of the bishop. Legend also claims that a quartered corpse in the water is said to have miraculously grown back together.

In 2008 an **Altar of the Third Millennium** was inaugurated on the site, which was dedicated to St Adalbert who was murdered in 997, St Stanisław (Stanislaus) as well as Pope John Paul II who has also been canonised.

➕ 196 C2 ✉ Skałeczna 15
🕐 Crypt: daily 9am–5pm
🚊 Tram 6, 8, 70, 73 (Pl. Wolnica)
🎫 2.50 złoty

over by buildings, the Old Town Hall moved from being in the middle of the square to the south-west edge. The building was erected in the 15th century and received its current form with its Renaissance-style attic 200 years later. Since the end of World War II, it has contained the collection of the **Ethnographic Museum**. From the original 2,000 objects that the founder Seweryn Udziela brought into the museum at the beginning of the 20th century, the number of exhibits has grown to around the 80,000 mark. The largest section of exhibits are dedicated to the life of people in the region and in Poland; the permanent exhibition also shows everyday objects and folk art from other regions of the world.
➕ 197 D2

Ethnographic Museum
✉ Pl. Wolnica 1
☎ 124 305 575; www.etnomuzeum.eu
🕐 Tue–Sun 10am–7pm
🚊 Tram 6, 8, 70, 73 (Pl. Wolnica)
🎫 13 złoty (free on Sun)

Where to...
Eat and Drink

Prices
A main course (without drinks)
£ under 45 złoty   ££ 45–90 złoty   £££ over 90 złoty

RESTAURANTS

Ariel ££
Ariel has been serving Jewish dishes such as gefilte fish and carp prepared in the Jewish way since at least the end of the 1980s. In the dining rooms furnished with antique furniture and paintings, time seems to have stopped. In the evening people meet here for Klezmer concerts.
✚ 197 F4 ⊠ Szeroka 18
☎ 124 217 920; http://ariel-krakow.pl
⊙ Daily 10am–midnight

Barka £
The old Dutch barge is moored on the bank of the Vistula, right next to the new Bernatka pedestrian bridge. The cargo space below deck has been turned into a bar and a large comfortable dining area with wooden floors and a fireplace. In summer, the food and drinks taste even better on deck. The service is good, the seasonal menu small but ambitious. And it keeps what it promises.
✚ 197 E2 ⊠ Podgórska 16
☎ 668 820 454; www.barkakrakow.pl
⊙ Daily noon–midnight

Bottigliera 1881 ££
A more than 100-year-old and long-forgotten wine cellar is the centrepiece of this small but nice wine restaurant in which it is difficult to get a table in the evening unless you have reserved in advance. The wine selection comprises more than 100 varieties of all price categories. The wines come from different regions in France, Italy and Spain, but also from more exotic places. A small menu provides a choice of tapas or selected set meals.
✚ 197 E2 ⊠ Bocheńska 5
☎ 660 661 756; www.bottigliera1881.com.pl
⊙ Tue–Sat noon–11pm, Sun noon–8pm

Dawno temu na Kazimierzu £
Hanging on the outside walls are the old signs of Jewish shops, on the inside the restaurant's rough dark walls, pot-pourri of household goods, old round iron stove and dim candlelight underline the impression of being in another time. The café-restaurant is fittingly called "A long time ago in Kazimierz", and it serves traditional Jewish meals and on some evenings live Klezmer music.
✚ 197 E4
⊠ Szeroka 1 ☎ 124 212 117;
www.dawnotemu.nakazimierzu.pl
⊙ Daily 10am–9:30pm

El Toro ££
A bull's head in the logo and hams dangling from the ceiling – here it is easy to feel like you are in Spain. In glass cabinets at the bar, there is a selection of tapas and plates with *Jamón Ibérico* and *Queso Manchego*, a marvellous *paella* as well as a respectable selection of Spanish wines which you can enjoy in the small bar or in the medieval vaulted cellar.
✚ 197 E2 ⊠ Pl. Wolnica 9
☎ 124 214 733; www.eltoro-restauracja.pl
⊙ Sun–Thu noon–10pm,
Fri, Sat noon–midnight

Hamsa Restobar ££

Hummus & Happiness promises Hamsa Restobar, the only restaurant with contemporary cuisine from Israel and its neighbouring countries. The meals are not kosher but are very tasty. To be recommended are the Mezze plates with small portions of for instance Hummus, Falafel, various dips and salads. Besides two large dining areas insides, there is also a beautiful summer garden.

🕂 197 F4 ⊠ Szeroka 2
☎ 515 150 145; www.hamsa.pl
🕓 Mon–Fri 10am–midnight,
Sat, Sun 9am–midnight

Klezmer-Hois ££

In the former Jewish bathing house, you can now listen to Klezmer music. Traditional Jewish meals are served to go with it. The interior furnishing with period furniture, comfortable sofas, lace doilies, mirrors and old oil paintings transport the visitor back to the time prior to World War II (reservation in the evening is very important).

🕂 197 F4 ⊠ Szeroka 6
☎ 124 111 245; www.klezmer.pl
🕓 Daily 9am–10pm

Nova Krova £

A vegan burger sounds almost like an oxymoron. Yet the success of this little restaurant shows that the combination works. Various sorts are served in XXL format, filled for instance with tofu, quinoa or falafel. Complementing them are other vegan dishes such as soups, salads and delicious cakes.

🕂 197 D2 ⊠ Pl. Wolnica 12
☎ 0530 305 304
🕓 Sun–Thu noon–9pm, Fri, Sat noon–11pm

Pimiento ££

Excellent Argentine beef from the grill is the hallmark of Pimiento, which also has another restaurant in Ulica Stolarska (13) in the Old Town. Numerous other wines from Argentina and other Latin-American countries are served to go with it. The furnishing is modern, the service friendly and unobtrusive. The menu also contains some fish and noodle dishes.

🕂 197 E3 ⊠ Józefa 26
☎ 124 212 502; www.pimiento.pl
🕓 Daily noon–11pm

Plac Nowy 1 ££

The restaurant in a new building on Plac Nowy may deter some people because of its size, but it offers good service and across-the-board quality from pizza and burger to duck breast sous vide. There is beer from a range of different local breweries to go with the meal and a bowling centre in the cellar.

🕂 197 E3 ⊠ Pl. Nowy 1
⊠ 124 427 700; www.placnowy1.pl
⊠ Sun–Wed 9am–midnight,
Thu–Sat 9am–2

Rubinstein ££

In its glazed patio, the medieval vaulted cellar and the summer garden on the bustling Szeroka Street, this hotel restaurant serves not only Polish and European food but also some Jewish dishes.

🕂 197 F4 ⊠ Szeroka 12
☎ 123 840 000; www.rubinstein.pl
🕓 Mon–Sat 5pm–10pm, Sun noon–10pm

Sąsiedzy ££

"Sąsiedzy" is the Polish word for "neighbour", and you can feel like you're having dinner with a good neighbour here. The traditional Polish meals are served in a fitting setting. There is a pretty winter and summer garden above ground and below there are several rooms with brick vaulted ceilings that are full of atmosphere. At midday a lot of the people living in the area, the neighbours so to speak, come here to eat.

🕂 197 E4 ⊠ Miodowa 25
☎ 126 548 353; www.sasiedzi.oberza.pl
🕓 Daily noon–11pm

Kazimierz

Insider Tip

Studio Qulinarne ££

The former bus depot at the technology museum is one of Krakow's culinary hot spots. The owner and designer Katarzyna Grüning has transformed the historic hall with its wide window fronts into an impressive place to eat. The team around the chef Oskar Zazuń conjure up original fish or meat creations, in which the individual components nonetheless complement each other perfectly and unite to create a total work of art.

➕ 197 E3
✉ Gazowa 4
☎ 124 306 914; www.studioqulinarne.pl
🕐 Mon–Sat 6pm–10pm

Szara Kazimierz ££

The offshoot of Szara restaurant is on a par with the main restaurant on Rynek Główny. To be recommended are the reasonable lunch menus comprising of soup and a main dish for just 35 złoty. In the summer, you can relax outside in the quiet garden

➕ 197 F4
✉ Szeroka 39
☎ 124 291 219; www.szarakazimierz.pl
🕐 Daily 11am–11pm

PUBS AND BARS

Alchemia

An institution in Kazimierz. In 1999 this trendy pub, one of the first of its kind, opened its doors in a former dry cleaner. Since then, an international group of mainly student age meets there and stays until late in the night sitting at old wooden tables in the flickering candlelight. Among other things concerts take place in the large cellar rooms during the annual jazz festival. *Alchemia* or *kuchni* (small snacks) like burgers or falafel are available.

➕ 197 E3
✉ Estery 5
☎ 124 212 200; www.alchemia.com.pl
🕐 Mon 10am–4am, Tue–Sun 9am–4am

BARaWINO

Marek Kondrat, has had a successful career in the wine business for many years, and has created a beautiful combination of wine shop and cosy bar. His collection encompasses about 350 wines and bubblies from all around the world, of which about 40 are also served by the glass. The latter include red and white wines from the Stettin area, which despite the northern location taste delicious. You can clear the palate in-between with little cheese snacks.

➕ 197 E2 ✉ Mostowa 1
☎ 668 671 712; www.marekkondrat.pl
🕐 Sun–Thu noon–10pm,
Fri, Sat noon–midnight

Le Scandale

The large garden, covered and heated in winter, is one of the most popular meeting points on Plac Nowy. The young and beautiful flock there, especially at the weekends, in order to party until late in the night. The cocktails are among the best in the town, and there are tapas, grilled dishes, pizza and pasta to keep you going.

➕ 197 E3 ✉ Pl. Nowy 9
☎ 124 306 855; www.lescandale.pl
🕐 Daily from 8am

Singer

Singer takes its name from the sewing machine tables at which the guests sit. Singer was among the first student pubs in Kazimierz and has as yet managed to withstand all trends. The small guest area is always full of people in the evening, and the music is not too loud to start with, so that it is still easy to chat. However, this tends to change later on when the tables are pushed to one side to make space for people to dance.

➕ 197 E3 ✉ Izaaka 1
☎ 122 920 622
🕐 Sun–Thu 9am–3am, Fri, Sat 9am–6am

Stajnia
The pretty green passage may remind you of the film *Schindler's List*, since some of the scenes were filmed there. Young people feel at ease in the Mediterranean-style surroundings of the former stables, and at weekends party there till late in the night, dancing to Latin-American rhythms.

🚺 197 D3 ✉ Józefa 12 ☎ 124 237 202
🕔 Mon–Thu 11am–1am, Fri, Sat 11am–3am, Sun 11am–midnight

Stara Zajezdnia
In the post-industrial ambience of the former tram depot, beer now flows from the microbrewery that took over the location in 2012. Among its selection are apple and honey beers. The long rows of table are crowded with people in the evening and sports programmes are broadcast on large television screens. A restaurant and large beer garden complement the ensemble.

🚺 197 E3 ✉ św. Wawrzyńca 12
☎ 664 323 988; www.starazajezdniakrakow.pl
🕔 Mon–Thu 2pm–midnight, Fri 2pm–1am, Sat noon–1am, Sun noon–midnight

Ulica Krokodyli
The small, rather unprepossessing pub "The Street of Crocodiles" takes its name from a book by Bruno Schulz and is one of the veterans of Kazimierz. During the day you can enjoy coffee and cake there, in the evening a leisurely beer. The interior furnishing with old wooden tables is timeless, the guests a bit older than in the trendy bars around them.

🚺 197 F3 ✉ Szeroka 30
☎ 124 310 516 🕔 Daily 10am–midnight

Ursa Maior
When fog rises over the thinly populated Bieszczady in south-east Poland, the people there say that it is because the bears are brewing beer. In the small town Uherce Mineralne, the bear is called Agnieszka Lopata – a brew master who has created some of Poland's most original Craft beers. Little works of art adorn the labels on the bottles. Just follow the sign with the bears and try the un-conventional flavours in the little bar. Whatever you like, you can take home with you in pretty gift cartons. *Insider Tip*

🚺 197 E2 ✉ Pl. Wolnica 10
☎ 730 565 888; www.ursamaior.pl
🕔 Sun–Thu 1pm–midnight, Fri, Sat 1pm–2am

CAFÉS

Cheder
The organisers of the Jewish Culture Festival established a nice café on the ground floor of a former synagogue. Anyone wishing to read the paper or a book in a relaxed setting will not have to worry about being glared at by the waiter when he or she sips on his water and coffee there for an hour. The home-made hummus is a revelation.

🚺 197 E3 ✉ Józefa 36
☎ 515 732 226; www.jewishfestival.pl
🕔 Daily 10am–10pm

Les Couleurs
The French café has been an established name on Plac Nowy for years – a popular place for an early or late breakfast, for a coffee in between meals or in the evening and until late in the night for a couple of beers or so.

🚺 197 E3 ✉ Estery 10
☎ 124 294 270
🕔 Mon–Thu 7am–midnight, Fri 7am–2am, Sat 8am–2am, Sun 8am–midnight

Mostowa Art Café
Young, hip people meet in the little art café on the way between Kazimierz and Podgórze to enjoy an equally hip beer from a small, little-known Polish brewery or to sip on a coffee as they talk about the latest films or exhibition openings.

🚺 197 E2 ✉ Mostowa 8
☎ 730 480 477 🕔 Sun–Thu noon–10pm, Fri, Sat noon–midnight

Old Jazz Café

This little café not far from the Galicia Jewish museum offers a selection of homemade cakes as well as good coffee. On Saturdays, there is occasionally a jazz evening, and admission is free.

Insider Tip

➕ 197 F4 ✉ Dajwór 20 ☎ 124 221 725
◷ Mon–Thu 8am–6pm, Fri 8am–10pm, Sat 10am–10pm, Sun 10am–6pm

Where to...
Shop

Slightly hidden away from the district's main streets, you can find quite a few interesting shops in which you can browse Polish designer clothes or jewellery. A larger collection of small shops can be found in Ulica Józefa.

FASHION, ART AND DESIGN

Hipsters will find the shirts and hats they want at **The Hive**, a small fashion shop (ul. Bocheńska 7; tel: 512 316 856; Tue–Fri noon–7pm, Sat until 6pm). In the same building Anna Maria Kwiatek offers **Idea Fix** in her Concept Store a forum for young Polish couturiers, artists and designers. Here you can find original clothing and shoes, jewellery and also home accessories, photographs and paintings (tel: 124 221 246; www.ideafix.pl; Mon–Fri 11am–7pm, Sat, Sun noon–6pm).

In the photo gallery **Trzecie Oko** ("Third Eye"), you can both admire the photo art on the walls but also buy beautifully illustrated books, for instance about Kazimierz (ul. Bocheńska 5; www.trzecieoko. com; Wed–Fri 4pm–7pm, Sat, Sun 2pm–5pm).

Józef Chorąży comes from a long established Krakow family of milliners. In his shop **Czapki i Kapelusze**, he sells traditional hats and caps for men (ul. Krakowska 35a; tel: 608 282 631; www.czapki chorazy.prv.pl; Mon–Fri 10am–6pm, Sat 9am–2pm).

High Fidelity is a treasure trove for those who love old records and CDs. The owner

Insider Tip

regards his shop a bit like a living room and does not like it when people start rummaging through the records as soon as they arrive (ul. Podbrzezie 6A; Mon–Fri 10am–4pm, Sat 11am–2pm).

The team from **Boogie Flowear** started with their hip fashion in Kielce and worked their way on to Krakow. The shop stocks shirts, shoes and other clothing from independent Polish designers which does not only appeal to skaters and break dancers (ul. Joselewicza 15; tel: 694 504 727; www.boogie flowear.com; Mon–Fri 11am–7pm, Sat, Sun until 5pm).

A good address for postcards and posters with old black-and-white motifs of Krakow as well as modern photo can be found in Galerie **LueLue** If you wish you can have your own photos printed on paper or fabric (ul. Miodowa 22; tel: 728 551 024; www.luelue.pl; 11am–7pm).

Numerous little shops and galleries line Ulica Józefa. Toumai Tabaz offers modern and antique handicraft from Iran and its neighbouring countries at his **Galeria Persja** (no. 13), including carpets, colourful fabrics, jewellery and deco articles (tel: 600 037 060; www. persja.pl; Mon–Sun 11am–6pm).

As its names indicates **Galerie d'Art Naif** (Hausnr. 11) focuses on naive art. Founder and collector Leszek Macak shows works there by well-known Polish artists such as Nikifor, but also by many undiscovered painters and sculptors (tel: 124 210 637; http://artnaive. sky.pl; Mon–Fri 11am–5pm, Sat, Sun until 3pm).

Women's fashion in retro style of the 1940s–60s, with matching accessories are available at **Vintage Classics** (no.11; tel: 509 626 818; www.vintage classics.pl; Mon–Sat 11am–7pm, Sun 10am–4pm).

PAON nonchalant brings together under one roof women's fashion, shoes and accessories from small Polish labels (tel: 124 446 074 and tel: 534 484 399; Mon–Sat 10am–6pm, Sun until 4pm).

At **Blazko Jewellery** (also at no. 11), jewellery designer Grzesiek Błażko showcases his colourful jewellery collection (tel: 508 646 298; www.blazko.pl; Mon–Fri 11am–7pm, Sat, Sun until 3pm).

Young fashion for women is the work of **Boutique Nuumi** (no, 14; tel: 881 762 366; daily 11am–7pm).

The work of various Polish designers can be found at the **Marka Concept Store** at no.5. The collection comprises among other things textiles, ceramics and jewellery (tel: 124 222 965; www.marka-concept store.pl; Mon–Fri noon–6pm, Sat 11am–5pm, Sun 11am–4pm).

Limitless shopping pleasure is the promise of **Galeria Kazimierz**, a shopping centre on the eastern edge of Kazimierz. Around 150 shops sell clothes, shoes, leatherware, jewellery, accessories, books and much more by Polish and international manufacturers (ul. Podgórze 38; tel: 124 330 101; www.galeria kazimierz.pl; Mon–Sat 10am–10pm, Sun until 8pm).

CULINARY TREATS

Regional products without any chemical additives from small-scale agricultural producers are available in the well-stocked grocery **Bacówka** on Plac Wolnica (► 130). The ranges comprises numerous meat and ham products, goat and sheep's cheese as well as jam and honey (tel: 607 421 584; www.bacowka towary.pl; Mon–Fri 7am–7pm, Sat 8am–3pm).

Bombonierka is a paradise for those with a sweet tooth: sweets,

lollipops and chocolate fruit in all shapes and colours (ul. Dietla 45 A; tel: 602 216 826; www. sklepbombionerka.pl; Mon–Fri 11am–6pm, Sat until 3pm).

The Benedictine monks in Tyniec sell high-quality cloister products in their shop. If you do not have time for an excursion to Tyniec (► 171) then look by **Produkty Benedyktyńskie**. In the small shop you will find quality foodstuffs, cosmetics, medicinal herbs, teas and various cloister liqueurs (ul. Krakowska 29; Mon–Fri 9am–6pm, Sat until 2pm; tel: 124 220 2176; www.produkty benedyktynskie.com.pl).

Insider Tip

At **Regionalne Alkohole** you are spoilt for choice with the variety of regional beers, wines and spirits (Miodowa 28a; tel: 533 593 335; www.regionalnealkohole.pl; Mon–Wed noon–10pm, Thu–Sat 10am–midnight, Sun noon–9pm).

Where to…
Go Out

In the evenings, the sound of Klezmer music can be heard all around Plac Szeroka in the heart of Kazimierz. For many tour groups, a visit to such a concert is part of the standard program. Young people out on the town tend to prefer to start the evening in the pubs around Plac Nowy (► 121) and then go off to the disco clubs where the parties last until early in the morning.

KLEZMER LIVE

Many of the restaurants and cafés around Plac Szeroka not only woo customers with their Jewish food, but also with invitations to listen to Klezmer concerts over dinner. The generally cheerful but sometimes melancholic music plays for example every evening in the **Klezmer-Hois** (➤ 133) or in the Ariel restaurant (➤ 132). A living legend is pianist **Leopold Kozłowski**, born in 1918, who at well over 90 continues to give pleasure to his audience in the Klezmer Hois and at the Jewish Culture Festival; he also had a small role in the Spielberg film *Schindler's List* (➤ 145).

Szeroka Street is where the Krakow band "Kroke" did its first gigs. With its jazzed-up version of Klezmer music, the three musicians act like Krakow's ambassadors and have in the meantime acquired a growing international audience.

NIGHTLIFE

Cocon Music Club

Founded in 2001, it is regarded as one of the oldest and best-known gay clubs in Poland. Besides the large dance floor, there is also a covered winter garden for smokers, a smaller second dance floor, a quiet lounge as well as three bars. People don't only go to Cocon at the weekends to party to the music of well-known DJs or for Karaoke on Thursday; talks, readings and theatre performances also take place there.

➕ 197 E2 ✉ Gazowa 21
☎ 126 322 296; www.klub-cocon.pl
🕐 Thu 9pm–5am, Fri, Sat 10pm–5am

Club Kabaret

With Poland's, as yet only, Drag-Queen revue "Love me", Lady Brigitte, Papina McQueen and Pussy Cat churn up the emotions of their audience with their love songs. The club is also a meeting point for salsa and tango dances and organises rock and jazz evenings as well as cabaret evenings.

➕ 197 D3 ✉ Krakowska 5
☎ 501 747 418; www.klubkabaret.pl
🕐 Tue–Sun from 6pm

Club Piękny Pies

The "Pretty Dog" is the meeting place of artists and students who tend to be in jeans and trainers as opposed to high heels or jacket and tie. People meet here for a beer or a cocktail to the sound of rock, punk, independent and electro music. At the weekends, concerts often take place or DJs play in the basement.

➕ 197 D3 ✉ Bożego Ciała 9
🕐 Sun–Thu 4pm–3am, Fri, Sat 4pm–5am

LaF

In the small, rather discreetly located club, women come together who want to meet other women, but the crowd also includes homosexual men and heteros. They dance to the classics of the 60s to 80s and to hip hop. The entrance to the cellar rooms is through Café Młynek.

➕ 197 E2
✉ Pl. Wolnica 7
☎ 607 307 121
🕐 Fri, Sat 10pm–4am

Opium Music Club

The predominantly young crowd here meets from Sunday to Thursday to listen to chillout music; by 9pm on Friday and Saturday the dance floor is full. A popular meeting place during the summer months is the large garden with beer tables and comfortable lounge furniture.

➕ 197 E4
✉ Jakuba 19
☎ 124 219 461; www.opium.krakow.pl
🕐 Mon–Fri from 2pm, Sat, Sun from 10am

Taawa

Whilst in most of the pubs in the surrounding area, there is a foible for vintage style, Taawa is more in favour of gleaming chrome, glass and leather. A chic ambience for an equally chic crowd. The bouncers make sure that this match is maintained

➕ 197 E3
✉ Estery 18
☎ 608 503 080; www.taawa.pl
🕐 Fri, Sat 9pm–5am

Podgórze & Surroundings

 **Little Treats**

Street Art
An overly large bell on a house wall in Ulica Piwna (no. 3) stands for the influence of the church in Poland – discover the numerous **wall paintings** in the Podgórze district.

Culinary Excursion into History
Do want to eat as they did in the 17th century? Go to the **Ogniem i Mieczem restaurant** (► 157), which also offers authentic rustic flair to go with the hearty dishes.

Sunbathe by the Lake
You can't swim in **Zakrzówek** Lake, but the rural idyll is an inviting place to have a picnic and to relax in the sun (from Podgórze with tram 11 or 23 to Norymberska).

Getting Your Bearings

Podgórze is the Polish word for foothills, and in fact the part of town on the south side of the Vistula does indeed nestle against white chalk cliffs. The Habsburgs founded the town in 1784 and called it Josefstadt after Emperor Joseph II. It is only since 1915 that Podgórze has been part of Krakow. The Nazis created a ghetto there for Krakow's Jewish population and later in Płaszów, located to the south, a concentration camp. In the former enamelware factory of Oskar Schindler there is an exhibition about the German occupation. Established here too is Krakow's top address for contemporary art, the MOCAK Museum.

Podgórze is a district in transition. Springing up among the dilapidated buildings are a growing number of freshly renovated historical residential buildings or new modern apartment blocks. Especially in the area by the Vistula more and more luxury flats are being built.

47 Muzeum Sztuki i Techniki Japońskiej Manggha

Most Grunwaldzki

Rondo Grunwaldzkie

ICE Kraków Congress Centre **48**

Marii Konopnickiej

Wisła

Karola Rollego

Buildings rcpresenting modern Krakow include the new Cricoteka, dedicated to documenting the art of Tadeusz Kantor, the Congress and event centre located further west, ICE Krakow and the Manggha Museum of Japanese Art and Technology.

Since a pedestrian bridge has connected Podgórze with Kazimierz, the district to the south of the Vistula has been developing into an area to eat out, with smart restaurants and pubs. Young people tend to make a beeline for the neighbouring district of Dębniki and the Forum directly on the Vistula, once a hotel that stood empty for more than ten years before evolving into one of the most popular party locations of the city and a place where young Polish couturiers and designers sell their products.

Getting Your Bearings

TOP 10

⭐ Fabryka Schindlera
   (Schindler's Factory)
   ➤ 144

Don't Miss

At Your Leisure

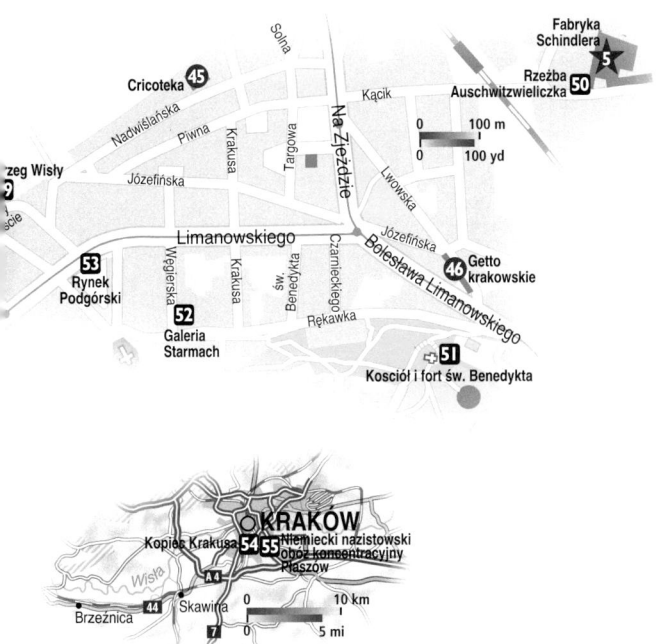

The Perfect Day

An abundance of history and art awaits you in the Podgórze district. If you follow our itinerary for the day you will take in the most important sight in the districts south of the Vistula.

🕘 9:30am

Start your discovery tour of Podgórze on the **Plac Bohaterów Getta**, the square dedicated to the heroes of the ghetto. There, an installation consisting of lots of chairs commemorates the district's sad history (photo right). In **Apteka Pod Orłem** (► 151) you will find a small exhibition about the time of the 46 **ghetto** (► 150).

🕚 11:00am

You can learn more about life in Krakow during the time of the German occupation in the former ⭐**enamelware factory of Oskar Schindler** (picture right above; ► 144). Take a bit of time for the multimedia exhibition, which is very well done.

🕧 12:30pm

In an old industrial warehouse, right next to the Schindler factory, you can eat delicious meals in the modern restaurant **Industrial** (► 156) and admire the artworks on the ceiling at the same time.

🕑 2:00pm

More modern art is on view next door in **MOCAK** (► 146), Krakow's museum for contemporary art. It focuses mainly on Polish works from the time of the political turnaround.

47 **Muzeum Sztuki i Techniki Japońskiej Manggha**

48 **ICE Kraków Congress Centre**

Fabryka Schindlera

Rzeźba Auschwitzwieliczka 50

45 Cricoteka

49 Brzeg Wisły

Getto krakowskie 46

Rynek Podgórski

Galeria Starmach 52

53

0   200 m
0   200 yd

Kościół i fort św. Benedykta 51

Wisła

⏰ 4:00pm

Take a look at the **Centrum Szkła i Ceramiki** (➤ 159) right opposite. There you can not only view the work of modern glass and porcelain artists, you may even find a nice souvenir to take home.

⏰ 6:00pm

Walk along the **49 south bank of the Vistula** (➤ 153) to **Forum Przestrzenie** (➤ 158) and take an evening aperitif lying on one of the lounge chairs.

⏰ 7:30pm

Go on a culinary excursion to the Far East today: in the **Tao** restaurant (➤ 157), which is very near the Bernatka pedestrian bridge (photo below) you can order fine Asian food. The selection includes Japanese *teppanyaki* dishes, which are prepared directly at your table – and when the weather is good in the beautiful garden.

⭐5 Fabryka Schindlera
(Schindler's Factory)

**The rather unprepossessing exterior of Oskar Schindler's former
factory is top of the list for visitors to Krakow on the south side
of the Vistula. Located in the old office buildings is the exhibition
about Krakow during the occupation from 1939 to 1945, which is
well worth seeing. Right next door in the old factory halls, the MOCAK
Museum exhibits contemporary art.**

It was just after the beginning of the German occupation of
Poland that Oskar Schindler took over the small enamelware
factory built in 1890 and located in the industrial district of
Zabłocie (ul. Lipowa 4). There he initially produced china,
which he mainly sold to the army, later he produced shell
cases and other armaments. On the black market he soon
amassed a fortune, securing his influence with bribes. He
used both later to save Jews from elimination.

From Playboy to Life Saver

Schindler's factory already employed 250 workers after just
a few months and this number increased to 800 workers
by the end of 1942, almost half of which were Jews from
the ghetto in Podgórze. When this closed in March 1943,
Schindler received permission to accommodate his Jewish
workers in their own camp on the factory grounds. Although
the factory's camp was run like an offshoot of the **Płaszów
Concentration Camp** (▶ 155), the Jewish workers there
lived under better conditions and were protected from the
despotism of the SS guards.

Visitors in
front of the
entrance to
the exhibition
in the
former office
buildings
of Oskar
Schindler's
enamelware
factory

Fabryka Schindlera

Oskar Schindler, who became a member of the Nazi party for opportunistic reasons in 1939, metamorphosised from a playboy and war profiteer to saviour of numerous Jews. When it became known in summer 1944 that the camp in Płaszów was to be closed down, he managed to get his factory transferred to Mähren. He received permission to take with him around 1,100 Jewish workers from his factory and the Płaszów concentration camp, thus saving them from certain death at the extermination camp.

Just before the end of the war Schindler fled to Germany, where his lifestyle after the war was very modest. **Steven Spielberg's** film **_Schindler's List_** (1993) made a wide audience aware of the factory owners commitment and fate. Schindler was awarded "The Righteous Among the Nations" honorific by the state of Israel because he had put his own life at risk to save Jews from murder.

Schindler's former enamel factory was nationalised after 1945 and produced telecommunications systems until the turnaround. It subsequently stood empty until the city of Krakow took over the land in 2005 and soon afterwards started transforming the old enamel factory into a museum.

Krakow at the Time of the Occupation 1939 to 1945

In the three-storey office buildings a new **Branch of the Historical Museum** opened in 2010 that focuses on the history of the town and day-to-day life of its citizens in the years from 1939 to 1945 (photo ► 143). At the start of the exhibition, the world is still in order; photos show a summer day in Krakow in 1939. It is the last summer before the War and happy people are out and about on the streets. What follows is an impressive walk through 45 stations of the town's history: first decrees by the German occupiers, the renaming of streets, first restrictions for the Jewish population, first atrocities.

On their way through the exhibition, visitors are witnesses of despotism and oppression, they are made aware of the conditions under the occupying army. They are present when the ghetto is set up in Podgórze and later accompany the Jewish population on the way to Płaszów. They receive an impression of the inhuman conditions there, hear the commands from the loudspeakers during the later eviction. Dogs bark and there are the sounds of shots. At the end of the route, the last surge of the German occupiers, the retreat and the arrival of the Soviet Army, a portrait of Stalin and the information that another difficult time was about to begin for Poland.

The explanations in English and Polish are often un-necessary, the photos and film recordings, the documents, installations and replicas speak for themselves, impressively conveying an idea of the years of the occupation and the everyday life of the people during this time. The former office of Oskar Schindler, still with the furnishing of the war years, is integrated into the tour; an installation lists the names of the Jews that were saved by him.

Podgórze & Surroundings

Muzeum Sztuki Współczesnej w Krakowie

It would be difficult to find a bigger contrast: while in the branch of the Historical Museum, you walk along the narrow aisles between the dark years of Krakow's history, the neighbouring **Museum of Contemporary Art Kraków** (**MOCAK**) with its large glass façade and light-flooded, spacious room stands as a symbol for the present and future. The Italian architect Claudio Nardi converted six halls of the former enamel factory and added a modern extension. His design gives the rather sober industrial architecture a certain Mediterranean flair.

The MOCAK was the first new art museum to be built after World War II, and it displays one of the country's most extensive collections of Polish and international contemporary art.

In the entrance area of the exhibition is a provocative installation by the Polish artist Grzegorz Klaman, comprising of a metal sign bearing the words *Kunst Macht Frei* (*Art Sets You Free*) – a clear reference to the sign above the entrance to Auschwitz *Arbeit Macht Frei* (*Work Sets You Free*). With this installation, the museum not only brings up the subject of the country's history, which we cannot and do not want to avoid in such a historic place, but also makes it clear that its aspiration is to be a place that supports the freedom of art. That is why time and again among the exhibited works visitors see exhibits that lead to intense discussion, such as Tomasz Bajer's installation, which depicts a cell in the Guantanamo prison camp, or the photo triptych by Katarzyna Górna entitled *Fuck me, fuck you, peace*, depicting young women in various phase of their life in explicit poses.

Since the museum opened in 2011, it has gradually extended its collection, which in the meantime now encompasses more than 4,000 works. Among these are works by high-profile Polish artists such as Paweł Althamer, Katarzyna Kozyra and Wilhelm Sasnal, but also from international greats such as the Chinese artist

Insider Tip

INSIDER INFO

- **Tickets** for the branch of the Historical Museum in **Schindler's Factory** cost 21 złoty and for the **MOCAK** 10 złoty for adults. It is better to buy the **Combined Ticket**, which includes a visit to the exhibition about "Krakow during the years 1939 to 1945" and the collections at the MOCAK. It only costs 22 złoty. It is even cheaper on museum days: on Mondays you can visit the Historical Museum in Schindler's Factory free-of-charge, and the same applies for MOCAK on Tuesdays.

- There is a helpful **mobile App** for people visiting the MOCAK exhibitions, which has been conceived specially for Android and iOS Smart phones. You can call up information about the individual artworks in English using iBeacons or QR codes (download links can be found at www.mocak.pl).

- Most of the books at the **MOCAK's Museum Shop** are available in both Polish and English, and the shop also sells pretty souvenirs such as art postcards, printed art reproductions, notepads and games.

This photo installation by Swiss artist Beat Streuli is one of the exhibits on show at the MOCAK

Ai Weiwei. The museum presents parts of its collection in a changing programme of exhibitions. Besides that, other works are on display in the many temporary exhibitions it organises.

TAKING A BREAK

After your museum tour, you can relax and build up your strength again on comfortable sofas in the modern interior of **Café Mocak** or between the props and documents from *Schindler's List* in the Historical Museum's **Filmcafé**.

➕ 198 C2 ✉ ul. Lipowa 4
☎ Fabryka Schindlera: 122 571 017; www.mhk.pl;
MOCAK: 122 634 000; www.mocak.pl
🎟 Fabryka Schindlera: April–Oct Mon 10am–4pm, Tue–Sun 9am–8pm;
Nov–March Mon 10am–2pm, Tue–Sun 10am–6pm;
MOCAK: Tue–Sun 11am–7pm
🚋 Tram 3, 19, 24 (Pl. Bohaterów Getta); Tram 6, 11, 13, 23 (ul. Limanowskiego; each with a 5 min walk at the end); Tram 9, 20, 50 (Zabłocie)
✋ ➤ Insider Info

THE PHOTOGRAPHER FROM AUSCHWITZ

Among the first works at MOCAK is a book about **Wilhelm Brasse** (1917–2012), a photographer from Żywiec (Saynbusch). He was deported to Auschwitz in 1940, and the Gestapo assigned him the task of photographing the prisoners for the camp files. Shortly before the camp was liberated, he was told to destroy the pictures, but he was able to save the negatives of almost 40,000 prisoners. The book *Wilhelm Brasse: Photographer* and the enclosed DVD – available from the museum shop – is based on conversations that the MOCAK Director Maria Anna Potocka had with Brasse just before his death. The book and DVD contain many of his photographs.

⑮ Cricoteka

In the list of favourite photo motifs in Krakow, the unusual new Cricoteka building located directly by the Vistula earned a place right at the top soon after it was unveiled. The Museum and Documentation Centre is dedicated to the work of Tadeusz Kantor (1915–1990), Krakow's most well-known theatre director.

An imposing structure made of reinforced concrete, covered in corroded and perforated steel arches over the old power station on the bank of the Vistula. Defiantly, the tower of the little factory building stretches up between the two wings of the new building. During the day, sunlight shines down inside through the thousands of little holes; in the evening the light inside illuminates the shell of the massive building.

Two firms of architects based in Krakow took their inspiration for the museum design from a pencil sketch by Tadeusz Kantor of a stooped man transporting a table. They carved into one side of the imaginary table then put the now V-shaped construction on the back of the old power station. The two long arms of the steel structure contain the exhibition rooms, which can be reached via the foyer in the basement.

Exceptional architecture to house exceptional work; the Cricoteka is dedicated to the theatre director Tadeusz Kantor

The new Cricoteka was opened at the end of 2014 in good time to celebrate the 100th birthday of Tadeusz Kantor and is dedicated to his artistic work. Kantor who grew up in a small Galician village headed an underground theatre in Krakow during the time of the German occupation, and later founded his theatre "Cricot 2" there in 1955.

He directed and adapted his experimental, visually commanding plays himself for the stage. Kantor became one of the most important theatre producers,

Kantor's art is on show in spacious exhibition rooms

critically monitored by the powers at be in Poland, and celebrated abroad. He also earned a name for himself as an artist and theatre critic. In December 1990, during a rehearsal shortly before the opening night of his last play *Today is My birthday*, Kantor died.

Kantor had already set up Cricoteka in 1980. Located in the Old Town, it was conceived as the headquarters of his theatre and archive for his many stage objects and props. This extensive collection now has its place in the exhibition centre by the Vistula.

In the spaciously arranged rooms, visitors are able to feel what it is like to be on stage and thus really take in the effect of the props. There are hundreds of objects and costumes, films and video recordings as well as sketches and theoretical drafts by Kantor. His career as an artist is recounted at seven stations – from his underground theatre through to his "Theatre of Death" towards the end of his career.

The cultural centre also offers space for temporary exhibitions of contemporary art, is used for theatre performances and is home to an educational centre as well as a library.

TAKING A BREAK

Crico Café on the 4th floor of Cricoteka offers a beautiful view. You can look out through the perforated exterior of the building towards the Vistula and Wawel.

---

198 A2 ✉ Nadwiślańska 2–4
☎ 124 427 770; www.news.cricoteka.pl
🕐 Tue–Sun 11am–7pm
🚌 Tram 3, 19, 24 (Pl. Bohaterów Getta); Tram 6, 8, 11, 13, 19, 23 (Korona)
💰 10 złoty (free on Tue)

46 Getto krakowskie
(Krakow Ghetto)

An installation of 70 large metal chairs placed singly or in small groups occupies a vacant space on Plac Bohaterów Getta. They commemorate the many thousands of Jews deported from here to the extermination camps. Located on the square was one of the entrances to the former ghetto. There is little evidence of it today.

The Nazis had made it clear that they wanted to make Krakow "free of Jews". From mid-1940 tens of thousands of Jews had already been forced to leave the town. On 6 March a ghetto was set up on the south side of the Vistula in Podgórze. It covered an area of 400m × 600m (1310ft × 1970ft) between the Rynek Podgórsky and the Plac Zdody, today's **Plac Bohaterów Getta** ("Heroes of the Ghetto Square"). Up to 18,000 Jews were crammed into a space in which about 3,000 people used to live. The non-Jewish inhabitants had to leave the area.

The empty chairs on Plac Bohaterów Getta remind people of the Jews that were deported from here to the extermination camps.

A Wall in the Shape of Tombstones
A high wall, which not coincidentally resembled Jewish tombstones, surrounded the ghetto. Anyone who left it without permission risked the death penalty. The ghetto inhabitants were forced to work at factories inside and out-side the ghetto. Food was strictly rationed and a **Judenrat** (Jewish Council) was in charge of maintaining order. From May 1942 thousands of people, predominantly the elderly, ill, women and infants were transported to the extermination camps in Belzac. Hundreds of Jews met their death through the SS during the massacre. On 13 and 14 March 1943 the ghetto was liquidated. Those capable of work were taken to the camp in Płaszów (► 155), the rest were deported to Auschwitz or shot straight away.

Hardly anything from that period still exists to remind people of the area's tragic history. Behind a primary school in Ulica Limanowskiego (no. 62), there is still a small piece of the former ghetto wall, as there is at Ulica Lwowska (nos. 25 to 29). Since 1983, it has borne a commemorative plaque to remind people of the ghetto inhabitants: "Here they lived, suffered and perished at the hands of Hitler's executioners." Signs on some of the buildings indicate which Jewish establishments were located there during the ghetto period, In Ulica Józefińska, there was a Jewish orphanage at no. 12, and next door at no. 14 the Jewish hospital. A commemorative plaque on a house in Ulica Piwna (no. 27) has informed its readers since 1948 that it was there that the members of the **Żydowska Organizacja Bojowa**, ("Jewish Combat Organisation") met and organised various acts of sabotage. Many of their members were caught by the Gestapo and murdered.

Since the end of 2005, 70 chairs have stood on the Plac Bohaterów Getta in memory of the fate that awaited many thousands of Jews who were transported from there to the extermination camps. **Roman Polański** was among the first people to provide money for the installation by **Piotr Lewicki**. The director had lived with his parents in the ghetto of Podgórze. Polański's mother was murdered at Auschwitz, his father survived the War in Mauthausen Concentration Camp, he himself was able to escape when the ghetto was being liquidated and found refuge with Polish families until the end of the war. A large sum for the memorial also came from a foundation set up by the director **Steven Spielberg**.

TAKING A BREAK

Showing off the diverse cuisine of the former multi-ethnic state of Galicia is the aim of the **Galicja Po Kolei restaurant** (ul. Lwowska 4; ➤ 156).

Insider Tip

✚ 198 B/C1 ✉ Pl. Bohaterów Getta 18
☎ 126 655 625; www.mhk.pl 🕐 Mon 10am–2pm, Tue–Sun 9am–5pm
🚊 Tram 3, 19, 24 (Pl. Bohaterów Getta)
✋ 10 złoty (free on Mon)

PHARMACY UNDER THE EAGLE

Tadeusz Pankiewicz was the only non-Jewish citizen allowed to continue living in Podgórze during the time it was a ghetto. He risked his life to help the Jewish inhabitants, ran the **Apteka pod Orłem**, the "Pharmacy under the Eagle", on what is now Plac Bohaterów Getta and later wrote a book about the atrocities he experienced there. Like Oskar Schindler, he was awarded "The Righteous Among the Nations" honorific. A small museum was set up in his former pharmacy in the 1980s. Since 2013, a department of the Historical Museum has also been located there. The rooms have been preserved, the shelves in the entrance area are still stacked with old medicines. It is a small exhibition that is well worth seeing, because it gives visitors an idea of what life was like for Jews in the ghetto and of the fate that awaited them in the Płaszów Concentration Camp as well as of the commitment of Tadeusz Pankiewicz.

At Your Leisure

47 Muzeum Sztuki i Techniki Japońskiej Manggha (Manggha Museum of Japanese Art and Technology)

The roof of the art museum built on the bank of the Vistula in 1994 takes its inspiration from the waves of the river. It houses the extensive collection of Japanese art that **Feliks "Manggha" Jasieński** donated to the National Museum in 1920. Around 70 years later, the benefactor's wish was fulfilled when a special place was created for them. The project was supported by the film-maker Andrzej Wajda, who came into contact with Japanese art for the first time when he saw Jasieński's collection as a young man. He donated the prize money for the renowned Kyoto Prize, which he received in 1987 for the construction of the museum. Wajda also later endowed his own extensive archive to the museum. On show at the museum are temporary exhibitions on art and design from the Far East.

INSIDER INFO

In summer, from the terrace of the **Café Manggha** you can enjoy the view across the Vistula to Wawel Hill over a cup of authentic Japanese tea, sushi or sashimi (www.cafe manggha.com.pl; Tue–Sun 10am–5pm).

Also located on the museum estate is Poland's only Japanese school.

➕ 196 A3 ✉ M. Konopnieckiej 26
☎ 122 672 703; www.manggha.pl
🕐 Tue–Sun 10am–6pm
🚊 Tram 6, 8, 18, 70, 73 (Wawel; 10 min. on foot); Bus 124, 144, 164, 169, 173, 179, 194, 229, 304, 424, 608 (Konopnieckiej)
💰 20 złoty (free on Tue)

48 ICE Kraków Congress Centre

The curved silhouette, pixelated facade and broad window fronts of the modern ICE Kraków building set a distinctive urban accent in the south of Krakow.

An excursion ship chugs sedately past the Manggha Museum

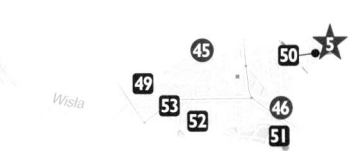

The structure located by the Vistula and opened at the end of 2014 has acted like a magnet: several new business hotels have developed in the direct vicinity. The new building not only offers space for large conferences but also for concerts, fashion shows, trade fairs, exhibitions and large banquets.

The building erected for the town and managed by the municipal festival office is equally successful in both its functions, namely as a business and cultural centre.

🏠 196 A2 ✉ M. Konopnieckiej 17
☎ 123 542 300; www.icekrakow.com
🚋 Tram 12, 18, 22, 52, 62 (Centrum Kongresowe)

49 Brzeg Wisły (Vistula Bank)

For a leisurely stroll, the boulevards on both sides of the Vistula offer a perfect choice. The south bank is quieter than, for instance, the Wawel area. An exception is the area by **Forum Przestrzenie** (➤ 158). The club that opened in 2013 is one of the in-places for Krakow students. Once you get a few paces past it

though, peace returns. Cyclists can continue the excursion along the river to the edge of town and on to the Benedictine Abbey of Tyniec (➤ 171).

🏠 197 E1 🚋 Tram 6, 8, 11, 13, 19, 23 (Korona); Tram 12, 18, 22, 52, 62 (Centrum Kongresowe)

50 Rzeźba Auschwitzwieliczka (Auschwitzwieliczka Sculpture)

Anyone on the way from Plac Bohaterów Getta (➤ 150) to Oskar Schindler's Factory (➤ 144) through the 17m (56ft) long and 3m (10ft) tall concrete passageway only notices on second glance that it is actually a work of art. Letters, cut into the ceiling form the word AUSCHWITZWIELICZKA. The Polish sculptor Mirosław Bałka (born 1958) took the inspiration for the sculpture from the often very garish advertising done by local travel agencies for their tours to Auschwitz and the

The ICE's glass palace soon became a major attraction

Podgórze & Surroundings

Wieliczka salt mines (➤ 163), marketing the former extermination camp as if it were Disneyland.

🚹 198 C2 🚊 Tram 3, 19, 24 (Pl. Bohaterów Getta); Tram 6, 11, 13, 23 (ul. Limanowskiego; 5 min. walk in each case); Tram 9, 20, 50 (Zabłocie)

🟥51 Kościół i fort św. Benedykta (St Benedict Church and Fort)

On the **Krzemionki mountain range**, which borders Podgórze to the south, Benedictine monks built a small Romanesque church in the 12th century. Little is known about its beginnings, the original form was lost during later building work. The interior, now designed in the Baroque style, is only on view once a year when, as is tradition, a mass takes place there on the Tuesday after Easter. Only a few steps away, the Habsburgs had one of three forts built here in the mid 19th century, the purpose of which was to protect Podgórze from attacks. St Benedict Fort is the only fort to have survived the test of time, but the polygon-shaped brick building has been empty for a long time.

Insider Tip

🚹 198 B/C1 🚊 Tram 3, 6, 11, 23, 24, 69, 73, Bus 127, 158, 174, 178, 643, 669 (Powstańców Wielkopolskich)

🟥52 Galeria Starmach

This little red-brick building built at the end of the 19th century with its three gables and large window fronts was once a Jewish prayer house. It was turned into a large shop during the German occupation and later used as a factory. In 1996 the art collectors **Teresa and Andrzej Starmach** bought it and transferred their gallery from Krakow's Main Market Square to the new location. In the large exhibition room, they present changing exhibitions on contemporary Polish and international artists. The "Krakow Photo Month" is opened there every year in May.

🚹 198 A1 ✉ Węgierska 5
☎ 126 564 915; www.starmach.com.pl
🕐 Mon–Fri 9am–6pm
🚊 Tram 6, 8, 11, 13, 19, 23 (Korona); Tram 6, 11, 13, 23 (ul. Limanowskiego)
✋ Free

🟥53 Rynek Podgórski (Podgórze Market Square)

Markets only take place on Podgórze's triangular, cobbled market square very occasionally these days, for example just before Christmas. It is worth taking a closer look at the old town hall on Rynek Podgórski (no. 13). In 1844/45, the former private residence Pod Czarnym Orłem ("Under the Black Eagle") was adapted in the Historicist style to serve the municipal authorities of the then independent town. During the time of the ghetto, the **Judenrat** (Jewish Council) had its base here. Today it accommodates parts of the Krakow city administration. Towering over the south side of the square is the neo-Gothic **Kościół św. Józefa (St Joseph's Church)** built between 1905 and 1909.

🚹 197 F1 ✉ Rynek Podgórski
🚊 Tram 6, 8, 11, 13, 19, 23 (Korona)

🟥54 Kopiec Krakusa (Krakus Mound)

The 16m (52.5ft) high mound with a diameter of 57m (187ft) is closely associated with the legends of the mystical King Krakus, the founder of Krakow. People have even looked for his grave there. According to serious archaeological research, the artificial mound was apparently erected between the 7th and 10th

The fabled Krakus Mound offers a panoramic view of Krakow

centuries, some researchers believe it may be even older. The mystical place is a popular meeting place for young people at night, who as they pause from their partying enjoy the view on the illuminated town below.

✚ 198 south C1 🚋 Tram 3, 6, 11, 23, 24, 69, 73; Bus 127, 158, 174, 178, 643, 669 (Powstańców Wielkopolskich)

55 Niemiecki nazistowski obóz koncentracyjny Płaszów (German National Socialist Concentration Camp Płaszów)

In the summer of 1940 a forced labour camp was set up in Płaszów in the south of Krakow, which later became a concentration camp. At times up to 25,000 people lived behind the heavily guarded electric fences. Thousands died as a result of hunger, overwork, mistreatment or execution, many were deported to other extermination camps. Only about 2,000 people survived the evacuation of the camp, of which little remains to remind us. The wooden barracks disappeared; the remains of the fence and the camp road paved in tombstones are simply props from the film shooting for *Schindler's List*

(➤ 145). Neighbours take their dogs for a walk here.

The camp commander Amon Göth, notorious for his cruelty, was hung in Krakow in 1946. His former villa stands between other residential houses in Ulica Heltmana (no. 22), in recent years run-down and up for sale. Even the neighbouring "Grey House" in Ulica Jerozolimska (no. 3), whose cellars once served as a prison and place of torture remained intact and is now a normal residential house. There are several memorials to the former concentration camp, and there is a large wooden crucifix as a reminder of the past terror.

✚ 198 southwards C1
🚋 Tram 3, 6, 11, 13, 23;
Bus 107, 143 , 243, 643, 669 (Dworcowa; from there it is about 5 min. by foot along Ulica Abrahama to Ulica Hetmana)

Where to...
Eat and Drink

Prices
A main course (without drinks)
£ under 45 złoty   ££ 45–90 złoty   £££ over 90 złoty

RESTAURANTS

Churrasco 1st unlimited ££
Since the redevelopment of the former Optima chocolate factory, one section of the building has become a new address for meat lovers. In Churrasco you can eat skewers of grilled meat galore, prepared in authentic Brazilian style, but there are also burgers, pizza and other choices on the menu.

✚ 198 A1 ✉ Krakusa 11
☎ 791 001 522 🕐 Mon–Fri 10am–midnight, Sat–Sun 11am–midnight

Delecta £
The trattoria offers a large selection of tasty pizzas with thin crispy pastry bases, cooked in a stone oven and available in two sizes. The menu also features home-made pasta, risotto as well as a range of well-prepared fish and meat dishes.

✚ 198 A2 ✉ Limanowskiego 11
☎ 124 235 001; www.restauracja-delecta.pl
🕐 Sun–Thu 11am–10pm, Fri–Sat 11am–11pm

Galicja Po Kolei £
This rather unimposing restaurant specialises in traditional dishes from the former Habsburg Empire. Besides *Wiener Schnitzel*, it also serves national dishes from Hungary, Romania, Ukraine and Poland, all at a reasonable price.

✚ 198 B2 ✉ Lwowska 4
☎ 122 962 413; www.galicjapokolei.pl
🕐 Mon–Fri 11am–9pm, Sat, Sun noon–10pm

Industrial Resto & Bar ££
The bare concrete and heavy steel girders of a former production hall stand in direct contrast to the furnishings and the large-scale paintings, The restaurant picks up the industrial theme of the Zabłocie district and at the same time creates a link to the neighbouring museum MOCAK (► 146). The fish and meat dishes prepared in the open kitchen are little works of art.

✚ 198 C2 ✉ Lipowa 4 a
☎ 122 638 626; www.restoindustrial.pl
🕐 Mon–Thu noon–10pm, Fri, Sat noon–11pm, Sun noon–9:30pm

Jadłodajnia Wcoraj i dziś £
Some of the meals still use the recipes of the first owner Maria Polewkowa, who founded the guesthouse in 1934. Since this time, it has, except – for a short phase in the 1950s – been run by the family. The menu of the "Caféteria of yesterday and today" features Polish meals that are freshly prepared. Enjoy the delicious soups such as *żurek* und *barszcz czerwony* or the homemade *pierogi*.

✚ 198 B2 ✉ Pl. Bohaterów Getta 10
☎ 126 562 057; www.jadlodajnia.com
🕐 Mon–Fri 10am–6pm, Sat 10am–5pm

Makaroniarnia £
With untreated walls and old photographs from Bella Italia, the Makaroniarnia makes an inviting and relaxed impression. The dishes served are as under-stated as the furnishings and the service: reasonably priced pizza

and pasta as well as a selection of fish and meat dishes. Don't come with any great expectations, and you will leave satisfied.

✚ 197 B1 ✉ Brodzińskiego 3
☎ 124 300 147; www.makaronarnia.com
⏰ Mon–Thu 10am–10pm,
Fri, Sat 10am–11pm

Restauracja Ogniem i Mieczem ££

Take a trip through the time of the Polish Aristocratic Republic. The name "With Fire and Sword" is taken from a novel by literature Nobel prize winner Henryk Sienkiewicz, which takes place in the 17th century. The rich hearty meals that arrive on the table are also based on recipes from that time. The rooms look like a scene out of a historical film, with huge timber beams, long wooden tables and large open fireplaces. You must try the honey vodka.

✚ 197 south D1 ✉ Pl. Serkowskiego 7
☎ 126 562 328; www.ogogniemieczem.pl
⏰ Mon–Sat noon–11:30pm, Sun noon–10pm

Tao ££

Are you looking for a change from Polish meals and the omnipresent pizza? Then try the traditional Japanese Teppanyaki meals, sushi or Thai curry served at the Tao restaurant, where everything prepared is absolutely fresh and delicious. In the summer you can enjoy the garden in the evening and in the winter the fireplace. Tip: Relax beforehand with a Thai massage in the Tao spa. *Insider Tip*

✚ 197 F1 ✉ Józefińska 4
☎ 725 880 304; www.taogarden.pl
⏰ Daily noon–11pm

Twój Kucharz ££

Presenting cooking as a passion: in the open kitchen, you can look over the shoulders of the chefs. Anyone who wants to learn more can take part in a culinary workshop. The menu changes every week. Polish food is cleverly refined in Mediterranean or Asian style. Slow Food principles are followed in the kitchen, mainly using regional and organic products. Meals are paired with appropriate organic wines from small European producers.

✚ 198 C3 ✉ Ślusarska 3
☎ 123 530 104; www.twojkucharz.pl
⏰ Tue–Sat noon–10pm, Sun noon–8pm

Zabłocie 13 ££

A gem in the industrial district of Zabłocie as is reflected in its name. On the outside the little building with its wooden shutters and dormers looks very friendly, and inside there is a timelessly modern air. The menu is like a trip around the world and includes Polish dishes as well as Mediterranean fare and burgers.

✚ 198 B3 ✉ Zabłocie 13
☎ 509 215 038; http://zablocie13.pl
⏰ Daily 10am–10pm

Zakładka Food & Wine ££

The bistro with three dining rooms is in one of the most beautiful Baroque buildings in the district. The atmosphere is relaxed, the service good, and the menu features classic French specialities such as snails and *foie gras*. To accompany the meals, there are several kinds of Champagne and around 100 well selected wines from all over the world, which you can also enjoy at the bar.

✚ 197 F1 ✉ Józefińska 2
☎ 124 427 442; www.zakladkabistro.pl
⏰ Mon 5pm–11pm (summer only),
Tue–Thu noon–11pm, Fri, Sat noon–midnight,
Sun noon–10pm

Zayka £

A modern, relaxed restaurant with authentic Indian cuisine. On offer are pleasantly spicy fish, meat and vegetarian dishes. During the week, there is also an inexpensive lunch menu, either with or without meat.

✚ 198 B1 ✉ Limanowskiego 46
☎ 508 786 855; www.zayka.pl
⏰ Tue–Sun noon–9pm

Podgórze & Surroundings

PUBS AND BARS

Forum Przestrzenie

Planned as a model Socialist hotel and opened in 1989, the luxury Forum hotel by the Vistula stood empty for several years from 2002, serving solely as an enormous advertising space. Today it is a hot spot for Krakow's trendy young crowd – café, pub and club all rolled into one. On chic sofas in the former lobby, you can enjoy hip soft drinks or wine served in classical beer bottles; in the summer, the deckchairs in front of the restaurant are very popular. Breakfast is served until 4pm and pizza until late in the night; in the evenings there is a DJ.

✚ 196 B1 ✉ Marii Konopnieckiej 28
☎ 515 544 097; www.forumprzestrzenie.pl
🕓 Daily from 10am

Krako Slow Wines

If the sweet Amselfelder is the only name that occurs to you when you think about wine from Central and Eastern Europe, then test the fine wines from Armenia, Georgia, Rumania, the Czech Republic, Slovakia and Poland. Some of them are the product of organic cultivation. Krako Slow Wines is a wine shop and cosy bar rolled into one. To accompany them, you can order Hungarian Salami, Bulgarian *schopska* salad or Polish *bigos*. There is occasionally live music in the evenings.

✚ 198 C2 ✉ Lipowa 6 F
☎ 669 225 222; http://krakoslowwines.pl
🕓 Sun, Mon 10am–9pm, Tue–Thu 10am–10pm, Fri, Sat 10am–midnight

CAFÉS

Bal

The café in an old rather soberly furnished warehouse in the former industrial area of Zabłocie is mainly popular with young team members from the surrounding start-up companies. Besides coffee and breakfast, there is also a lunch menu with and without meat, and the brunch buffet at the weekend is very popular.

✚ 198 C3 ✉ Ślusarska 9
☎ 734 411 733 🕓 Daily 8:30am–9pm

Boulevard 11 Bistro & Wine

The small, modern café in the new apartment block by the Vistula is a favourite with the employees working at the offices nearby as well as visitors to the Cricoteka. Coffee is served from early in the morning, and the menu includes a small but fine range of breakfast choices, midday soups, salads and other light meals as well as a selection of homemade cakes.

✚ 197 F2 ✉ Nadwiślańska 11
☎ 512 437 377 🕓 Mon–Fri 8am–7pm, Sat 9am–7pm, Sun 9am–5pm

Cawa

A cosy café with an outdoor terrace for the entire day. In the morning, it serves a good breakfast, during the day only a few but very tasty meals, and in the evening there is a great choice of open wines or something sparkling. The younger generation hangs out here and chills to the music.

✚ 197 F1 ✉ Nadwiślańska 1
☎ 126 567 456; www.cawacafe.pl
🕓 Mon–Fri 8:30am–10pm, Sat, Sun 9:30am–11pm

Cinema Paradiso

From the outside, the Cinema Paradiso is not very spectacular and it is not particularly remarkable inside either, but the friendly Polish-Mexican couple who run it serve very good coffee. There is a small breakfast selection, and you can order tortillas and nachos throughout the day. In the evening, the films in the cinema auditorium are free of charge, and are often in English or Spanish, or Polish with English subtitles.

Insider Tip

✚ 197 south E1
✉ Pl. Niepodległości 1 ☎ 122 963 696

Ⓒ Mon–Thu 10am–midnight, Fri 10am–2am, Sat 8am–2am, Sun noon–midnight

Clubokawiarnia Kącik 6

The small alternative café is a good stop on the way to Schindler's Factory (➤ 144). Besides various coffee specialities there are also simple meals such as wraps, burgers and *pierogi*.

✚ 198 B2 ✉ Kącik 6 ☎ 602 761 054 Ⓒ Mon–Sat 10am–midnight

Rękawa

In this small, cosy restaurant, you can try all sorts of coffee from many different areas in the world. If you like it, you can also buy the coffee beans there and "brew" a pot yourself at home. To accompany your coffee at the restaurant, you can order from a selection of delicious cakes and fresh salads.

✚ 197 F1 ✉ Brodzińskiego 4 B ☎ 122 962 002 Ⓒ Mon–Fri 9am–10pm, Sat, Sun 10am–10pm

Stopkladka

🚼 This pretty café is particularly popular with children because it not only has a play corner it also offers regular chocolate workshops. Adults appreciate the good coffee and delectable apple cake.

✚ 197 F1 ✉ Brodzińskiego 8 ☎ 796 052 070 Ⓒ Mon–Fri 8:30am–10pm, Sat, Sun 9am–10pm

Where to…
Shop

The southern town districts do not have your typical boulevards for browsing and shopping. There are a few pearls spotted around, which you have to specifically aim for – but when you do, you may find yourself travelling home with a one-of-a-kind piece by a Polish designer or couturier.

In the **Centrum Szkła i Ceramiki** (Centre for Glass and Ceramics, ul. Lipowa 3; www.lipowa3.pl), vis-à-vis Schindler's Factory (➤ 144), you can watch the glass blowers at work, see the glass and ceramic exhibitions and also buy beautiful souvenirs made of glass and ceramic. The exhibitions and sales rooms are open from Mon–Fri 9am–5pm and Sat 10am–2pm.

What looks at first glance to be a crushed paper cup is actually made of porcelain and is part of the **Manufaktura Porcelany collection** (Porzellanmanufaktur, ul. Węgierska 7/2; www.manufaktura porcelany.pl). The company offers original cups, bowls and salt shakers as well as earrings made of porcelain. Tours can be arranged by contacting the owner Liliana Sztybel at tel: 880 509 414.

Small regional farmers sell their food products at the **Targ Pietruszkowy** (ul. Kalwaryjska 9–15; Tram Korona; www.targ pietruszkowy.pl) on Saturdays from 8am–1pm and Wednesdays from 2pm–6pm. A lot of the stallholders have organic farms. In addition to meat joints and sausages, fruit and vegetables, you can also buy cheese, wine, soft drinks and jams.

Are you looking for an alternative to wines from Italy or Spain? Then pop into Paweł Woźniak's wine shop **Winnacja** (ul. Lipowa 6 e; www.winnacja.pl; Mon–Fri 10am–7pm, Sat until 5pm). He offers a large selection of fine wines, mainly from smaller vineyards in Armenia, Georgia, Moldavia, Romania, Poland and other countries from Central and Eastern Europe. You can test the wines as well of course.

FASHION AND DESIGN

Dozens of young Polish fashion designers present their clothing, jewellery and accessories, mainly for women, in the **Forum Mody**, the former luxury hotel Forum. You can find really unique, inexpensive pieces there which are sure to make your friends green with envy when you travel home (Marii Konopnieckiej 28; tel: 530 789 541; Mon–Sat 11am–8pm, Sun 11am–5pm).

Now set up in the former kitchen of the deserted hotel is the **Forum Designu**, a showroom for design made in Poland. Young artists and designers present their furniture and lamps, textiles, decorative products, tableware and much more (Mon–Sat 11am–8pm, Sun until 4pm).

If you are looking for an unusual doll's house for your children, pop into 🏠 **boominy & friends**, which has a factory outlet at no. 11 ul. Nadwiślańska (www.boomini.com). The high-quality wooden houses have been awarded design prizes, and the luxury versions cost almost as much as a summer house. There is a choice of all sorts of accessories, different dolls, wooden toys and children's clothing.

Where to...
Go Out

On the south bank of the Vistula the venues for cultural entertainment in the evening used to be fairly limited. That has all changed since the opening of the modern International Congress Centre ICE Kraków. Large rock, pop and classical concerts now take place in the multifunctional rooms.

While the well-known Club Fabryka in the old industrial area of Zabłocie had to close at the end of 2015, and the future of the city beach with its bar, restaurant and club is still up in the air, there are – given the speed at which nightlife changes in Krakow – sure to be some new hot spots in the southern districts very soon.

MUSIC

Drukarnia
The Drukarnia is the trendsetter in Krakow. Originally opened at an old printers in the Old Town, it later became one of the top addresses in Kazimierz before moving to the other side of the Vistula to Podgórze. The concept has remained the same: during the day it is a cosy café, in the evenings a wonderfully laid-back pub. Jazz is often played in the spacious cellar, and at the weekend there are dance parties.
➕ 197 F1
✉ Nadwiślańska 1
☎ 126 566 560; www.drukarniaclub.pl
🕐 Daily from 10am

ICE Kraków
Since it was opened at the end of 2014, the ICE Kraków has also become one of the city's most important event venues. In the main auditorium, with its excellent acoustics, star violinist Nigel Kennedy, the tenor Roman Vargas and the Fado singer Mariza have all graced the stage. Opera, ballet and musicals are performed before an audience of up to 2,000 people. Concerts also take place there as part of the Summer-Jazz Festival or the Sacrum Profanum Festival.
➕ 196 A2
✉ Marii Konopnieckiej 17
☎ 123 542 300; www.icekrakow.pl
🚋 Tram 12, 18, 22, 52, 62 (Centrum Kongresowe)

Excursions

Excursions

Krakow is not the only UNESCO World Heritage Site in this area. Several other can be found dotted around the former city of kings in Woiwodschaft Małopolska (Lesser Poland Voivodeship), and they could hardly be more diverse. What is more, stretching out in front of the gates to the city is Poland's smallest national park which is full of exceptional rock formations.

In 1978, the more than 700-year-old **Wieliczka salt mine** was declared a World Heritage Site. You can experience the fascinating world of salt on the normal tourist route or the adventurous miner's tour. Another insider tip is the Bochnia salt mine, which is also a UNESCO site.

Whilst we can enthuse about the technical and artistic achievements of past generations, the dark side of human existence shows its ugly face in the former **Nazi Concentration Camp Auschwitz-Birkenau**.

Also a UNESCO site is the **Calvary Hill in Kalwaria Zebrzydowska**, which Karol Wojtyła used to enjoy visiting even as a young man. His birth house in nearby Wadowice has been turned into a museum to commemorate the Polish man who later became Pope John Paul II.

You can reach the **Benedictine Abbey of Tyniec** either by bike or gondola. There, you can try the delicious monastery products.

You can discover the medieval forts on "The Trail of the Eagle's Nest" through the **Jura Krakowsko-Częstochowska** or the Polish Jura. Nature has formed exceptional limestone formations, which exercise a magical appeal on climbers.

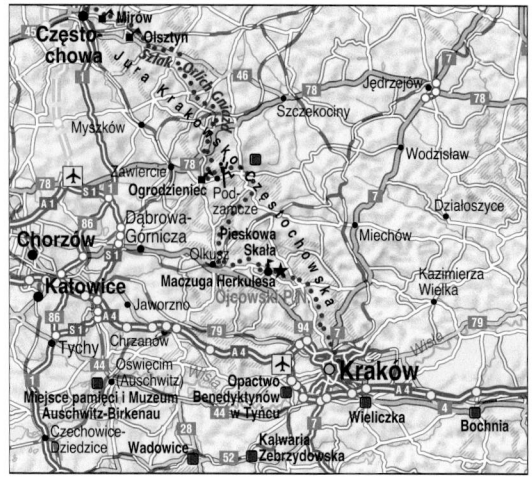

Wieliczka and Bochnia Royal Salt Mines

Salt has been mined to the south-east of Krakow since the 13th century, and in the Middle Ages it was worth as much as gold. Visitors to the subterranean world of Wieliczka und Bochnia today discover magnificent chambers in which everything is made of salt and where they can party and even stay the night.

Salt was mined in Wieliczka for more than 700 years, and had to be laboriously transported to the surface from the innumerable chambers and tunnels that over the years reached a total length of around 300km (185mi).

Even the magnificent chandeliers in the huge Kinga Chapel are made of salt

The guide receives guests with the traditional, regional greeting *"Szczęść Boże"* ("God Bless you"), then it is off down the first 380 steps below ground together. On winding paths, the around 3km (1.8mi) tour descends ever deeper, past subterranean lakes, old mining equipment and numerous sculptures that the miners carved from salt over the centuries. Sometimes the groups move from chamber to chamber every minute, because the Wieliczka salt mine ranks as one of the largest tourist attractions and over a million people visit it each year.

Even Goethe was in Wieliczka
Since 1978 the mine has been listed as a UNESCO World Heritage Site, but it was already an attraction long before then. In 1790, for example, Johann Wolfgang von Goethe

Excursions

Those so inclined can create their own "salty souvenirs" at the end of the salt mine tour

visited it and there is a salt statue of the great poet in front of the **Weimar Chamber** which commemorates the occasion. The most beautiful subterranean chamber has to be **The Chapel of St Kinga**, 54m (177ft) long, 18m (59ft) wide and 12m (39ft) high. From the flooring to the artistically designed altar and magnificent chandeliers, everything is made entirely of salt. Generations of miners worked on it. Salt reliefs depict scenes from the Old and New Testament. Even Leonardo da Vinci's *Last Supper* was intricately copied in salt. To this day, holy mass is celebrated in the chapel, weddings take place here as do concerts.

Insider Tip

If you prefer a bit of adventure and don't want to encounter other groups every step of the way, then opt for the Miners' Route. Slip into miner's gear and experience first hand how hard the day-to-day work was. In the light of a miner's lamp, you move along narrow paths, have to climb up ladders or creep through tunnels, detect by smell a fire that has just begun to smoulder and experience how the earth begins to quake. In the end, you can also find out for yourself just how hard it is to form a figure out of salt stone and make yourself a little souvenir at the same time.

Bochnia, also a National Heritage Site

Although the nearby Bochnia salt mine is a few years older – the "white gold" was mined there from 1248, it has stood in the shadow of Wieliczka for a long time. However, that is now changing since Bochnia obtained UNESCO-World Heritage status in 2013. Although some of the subterranean tunnels are also open to visitors in Bochnia, things are a bit more relaxed there. As in Wieliczka there is a tour to the most beautiful chambers. The history of mining rock salt is recounted in a diverse and entertaining way using multimedia. One part of the route is done on the pit train and in a boat; it is a very adventurous route which leads into the oldest parts of the mine.

Wieliczka and Bochnia Royal Salt Mines

Football and relay races below the soil

With its gigantic dimensions the **Ważyn Chamber** at a depth of 250m (820ft) is the largest attraction in Bochnia. It is the sports "field", conference centre and dormitory all in one and can be reached via a staircase or a 140m (460ft) long **slide**. The 2,500m² (27,000ft²) chamber is the goal of young groups. They play basketball or football there, dance beneath the flashing disco ball and then withdraw to the dormitory with more than 200 beds. Company events and sports events also take place there. Even a half marathon has been organised in the subterranean world of salt, and every year in March 60 teams compete against each other in a 12-hour relay race.

Classical concerts and lively New Year parties take place in Bochnia and Wieliczka deep down below the Earth's surface. And since the air there is particularly clean and the micro climate relieves skin illnesses and respiratory symptoms, spa facilities are also available at both mines.

Kopalnia Soli Wieliczka (Wieliczka Salt Mine)
✉ ul. Daniłowicza 10, 32-020 Wieliczka
☎ 122 787 302; www.salzbergwerkwieliczka.de
🕐 Daily 7:30am–7:30pm; Nov–March 8am–5pm
💶 55 złoty; foreign-language tour 84 złoty

Kopalnia Soli Bochnia (Bochnia Salt Mine)
✉ ul. Campi 15, 32-700 Bochnia
☎ 146 152 460; www.salzbergwerk-bochnia.eu
🕐 Mon–Fri 9:30am–3pm, Sat, Sun 10:15am–3pm
💶 35 złoty (45 złoty in summer); English language tour 70 złoty

INSIDER INFO

- **Individual tours** in English on the "Tourist Route" in Wieliczka: daily all year round, every 30 min. from 9am–5pm. In Bochnia there are tours in English daily at 3pm.
- The salt mine in Wieliczka has an **information office** in Krakow, in which besides information and tickets you can also receive information and tickets as well as all kinds of products such as rock salt, bath salts and salt lamps (ul. Wiślna 12a; Mon–Fri 9am–5pm).

Insider Tip

Insider Tip

- Make sure you wear sturdy, comfortable shoes and warm clothing. In the daytime, the temperature below ground is between 14 and 16 °C (57°F–61°F).
- In order to enjoy the healthy salty air, you don't need to go underground in Wieliczka. A few years ago a **graduation works was set up on the area**. Brine, which runs down the huge walls, creates a healthy, ocean-like climate in the surrounding area.
- In both salt mines, the tour ends in a **restaurant underground** in which you can buy something to get you up and going again.

Directions You can reach Bochnia and Wieliczka comfortably by regional train from Krakow. With the car to Bochnia (50km/30mi east) you will need approx. 45 min., to Wieliczka (approx. 15km/9mi south-east.) around 30 min. In Krakow numerous excursion trips are offered to Wieliczka.

Former Concentration Camp Auschwitz-Birkenau

In 1979 UNESCO put the former concentration camp Auschwitz-Birkenau on its list of National Heritage Sites, both to bear witness to the murderous policy of the Nazis but also to commemorate the strength of the human spirit in the face of the most horrific of human conditions.

Arbeit Macht Frei (*Work Sets you Free*) is inscribed over the entrance to the original camp, Auschwitz I in the town of Oświęcim, which the Nazis set up in what had formerly been a barracks in 1940. It is a cynical slogan, since in fact the inmates were then to be exterminated through inhuman working and living conditions.

The first trains brought political prisoners from Poland, later they mainly contained Jews from countries all over Europe, but also Sinti and Roma as well as Soviet prisoners of war.

In 1941, to cope with the mass deportation of Jews, the extermination camp Birkenau was set up 3km (1.85mi) away from the main camp. Those who were not immedi-

Visitors from all over the world remember the Nazi atrocities at Auschwitz-Birkenau

Former Concentration Camp Auschwitz-Birkenau

The cynical slogan over the entrance to the main camp (Auschwitz I)

ately murdered in gas chambers after their arrival were subjected to forced labour under extremely hard conditions. More than a million people lost their lives there. Only about 5,800 sick and debilitated prisoners could be liberated from the camp in 1945.

Impressive Exhibition in the Main Camp

An exhibition in the main camp, Auschwitz I, depicts the history of the camp and its prisoners. Suitcases, shoes and other personal objects bear testimony to the fate of many of the prisoners. Artistic work, done either illegally inside the camp or after liberation from the camp, symbolise the suffering, hope and will to live of the inmates. A distressing film shows recordings of the camp just after its liberation on 27 January 1945.

A tour leads to the former cells, "Death's Wall" where people were shot, and to the first gas chamber in which the Nazis performed their initial tests aimed at the systematic extermination of the Jews.

Rubble was all that remained of the extermination camp Birkenau, its gas chambers and crematorium at the end of the war. The SS blew up the camp before their retreat. When you walk over the huge complex surrounded by barbed wire and watch towers, you can only surmise the extent of the machinery of annihilation. Rails lead to the ramp on which the guards carried out the selection process; a solitary cattle truck stands there. What happened next is left to the imagination of the visitors.

In the Earlier Schtetl in Oświęcim

Around 1.5 million people from all over the world visit the former extermination camp each year, two thirds of whom are teenagers and young adults. Only a fraction of that number stops off in Oświęcim (in German Auschwitz), the town that gave the camps its name and currently has a population of 40,000 people. Prior to World War II, the majority of the inhabitants were Jews. Of the once 20 Jewish houses of worship only the **Chevra Lomdei Mishnayot Synagogue**, founded in 1913 remains. In 2000, it became part of the Jewish Museum. Its exhibition makes it possible to see what life was like during the time of the Schtetl.

Excursions

Państwowe Muzeum Auschwitz-Birkenau
✉ ul. Więźniów Oświęcimia 20, 32-603 Oświęcim
☎ 338 448 099; www.auschwitz.org
🕐 April, May, Sep daily 8am–6pm; June–Aug to 7pm; March, Oct until 5pm;
Feb until 4pm; Jan, Nov until 3pm; Dec until 2pm
💵 Free

The exhibition in Auschwitz I shows the gruesome fate of the camp inmates

Muzeum Żydowskie
✉ Pl. Jana Skarbka 5, 32-600 Oświęcim
☎ 338 447 002; www.ajcf.pl
🕐 Sun–Fri 10am–6pm, until 5pm in winter 💵 10 złoty

INSIDER INFO

■ From April till October, from 10am–3pm you can only visit the main camp Auschwitz I in groups. Individual visitors can join group tours. Information about the times and languages of the tours are on the website. The four-hour tour costs 45 złoty. Make sure you book online in advance.

■ Individual visits through Auschwitz I are possible outside of the above times. There is free access to Birkenau.

■ Plan enough time for your visit. You should allow three hours for the two camps.

■ **Shuttle buses** travel between the two camps and are free of charge.

■ **Café Bergson belongs to the Jewish Museum.** The house it is in once belonged to Szymon Kluger, the last Jewish inhabitant of Oświęcim. In addition to coffee and cakes, the café also serves vegetarian meals (Plac Jana Skarbka 2; daily 11am–7pm)

Directions Regional trains travel from the main station in Krakow to Oświęcim, which is located to the west (travel time: about 2 hours). There is a bus service between the station and the camp. With the car, you will need about 1.5 hours for the approximately 70km (45mi) journey. Numerous organised bus tours shuttle between Krakow and Auschwitz.

Kalwaria Zebrzydowska & Wadowice

Since the majority of 17th-century Poles could not afford to go on a pilgrimage to Jerusalem, the voivode of Krakow Mikołaj Zebrzydowski set up a Calvary Hill with a Chapel of the Crucifixion in Lesser Poland. Karol Wojtyła often made a trip there from his nearby home town of Wadowice.

In 1601 Mikołaj Zebrzydowski had a chapel built on the picturesque hills near Lanckorocka to the south-west of Krakow that was based on the model of the Calvary Chapel in Jerusalem. Three years later, building began on a monastery with a church that resembles the Church of the Sepulchre in Jerusalem. The building of a **Calvary Hill** continued over the following years. The result was a 7km (4.3mi) path with 42 chapels depicting the stations of the cross. In 1999 UNESCO added the entire ensemble from Kalwaria Zebrzydowska to the list of National Heritage Sites.

Passion Plays

The Bazylika Mariacka in Wadowice, in which Karol Wojtyła was baptised

The passion plays are a special highlight. They take place every year for a week during the Easter period and are watched by tens of thousands of visitors. It is a tradition that dates back to 1608. A second highlight is from 13–15 August when Mary is symbolically carried to her tomb and then ascends to heaven. Yet at other times of the year, too, the Calvary Hill is a popular destination for many people who combine a stroll through the green foothills with a spiritual experience.

Excursions

A frequent guest on Calvary Hill was John Paul II, who was born on 18 May 1920 in Wadowice, located 15km (9.5mi) away, the town in which he lived for the first 18 years of his life. Even as a child, he had often visited the pilgrimage site with his father, and he returned there in 1979 and 2002 when he was Pope.

Birthplace of the Pope

In his home town in Wadowice, in which the family owned a little flat, a small exhibition was initially opened in 1984, which by 2014 turned into a **museum** on four floors dedicated to the life and work of the Polish pope. The multimedia exhibition not only presents the theologian but also reveals the person that Karol Wojtyła was outside of his religious duties, a man who was an enthusiastic hiker and skier in his free time. Historical photos show the Wadowice of Wojtyła's childhood. Not far from there is the **Bazylika Mariacka** (Basilica of the Presentation of the Blessed Virgin Mary), in which he was baptised.

As a boy, Karol liked buying *kremówki*, pastry slices filled with custard cream, from the bakery belonging to Karl Hagenhuber. Although the former bakery on Rynek (no. 15) is now a bank, it is still possible to buy *kremówka papieska*, the popular "Papal Cream Cake" from many bakeries in Wadowice.

Klasztor oo. Bernardynów
(Bernardine Monastery in Kalwaria Zebrzydowska)
✉ ul. Bernardyńska 46, 34-130 Kalwaria Zebrzydowska
☎ 338 766 304; www.kalwaria.eu

Muzeum Dom Rodzinny Jana Pawła II
(John Paul II Family Home Museum)
✉ ul. Kościelna 7, 34-100 Wadowice ☎ 338 233 565; www.domjp2.pl
🕐 9–7; April, Oct until 6; Nov–March until 4 💵 20 złoty (free on Tue)

Insider
Tip

INSIDER INFO

- It is just not done to visit Wadowice and not eat a Papal Cream Slice. So go to the **Cukiernia Wadowice**, which also has all sorts of other sweet temptations in the window (ul. Kościuszki 21; daily 9am–7pm, until 6pm in winter). If you acquire a taste for them, there is also a branch in Ulica Grodzka (28) in Krakow.
- Combine your trip with a visit to **Lanckorona**, which is not far from Kalwaria Zebrzydowska. The village market square is surrounded by attractive 19th-century wooden houses. You can spend the night at the **Willa Tadeusz** (£), opened in 1924, one of Poland's first private guest houses. Well-known artists like Sławomir Mrożek and Andrzej Wajda were guests there (Lanckorona 46; tel: 338 763 592; www.willatadeusz.com).

Directions From the main station, you can take a train (changing at Kraków-Płaszów) to Kalwaria Zebrzydowska and Wadowice (journey time 70 min. or 1.5 hr.). The drive to Wadowice (approx. 50km/30mi south-west) takes a good hour.

Benedictine Abbey of Tyniec

About 15km (9mi) south-west of Krakow, enthroned on a limestone cliff high above the Vistula, is the Opactwo Benedyktynów w Tyńcu (Abbey of Tyniec). Benedictine monks from Rhineland began building the monastery and church in the mid 11th century. The abbey is a popular destination for tourists wishing to take a trip out into the countryside surrounding Krakow.

A millennium of monastery life in the Benedictine Abbey of Tyniec at the gateway to Krakow

he Gothic, twin-towered church was redesigned in the Baroque style during the 17th and 18th century. At the end of the 19th century, it received three stained glass windows by the Art Nouveau artist Stanisław Wyspiański (▶ 16). The monastery building destroyed by a fire in 1831 – the church only suffered damage to the roof – was not rebuilt until 1947. The oldest traces of the church date back to the Romanesque period. Commemorative plaques in the south wing of the cloister reconstructed in 1989 recount the history of the monastery, starting with its foundation in 1044 and covering the period until the return of the Benedictine monks to the deserted monastery in 1939. The **monastery museum** shows liturgical artefacts and texts from past centuries. In the **monastery restaurant**, you can try out meals prepared according to traditional Benedictine recipes.

✉ ul. Benedyktyńska 37, 30–398 Kraków. Gondolas set off from the Wawel and reach the monastery upstream in about one and a half hours. It takes a good hour on the bike; most of the route runs along the left bank of the Vistula.
☎ 126 885 450; www.tyniec.benedyktyni.pl ⊙ Museum: 10am–4pm. Shop: 9:30am–6pm. Restaurant: noon–6pm. Monastery tours: Mon–Fri every hour 9am–noon, 2pm and 3pm, Sat 9am–noon, 2pm, Sun 10:15am, noon–3pm
💶 10 złoty (combined ticket to visit the monastery and museum)

Jura Krakowsko-Częstochowska

On the "Trail of the Eagles' Nest" white castles perched on equally white rocks follow one after another as if on a chain of pearls. Leading through the Jura Krakowsko-Częstochowska (Polish Jura or Polish Jurassic Highland), this excursion and recreation area is just outside Krakow.

The curious rocky landscape to the north-west of Krakow stretches towards the Polish pilgrimage site of Częstochowa. Millions of years of wind and weather have taken their toll on the limestone and created original rock formations.

The most well-known is **Maczuga Herkulesa** (Bludgeon of Hercules), an around 12m (39ft) high monolith, found

The castle ruins of Ogrodzieniec is one of the most impressive "eagle's nests" in the Polish Jura

INSIDER INFO

The most beautiful caves in the national park include the around 320m (1050ft) long **Grota Łokietka** near **Ojców** and the slightly smaller **Jaskinia Ciemna** near **Czajowice**, which has the more attractive dripstone formations. According to legend, the Polish King Władysław Łokietek hid in the Łokietka Grotto as he was fleeing from the Bohemian troops. Both caves can be visited every day from April to November or October (www.grotalokietka.pl; www.ciemna.ojcow.pl).

not far from the Renaissance castle of Pieskowa Skała. There are around **1,000 caves** along the plateau. Some of them provided man with protection in the Stone Age.

Pieskowa Skała Castle was erected in the 14th century as a defensive stronghold and then later in the 16th century extended and remodelled in the Renaissance style. Its arcaded courtyard is reminiscent of the one at Krakow's Wawel. Renovated in 2016, the castle now accommodates part of the collection from Wawel Museum. These encompass 15th to 19th-century artworks.

Ojców National Park

The Jura's most precious natural landscapes are protected in the **Ojcówski Park Narodowy** near Ojców, about 16km (10mi) north of Krakow. Poland's smallest national park not only awaits you with scenic beauties but also with an enormous diversity of species. Around 11,000 species can be found there, including for instance at least 17 different kinds of bat.

Trail of the Eagles' Nest

The rock formations of the Krakow-Częstochowa Upland have provided mankind with protection for centuries. King Kazimierz Wielki (Casimir III the Great) had up to 30m (100ft) high border castles built on the rocks, now on the 163km (100mi) long **Szlak Orlich Gniazd** (Trail of the Eagles' Nest) tourist route. Their purpose was to secure Poland's border to what had become Bohemian Silesia as well as the trading route between Krakow and Breslau (Wrocła).

Impressive Castle Ruins

Only ruins remain of many of the former castles, which nonetheless still look impressive in terms of size and where they are located. One of the most well-known ruins is **Ogrodzieniec**, once Europe's second largest castle, cleverly conceived so that the walls blend into the surrounding rocks. The ruins of **Mirów** and **Olsztyn** are also impressive.

Climbing Areas

The Polish Jura is one of the most popular places to go climbing in Poland. Numerous routes for various levels of climbers have been prepared with climbing hooks.

Excursions

There are 500 marked routes around the village of **Podzamcze** alone, the most important climbing centre of the mountain range.

Centrum Edukacyjno-Muzealnym OPM
(Training Centre and Museum of Ojców-National Park)
✉ Ojców 9, 32045 Sułoszowa
☎ 123 892 005; www.ojcowskiparknarodowe.pl
⏰ Summer: Mon–Fri 9am–4pm, Sat, Sun 10am–4pm;
winter: Mon–Fri 9am–3pm

Zamek Pieskowa Skała (Pieskowa Skała Castle)
✉ 32-045 Sułoszowa
☎ 123 896 004; http://pieskowaskala.eu; www.pieskowaskala.pl
⏰ April, Oct Tue–Thu, Sat, Sun 10am–4pm, Fri 9am–1pm;
May–Sep Tue–Thu 9am–5pm, Fri 9am–1pm, Sat, Sun 10am–6pm;
Nov–March Tue–Sun only group tours (from 15 pers.) 🎫 11 złoty

Walking along the "Trail of the Eagles' Nest" to the ruined castle of Olsztyn

Directions For your excursion to the Polish Jura, you should use a car, since it is difficult to reach with public transport. You need a good half day to visit Ojców National Park, the castle ruins of Ojców and the nearby Pieskowa Skała Castle with the Hercules bludgeon. If you also wish to visit the castle ruins of Ogrodzieniec, then you should plan a whole day.

INSIDER INFO

Near the castle ruins of Ogrodzieniec, 60km (37mi) north-west of Krakow is the design hotel **Poziom 511**, whose glass facade blends perfectly into the landscape. In the restaurant you can enjoy regional cuisine as you look out at the limestone cliffs (ul. Bonerów 33, 42-440 Podzamcze; tel: 327 462 800; www.poziom511.com).

Walks & Tours

1 ON THE TRAIL OF JOHN PAUL II
Walk

DISTANCE: 3.2km (2mi) **TIME:** approx. 3 hours.
START POINT: Ulica Franciszkańska (no. 3); Tram 1, 3, 6, 18, 20, 69,
73 (Pl. Wszystkich Świętych) ✚ 195 D2 **END POINT:** Plac Jana Matejki;
Tram 2, 7, 8, 14, 18, 24, 69, 73 (Basztowa) ✚ 195 F5

Karol Wojtyła had close ties with Krakow for more than 59 years. He came here as a young man with his father; it was here that he became a man of the church, worked as a priest, bishop, archbishop and cardinal. As Pope John Paul II, he filled people with hope and courage during their stays in Krakow. Many sites are connected with his work.

❶–❷
Start your tour along the trail of the Polish Pope in Ulica Franciszkańska. From 1963 to 1978, Karol Wojtyla resided at no. 3 in the **Pałac Biskupi (Bishop's Palace** ➤ 104) as Archbishop of Krakow. He also stayed in the yellow Baroque building during his later visits as Pope. He spoke to the many Catholics who gathered in front of the building from the window on the first floor. Commemorating this emotional occasion is a picture of him in the "Pope's Window".

In the **Kościół Franciszkanów (Church of St Francis of Assisi**; ➤ 98), directly opposite, Wojtyła used to enjoy visiting holy mass even as a young theology student.

On the other side of Plac Wszystkich Świętych and Ulica Dominikańska you come to Ulica Poselska. At the 17th-century **Klasztor Sióstr Bernardynek (Convent of Bernardine Nuns**;

Karol Wojtyła lived for over 15 years in the building which is now the Archdiocesan Museum

ul. Poselska 21), Karol Wojtyła very often prayed at the adjacent **Kościół św. Józefa** that has an altarpiece that depicts St Joseph and Jesus as a boy.

❷–❸
From St Joseph's Church, continue along Ulica Poselska, then turn left into Ulica Grodzka and almost immediately right into Ulica Senacka. Then after a few metres turn left into **Ulica Kanonicza** (➤ 90), where many of the buildings belong to the Catholic Church. Some of them are used by the pontifical university that bears the name of John Paul II.

Karol Wojtyła lived from 1951 to 1967 at no. 19 and later in the house next door at no. 21. Today, both

buildings are joined together and house the **Muzeum Archidiecezjalne** (**Archdiocesan Museum**). Included in the collection is one of the rooms of the later pope with personal mementoes, including his first skis from 1954.

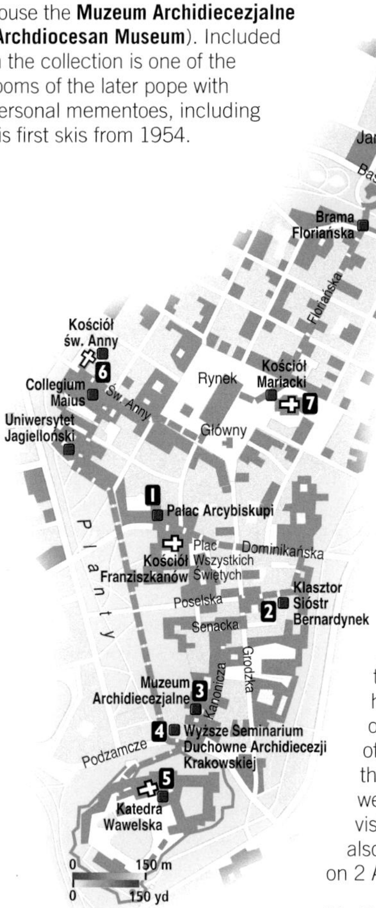

3-4

If you turn right at the end of Ulica Kanonicza, you will come to Ulica Podzamcze at the foot of Wawel Hill. After World War II, Wojtyła studied theology here at the **Archdiocesan Seminary** (no. 8); not even a decade later, he was teaching theology students there.

4-5

Directly opposite is the way up towards Wawel Hill. In **Wawel Cathedral** (▶ 85) Wojtyła served first as the bishop from 1958 and from 1964 as Archbishop of Krakow. It was there, too, that he actually held his first mass after his ordination in 1946 in the crypt of St Leonhard. The chime of the powerful Sigismund Bell welcomed the pope on his later visits to the town and they also sounded after his death on 2 April 2005.

5-6

After visiting Wawel Hill, walk over the Planty to the University District. It was at **Jagiellonian University** that Wojtyła began his degree in Polish philology in 1938, which he had to stop during World War II. During the time of the German Occupation, he took part at secret underground lectures in philology and theology. In 1948 he completed his doctorate in theology. In 1953, shortly before the theological faculty was closed by the Communist authorities, completed his postdoctoral qualification.

TAKING A BREAK

Take a break in Ulica Grodzka (no. 28), to enjoy something sweet from the Pope's home town. Besides cakes and tarts, the **Cukiernia Wadowice** also serves the famous *kremówka* (*cream slices*), which Karol loved, even when he was a boy (daily 9am–9pm).

Memorial plaque to Pope John II by St Mary's Church

As Pope, he was awarded an honorary doctorate in **Collegium Maius** (➤ 93) in 1982. Wojtyła often went to pray at the neighbouring **Kościół akademicki św. Anny** (Collegiate Church of St Anne; ➤ 96) as a student; in 1997 he gave a great speech there on the 600th anniversary of the theological faculty.

6 – 7

From the Church of St Anne continue along Ulica Świętej Anny to the Main Market Square. **St Mary's Church** (➤ 56) also has close ties with the Pope. Between 1952 and 1958, he worked there as a priest and confessor. When an attempt on his life was made in 1981, students organised the so-called "White March", which began on Błonia Park to the west of the city and led to St Mary's Church. Around half a million people took part. After the death of the pope in 2005, countless mourners joined a second "White March" this time from St Mary's Church in the centre to Błonia Park.

7 – 8

Cross Ulica Floriańska and go through **St Florian's Gate** (➤ 62) to reach the Kleparz district. Looming at the end of the extended **Plac Jana Matejki** is the Baroque **St Florian's Church**, where Wojtyła spent his first years (1949 to 1951) as a priest. A focal area for him there was his work with the students. He continued this work even when he was on sabbatical leave from the parish to complete his post-doctoral qualification.

The walk through the centre of the town ends in St Florian's Church, but you will also find numerous memorial sites to John Paul II in other parts of the town.

SHORT EXCURSION

If you would like to extend your tour a little, walk from Wawel Hill over the Vistula Bridge Most Dębnicki and then westwards to Ulica Tyniecka. At no. 10, the unprepossessing house is where Karol Wojtyła and his father moved in 1938. They lived there in two small rooms. Wojtyła's father died of a heart attack in 1941; his grave is in the Rackowicki graveyard to the north of the main station. Karol lived in his uncle's house, which can only be viewed from outside, until 1944.

2 THROUGH THE GREEN WEST
Cycling Tour

DISTANCE: ca. 15km (9mi) **TIME:** about 5 hours.
START/END POINT: Park Jordana (ul. Rejmonta; approx 2km (1.25mi)
west of Rynek Główny)

This tour takes you from the edge of the Old Town to the "Green West" of Krakow. Enjoy the dream view from Kościuszko Mound and experience the atmosphere at the zoo in the middle of the woods. As it is quite long, it is worth doing the excursion on a bike. Otherwise, you can also shorten the route and do it on foot.

1–2
From the direction of the Old Town, head west towards Ulica Krupnica, cross the broad Aleja Mickiewicza and continue along the Ulica Romana Ingardena past the buildings of the Jagiellonian University. You will come to **Jordan Park**, which was laid out on the initiative of the city councillor and doctor Henryk Jordan (1842–1907) in 1889. Jordan was of the opinion that

Flying kits on Błonia Park; looming in the background is the Kościuszko Mound

TAKING A BREAK
In the **Panorama Café** at the foot of the Kościuszko Mound, you can enjoy light meals such as soups or salads as well as coffee and cake with a view of the countryside (April–Oct Mon–Fri from 11am, Sat, Sun from 10am). The menu in the **Pod Kopcem** Restaurant right next door offers more choice (al. Waszyngtona 1, 126 622 029; http://restauracjapodkopcem.pl; Mon–Fri 9am–7pm, Sat, Sun 11am–8pm). The **Villa Decius** Restaurant in the house of the same name is very stylish (ul. 28 Lipca 1943 17A, 124 253 390; www.vd-restauracja.pl; daily noon–10pm).

physical exercise contributed to good health and created Europe's first public playground. In the midst of the parkland, he established 14 sports areas for team games, athletics and gymnastics. To this day the 22ha recreation area offers 🏃 sport and game areas, a skateboard park, a sledging slope and cycle tracks. A total of 36 memorials commemorate famous Poles from Fryderyk Chopin to John Paul II.

2–3
Pass the small lake with rowing boats to Aleja 3 Maja and continue your tour on the other side of **Błonia Park**. The former grazing ground for cattle is now a popular

Short break on the cycle tour to the Camaldolese Monastery of Bielany

leisure area for the people of Krakow. Pope John Paul II preached here during his trip to Poland in front of hundreds of thousands of Catholics. A 26 ton granite rock from the Tatra near Aleja 3 Maja commemorates him. It bears the inscription in Polish "You are a rock". Błonia Park was also one of the venues during the Catholic Church's World Youth Day at which Pope Francis preached to a huge congregation.

3–4

On the Ulica Focha cross the Rudawa, a small tributary of the Vistula and continue along the small road through the green city district of **Zwierzyniec**. Ulica Focha merges into Ulica Krolowej Jadwiga, from which about 300m

(1,000ft) farther on, Ulica Hofmana branches off to the left. Follow the Hofmana, which eventually merges into the Aleja Małeckiego.

Already visible in the distance is the 34m (112ft) high **Kopiec Kościuszki (Kościuszko Mound)**, which, completed in 1823, was modelled after the prehistoric Krakus Mound and commemorates national hero Tadeusz Kościuszko. Many of Krakow's citizens helped to construct the mound. The Habsburgs had a citadel built at the bottom of the mound in the mid-19th century, part of which is still to be seen. What remains is now home to a radio station as well as two cafés and a restaurant. Part of the fortifications includes a neo-Gothic chapel dedicated to Blessed

OPENING TIMES
Galeria Bronisława Chromego
✉ ul. Krańcowa 4
☎ 603 793 650; www.bronislawchromy.pl
🕐 Tue–Sun 11am–6pm 🎟 Free

Ogród Zoologiczny (Zoo)
✉ al. Żubrowa
☎ 124 253 551; www.zoo-krakow.pl
🕐 9am–6pm (summer) 🎟 18 złoty

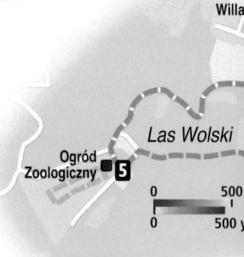

Autorska Galeria
Bronisława Ch

Willa

Las Wolski

Ogród
Zoologiczny 5

0   500
0   500 y

Bronislava. It is well worth climbing up to the top of the mound. When the weather is clear, there is a good view over the town and to the Tatra Mountains.

Insider Tip

4-5

From Kościuszkio Mound cycle about 4km (2.5mi) westwards through the rolling terrain of the **Las Wolski** forest to **Ogród Zoologiczny**, **Krakow Zoo**. Opened in 1929, the zoo is located in the middle of the forest. Covering an area of 15ha, it is home to around 1,300 animals from all over the world. About 100 of the species living there are in danger of extinction, and they include the snow leopard and Indian elephants. In 2016 a new basin was created for the equally endangered Humboldt penguins. The complex also has a 🧒 Mini Zoo, in which children are allowed to stroke and feed the animals.

5-1

From the zoo, cycle in a north-east direction through the forest to the **Decjusza Park**. In the northern section of the small park at no. 4 Ulica Krańcowa, you will find the **Galeria Autorska of Bronisław Chromy**, whose work includes the Wawel dragon (photo ▶86). There, you can walk through a magical **sculpture garden**. Around 200m (650ft) south as the crow flies is

KLASZTOR KAMEDUŁÓW, BIELANY

If you wish to extend your tour, take a little detour from the zoo by heading west to the Camaldolese Monastery atop Srebrna Góra (Silver Mountain). The Camaldolese monks behind the walls of the gleaming white monastery live a very secluded life in adherence with the strict rules of their Order. Women are only permitted to enter on eight feast days.

Growing on the slopes around the monastery, on an area measuring about 12 ha, are the grapes of the Srebrna Góra vineyard (ca. 4.2km/ 2.5mi; 30 min., not open for visits).

✉ al. Konarowa 1
☎ 124 297 610; www.kameduli.info
🕐 Doors open: daily 8am–11am, 3pm–4pm for half an hour each time

the **Willa Decjusza** (**Villa Decius**), which was built from 1530 to 1535 according to the plans of the Italian architect Bartolomeo Berrecci, and is one of the city's most beautiful Renaissance buildings. In the 19th century, the erudite Princess Marcelina Czartoryska invited guests to her literary salon; today the villa is once again an international meeting place for artists and scientists.

From there, the route returns over **Błonia Park** via **Jordana Park** and on to the Old Town.

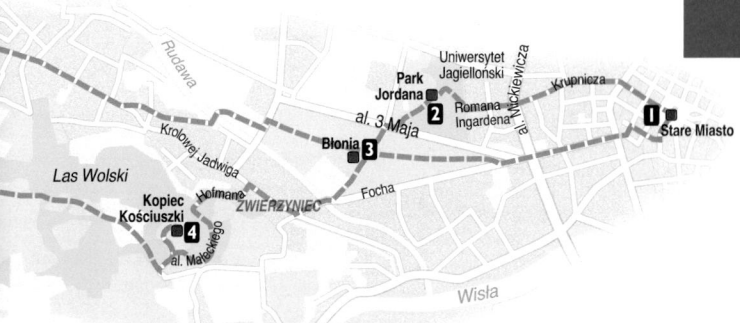

3 RETRO TOUR THROUGH NOWA HUTA
Walk

DISTANCE: approx. 8km (5mi) **TIME:** approx. 3 hr.
START POINT: Ulica Ujastek 1 (Tram 4 , 22 to Kombinat;
approx. 10km/6mi north-west of the Old Town)
END POINT: Ulica Obronczów Krzyża 1 (Tram 5 to Teatr Ludowy)

Nowa Hut was conceived as a model Socialist town to attract people from a working-class background to the outskirts of the bourgeois city of Krakow. However, instead, it turned into a hotbed of civil discontent. You can go on a hip retro tour of the district in a trabant, or explore it individually on foot.

❶–❷

From the "Kombinat" tram stop it is only a few steps to the first house on Ulica Ujastek. That is where you will find the **administration building of the steelworks**, which once bore Lenin's name. Almost 40,000 people used to work in the huge factory, which at peak times produced over

IN A TRABANT THROUGH NOWA HUTA
If you don't want to walk through Nowa Huta on your own, you can do a retro tour with **Crazy Guides**. In authentic style, you drive through the Socialist model town in a trabant, the tour including an earlier worker's home in the 1970s. Lunch is in an old milk bar with a glass of vodka (infos under ☎ 500 091 200; www.cracyguides.pl).

six million tons of steel per year – and heavily polluted the environment. Today the works belong to **ArcelorMittal** and employs not even a tenth of the number of workers. The huge administration building, constructed from 1952 to 1955, is typical for the style of the Nowa Huta, which combined Socialist Realism with Krakow Renaissance architecture. Thus the building's attic style is reminiscent of the Cloth Hall.

Broad green areas border the Aleja Solidarności. Follow this about 1km (0.5mi) westwards and turn right into the tranquil Ulica Wańkowicza. There was a **manor house** (no. 25) here long before the model town was set up. At the end of the 18th century, from 1791, it belonged to **Hugo Kołłątaj** (1750–1812), one of the authors of Poland's first constitution, and later the painter **Jan Matejko** (► 16), who wanted to escape from the hustle and bustle of the town. There is now a museum in the small **Dworek Jana Matejki** (Jan Matejko Manor House) and visitors can admire paintings by Matejko and other objects that used to belong to the earlier inhabitants.

Shortly before you reach the manor house, you will see an old 17th-century **wooden church** Kościół św. Jana Chrzciciela on the left-hand side of Wańkowicza Street. It has only been at this location since 1985; until then it was in the little village of Jawornik located about

Retro Tour Through Nowa Huta

TAKING A BREAK

The **Stylowa** restaurant offers
the perfect atmosphere for a
retro tour. The oldest establishment in
Nowa Huta is still furnished in 1970s
style. The prices have been adjusted
but are still extremely reasonable.
From Fridays to Sundays there is music and dance in the style of regimes
gone by (✉ osiedle Centrum C3,
near Park Ratuszowy, ☎ 126 442
619; http://stylowa-nowahuta.pl).

Insider Tip

30km (18mi) south of Krakow. The
little church is only open for church
services.

2–3

From the manor house walk a little
way back along Wańkowiczka
Street and turn off right. After about
200m (650ft) you will reach the
Dłubnia, a small tributary of the
Vistula which flows into a small
artificial lake. The lake laid out in
the late 1950s together with the
surrounding **Park Zalew Nowohucki**

is a popular recreation area in this
city district. Cross the park to Aleja
Solidarności. Continue south past
the allotment gardens, then along
Ulica Klasztorna to the **Cistercian
monastery of Mogiła**, whose history
stretches back to the early 12th
century. Look out for the 16th-cen-
tury wall paintings by the Cistercian
monk Stanisław Samstrzelnik, which
decorate the monastery church and
the library. The crucifix of Mogiłia is
thought to have miraculous powers,
having been the only object inside
the church to survive a fire in 1447.

3–4

A few steps to the west of the monastery is the **hospital** that is named
after the author **Stefan Żeromski**
(1864–1925). An imposing staircase
leads up to the building, which is
built in the style of Socialist Realism.

This adjoins the 50 ha park **Łąki
Nowohuckie** near an oxbow lake
once part of the Vistula. It is distinguished by a biodiversity of flora
and fauna and has been declared
a **Natura 2000 site**.

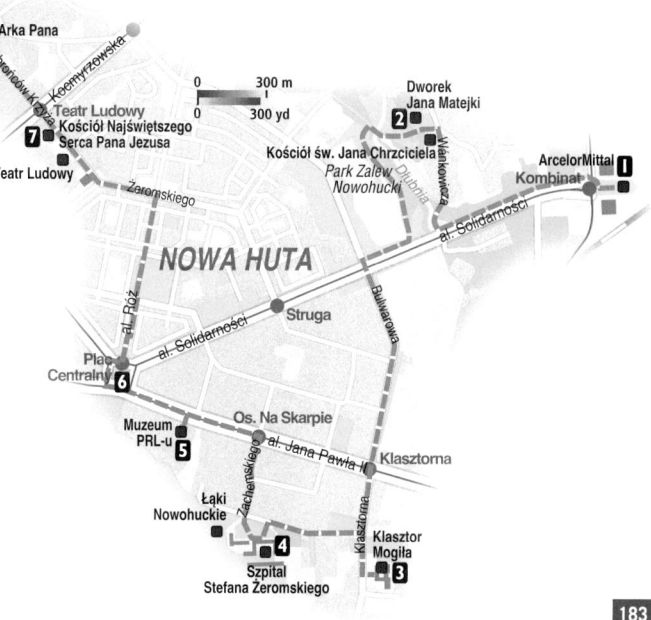

Walks & Tours

Muzeum PRL-u. focuses on the history of Socialist Poland

Just a few steps further on you will reach the small **Kościół Najświętszego Serca Pana Jezusa (Sacred Heart Church)**, built in 2001. Directly next to it is a wooden cross with which the inhabitants of the district protested in 1960 when the authorities did not fulfil their commitment and build a church for Nowa Hutta. This resulted in fierce confrontations between the police and demonstrators.

④–⑤

From Żeromski-Krankenhaus walk north along Ulica Zachemskiego and turn left into the Aleja Jana Pawła II. After about 150m (500ft) you will come to the former cinema "Światowid". Since 2013, a new **Muzeum PRL-u** has been based there. It focuses on Poland under the Communist regime and has already hosted quite a number of temporary exhibitions.

⑤–⑥

Further along Aleja Jana Pawła you will come to **Plac Centralny**. In a star-like formation, broad alleys branch out from the square which is now named after the former US President Roland Reagan.

The Soviet building style of Socialist Realism mixes here with elements from the Renaissance and Baroque periods.

⑥–⑦

Follow Aleja Róż to the north, then turn left into Ulica Żeromskiego and pass the **Teatr Ludowy** (community theatre), which performed avant-garde pieces during the Socialist period and, even now, attracts attention due to its innovative theatre projects.

⑦–⑧

After continuous protests, building was ultimately begun on the church **Arka Pana** ("The Lord's Ark") in 1967 to the north on Ulica Obrońców Krzyża (no. 1); it was finished ten years later.

Support came from all over the world for the futuristic work. Pope Paul VI sent a stone from Peter's grave as a foundation stone and astronauts from Apollo 11 brought a crystal from the moon for the tabernacle. During the time of martial law, 1981–1983, the church was a centre of the resistance.

OPENING TIMES
Dworek Jana Matejki
✉ ul. Wańkowicza 25 ☎ 126 445 674
🕐 Mon–Fri 10am–2pm 💵 5 złoty

Muzeum PRL-u
✉ osiedle Centrum E1
☎ 124 467 821; www.mprl.pl
🕐 Tue–Sun 10am–5pm
💵 9 złoty (free on Tue)

Practicalities

Practicalities

WHAT YOU NEED

		USA	Canada	Australia	Ireland	Germany	Ireland	Netherlands
● Required ○ Suggested ▲ Not required	Some countries require a passport to remain valid for a minimum period (usually at least six months) beyond the date of entry – check beforehand.							
Passport		●	●	●	●	●	●	●
Visa		▲	▲	▲	▲	▲	▲	▲
Onward or Return Ticket		▲	▲	▲	▲	▲	▲	▲
Health Inoculations		▲	▲	▲	▲	▲	▲	▲
Health Documentation (▶ 190, Health)		○	○	○	○	○	○	○
Travel Insurance		○	○	○	○	○	○	○
Driver's Licence (national)		●	●	●	●	●	●	●
Car Insurance Certificate		n/a	n/a	n/a	●	●	●	●
Car Registration Document		n/a	n/a	n/a	●	●	●	●

WHEN TO GO

High season   Low season

JAN	FEB	MAR	APRIL	MAY	JUNE	JULY	AUG	SEP	OCT	NOV	DEC
-1°C	1°C	6°C	13°C	18°C	21°C	23°C	22°C	18°C	14°C	6°C	0°C
30°F	34°F	43°F	55°F	64°F	70°F	73°F	72°F	64°F	57°F	43°F	32°F

☀ Sun   ☁ Cloud   🌦 Sunshine and showers

The given temperatures correspond to the **average peak temperatures** for the corresponding month. It is generally warm and sunny in the summer, but colder and wetter phases are possible. In April or May, the temperatures are often already very mild. You do not normally have to expect extremely cold weather in the winter; snow is possible but not certain. Krakow is a tourist destination **all year round**, although it is fuller in the summer months than the rest of the year. That is when a lot of open-air events take place. The long weekends are very popular with the Polish tourists, for instance around 1–3 May, Corpus Christi and Ascension. Good times to go are May, June and September.

GETTING ADVANCE INFORMATION

Websites
InfoKrakow
■ www.krakau.travel

Polish Tourist Office
■ www.polen.travel

In Krakow
InfoKrakow
Pl. Wszystkich Świętych 2
☎ 0048 12 6 16 18 86
(from abroad)
☎ 0 12 6 16 18 86 (in Poland)

GETTING THERE

By plane: Many international airlines fly to **John Paul II Airport** (www.krakowairport.pl) in the western suburb of Balice. There are direct connections from London, Bristol, Edinburgh and Manchester.

By train: There are no direct connections from the United Kingdom and you will need to change at least twice. However, by taking the Eurostar to Paris and then the **City Night Line** to Berlin and an express train to Warsaw, it is possible to organise a relatively fast and comfortable journey. Once a week there is a **EuroNight** Paris to Moscow service (https://rail.shop/realrussia) that takes 19.5 hours to Warsaw. Connections from Warsaw and Krakow to other Polish cities, to tourist goals in the regions such as Wieliczka or Zakopane as well as in the direction of Prague or Budapest are good.

By Bus: Buses from Eurolines (www.eurolines.de) travel from various German towns to Krakow. There are also direct connections from Berlin with PolskiBus (www.polskibus.com; also bookable via www.flixbus.de).

By car: The fastest connection from the UK is via Brussels (E314), Cologne and Görlitz (A4) via Wrocław (Breslau) and Katowice (Kattowitz). It has been completely renewed, but you will have to pay tolls on some of the motorways. You can pay at the toll stations with złoty or euros.

If you are travelling in a **motor home** you need to register with the **viaTOLL** system (see www.viatoll.pl).

TIME

Krakow lies within the **Central European time** zone (CET), i.e. one hour ahead of Greenwich Mean Time (GMT). Clocks are adjusted forwards one hour for summer time in March. They're put back again in October

CURRENCY & FOREIGN EXCHANGE

Currency: The złoty (PLN) is Poland's official currency; 1 złoty is 100 groszy.
The bank issues 10-, 20-, 50-, 100-, 200- and 500-złoty notes and 1-, 2-, 5-, 10-, 20- and 50-groszy as well as 1-, 2- and 5-złoty coins.
£1 = approx. 4.3 złoty; 1 złoty = approx. £0.23. It is not normally possible to pay with euros.

Credit Cards are accepted in most shops, restaurants and hotels. When paying with a credit card or withdrawing money from **cash machines** (*bankomat*), make sure that the calculation is done on the basis of złoty, because it is cheaper.

Exchange Banks generally offer the best rates for changing foreign currency and travellers' cheques. Commissions and exchange rates can vary wildly. You will need to present your passport when changing cash or travellers' cheques. You can also use credit and debit cards (Visa and Mastercard are the most widely accepted) for cash advance in banks and from cash machines (ATMs). You will usually be charged by your bank for the service.

POLISH NATIONAL TOURIST OFFICE ➤ www.polen.travel

In the UK
10–11 Heathfield Terrace
2nd floor, London W4 4JE
☎ 300-303-1813

In the US
5 Marine View Plaza #303b
Hoboken, NJ 07030
☎ 201-420-9910

Practicalities

WHEN YOU ARE THERE

NATIONAL HOLIDAYS

1 Jan	New Year's Day
6 Jan	Epiphany
March/April	Easter Sunday, Monday
1 May	State Holiday/Labour Day
3 May	Constitution Day
May/June	Corpus Christi
15 Aug	Assumption
1 Nov	All Saints' Day
11 Nov	Independence Day
25/26 Dec	Christmas

ELECTRICITY

The power supply is 220 volts AC. Sockets take two-pronged round continental plugs.

Visitors from the UK will need an adaptor, and visitors from the USA will need a transformer for 100–120 volt devices.

OPENING HOURS

○ Shops
● Offices
● Banks
● Post offices
● Museums/Monuments
● Pharmacies

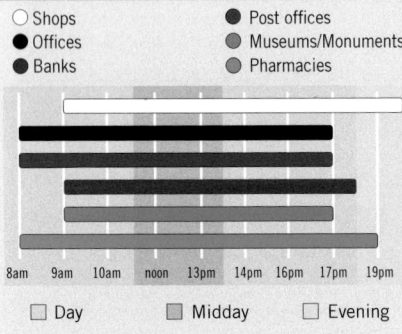

8am 9am 10am noon 13pm 14pm 16pm 17pm 19pm

☐ Day   ☐ Midday   ☐ Evening

The **shops** are generally open Mon–Sat from 9am–8pm, some on Sun as well; **shopping centres** and **department stores** sometime until 10pm; many **grocery stores** open at 6am. **Post offices**: Mon–Fri 9am–6pm, only a few open on Sat; many **museums** are closed on Monday, otherwise generally 9am–5pm, sometimes shorter hours in winter, in the high season much longer.

TIPS/GRATUITIES

Tips are expected in bars and restaurants; up to ten percent of the bill is usual. In taxis, round up the amount generously. It is usual to give small tips to porters and chambermaids. City guides also appreciated a little extra.

Taxi	Round up the bill
Guides	10–20 złoty
Hotel porters	3–8 złoty
Room service	Discretionary

ALCOHOL & SMOKING

Drinking alcohol in public, unless you are in a restaurant or recognised event location, is forbidden. Smoking is not allowed in restaurants outside designated smoking areas, on public transport, platforms, in theatres or museums.

TIME DIFFERENCES

Krakow (CET)
12 noon

←
London (GMT)
11am

→
New York (EST)
6am

→
Los Angeles (PST)
3am

→
Sydney (AEST)
9pm

Practicalities

STAYING IN TOUCH

Post You will see the red letterboxes of Poczta Polska all over the town. The main post office is on the corner of Ulica Staro-wiślna/Ulica Westerplatte (tel: 124 210 348; Mon–Fri 8am–8pm, Sat 8am–2pm). The post-age for a standard

letter (to 20 g)/postcard to an EU country Land is 5 złoty. A slightly faster service is as *Prioritetowa* letter or postcard for 6 złoty

Public Telephones: You need a telephone card for public telephones, which you can buy from kiosks or post offices. In Poland the area code has to be dialled even for local calls.
International Dialling Codes:
Dial 00 followed by

United Kingdom:	**44**
Republic of Ireland:	**353**
USA/Canada:	**1**
Australia:	**61**
Poland:	**48**

Mobile phones and services Krakow and the sur-rounding area has a very good mobile telephone service. Your mobile phone will automatically dial into one of the networks when you enable the function. From 15 June 2017, the roaming charges within the EU will be largely eliminated. You will then pay the same for them as you do for normal conversation and SMS in the UK. Consequently, it is generally no longer worth buying a prepaid card from a Polish provider.

WiFi and Internet In terms of free Internet provision, Poland is one of the leading countries in Europe. Almost all the hotels have free WiFi for their guest, and in restaurants and cafés too you can dial in to the network free. In the centre of Krakow there are many hot spots with free WiFi).

PERSONAL SAFETY

Krakow is a very safe town. CCTV monitors the roads and squares frequented by many tourists.

The crime level is much lower than for other European cities of a similar size; none-theless, you should observe the following precautions:

- Put your valuables into the hotel safe.
- Do not leave any valuables on view in your car; at night, where possible, use an underground car park or a supervised parking space.
- Keep an eye on your purse/wallet when you are at the main station or at busy tram stops.
- Ask ticket inspectors in the tram to show you their ID card with photo.
- If you are the victim of a crime, contact the police, for example at Rynek Główny (no. 29) or Kazimierz in Ulica Szeroka (no. 35).
- There is a Police Tourist Service Point at the Tourist Information Centre in Wawel (ulica Powiśle 11) from July till October.

EMERGENCY	112
POLICE	997
FIRE	998
AMBULANCE	999

Practicalities

HEALTH

 Insurance: On presentation of your European Health Insurance card (EHIC), EU citizens receive the necessary medical aid. An additional private travel insurance is still recommendable nonetheless.

 Dental Services: There are various emergency services that are open 24/7, including Denta-Med with practices in Ulica św. Gertrudy 4 on the fringe of the Old Town, in Ulica Augustiańska 13 in Kazimierz and Ulica Na Zjeździe 13 in Podgórze (www.denta-med.com.pl).

 Weather: It can be hot in Krakow in summer. When it is, you should wear suncream and stay hydrated.

 Drugs: The availability of chemists (*apteka*) in Krakow is very good; an emergency service plan is usually visible. The chemist in Mogilska 21, on the east side of the Old Town is usually open.

 Safe Water: All tap/faucet water is readily drinkable.

CONCESSIONS

Students, adolescents, senior citizens: Students carrying the International Student Identity Card (ISIC) or the Euro-26 card receive discounts at museums or other cultural institutions and on fares. This also applies to people over 65.

Museums: Many museums have one day a week where there is no entrance fee for anyone.

KrakowCard: You can buy it for two (100 złoty) or three (120 złoty) days and it provides free access to around 40 museums and other institutions as well as free use of local public transport (three-day tickets without free use of public transport cost only 70 złoty or 60 złoty for students). If you book online, it can also be used for the trip from the airport into town (www.krakowcard.com).

TRAVELLING WITH A DISABILITY

Entrances to public buildings, road crossings, hotels and restaurants are being increasingly designed to be barrier-free. Radio Taxi Partner; tel: 19 633, has taxis for wheelchair users. There is an information centre for people with disabilities in Ulica Krolewska 94, tel. 126 368 584; www.krakow-info.com/disabled.htm

CHILDREN

The Poles generally love children. Many hotels in Krakow have playrooms and special menus for kids.

Special attractions for children are also marked in this guide with the logo shown above.

CUSTOMS

EU regulations apply for importing goods from Poland, e.g. up to 800 cigarettes and up to ten litres of spirits are tax-free. It is necessary to apply for authorisation from the Voivodship Conservator of Monuments or the National Library in Warsaw if you wish to export art, books or antiques produced before 1949.

EMBASSIES & HIGH COMMISSIONS

UK (Krakow)
 12 421 70 30

USA (Krakow)
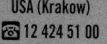 12 424 51 00

Ireland (Warsaw)
☎ 22 564 22 00

Australia (Warsaw)
☎ 22 521 34 44

Canada (Warsaw)
☎ 22 584 31 00

Useful Words and Phrases

The Polish language may initially seem very unfamiliar to you with its many sibilants. However, with a little practice, you will be able to master key words and phrases in Polish and impress your host. The written language uses a number of special characters:

ą nasal *o*	ł similar to the English *w*	ó like *u*
ć soft *tch*	ń soft *n* (as in Cognac)	ż soft *zh*
ę nasal *e*	ś soft *sh*-like sound	ź hard *zh*

The combination **cz** is pronounced *tch*, **rz** like a hard *zh* and **sz** like *sh*. In the case of the combination **ck**, the letters are spoken individually.

SURVIVAL PHRASES

Yes / No **tak / nie**
Please **proszę**
Thank you **dziękuję**
Excuse me **przepraszam**
Hello / Goodbye **cześć / do widzenia**
Good afternoon **dzień dobry**
Good evening **dobry wieczór**
Good night **dobranoc**
Help **pomoc**
How are you? **Jak się masz?**
I don't speak Polish! **Nie mówię po polsku!**
I don't understand **Nie rozumiem!**
Do you speak English? **Czy mówisz po angielsku?**
good/in agreement **dobry** (adjective)/ **dobrze** (adverb)
bad **zły** (adjective)/**źle** (adverb)
United Kingdom **Wielka Brytania**
America **Ameryka**
Poland **Polska**
What time is it? **Która jest godzina?**
Morning **rano**
Afternoon **po południu**
Evening **wieczorem**
Now **teraz**

Today **dzisiaj**
Yesterday **wczoraj**
Tomorrow **jutro**
Day **dzień**
Monday **poniedziałek**
Tuesday **wtorek**
Wednesday **środa**
Thursday **czwartek**
Friday **piątek**
Saturday **sobota**
Sunday **niedziela**

DIRECTIONS & GETTING AROUND

Where is…? **Gdzie jest…?**
Street **ulica**
Here / There **tu/tutaj / tam**
left/to the left **lewo/na lewo**
right/to the right **prawo/na prawo**
straight on **prosto**
near / far **blisko / daleko**
How do I get to/Where is the…?
  Jak dostać się…/Gdzie jest…
… station… **do dworca**
… toilet… **do toalety**
… airport… **na lotnisko**
… museum… **do muzeum**

NUMBERS

0 **zero**	11 **jedenaście**	30 **trzydzieście**
1 **jeden**	12 **dwanaście**	40 **czterdzieście**
2 **dwa**	13 **trzynaście**	50 **pięćdziesiąt**
3 **trzy**	14 **czternaście**	60 **sceśćdziesiąt**
4 **cztery**	15 **piętnaście**	70 **siedemdziesiąt**
5 **pięć**	16 **szesnaście**	80 **osiemdziesiąt**
6 **sześć**	17 **siedemnaście**	90 **dziewięćdziesiąt**
7 **siedem**	18 **osiemnaście**	100 **sto**
8 **osiem**	19 **dziewiętnaście**	101 **sto jeden**
9 **dziewięć**	20 **dwadzieścia**	1,000 **tysiąc**
10 **dziesięć**	21 **dwadzieścia jeden**	

Useful Words and Phrases

Tram / Bus **tramwaj / autobus**
Stop **przystanek**
Ship **statek**
Ticket **bilet**
Reservation **rezerwacja**
Departure / Arrival **wyjście / przyjazd**
Bicycle **rower**
Car **samochód**
Supervised parking **strzeżony**
I have broken down. **Mam awarię samochodu.**
Where is the nearest garage? **Gdzie jest tu w pobliżu warsztat samochodowy?**
Museum **muzeum**
Church **kościół**
Post / Bank **poczta / bank**
Tourist information **informacja turystyczna**
Exchange **kantor**

ACCOMMODATION

Hotel **hotel**
Accommodation **noclegi**
Room **pokój**
Bathroom / Shower **łazienki / prysznic**
Room available **wolne pokój**
Do you have a single/double room available?
Czy masz pokój jednoosobowy/ dwuosobowy za darmo?
I have reserved a room.
Mam zarezerwowany pokój.

How much does the room cost a night?
Ile kosztuje pokój za noc?
Room number **numer pokój**
Key for the room **klucz do pokoju**

SHOPPING

Where can I find…? **Gdzie znaleźć…?**
Shop **sklep**
Butcher **sklep rzeźniczy**
Food store **sklep spożywczy**
Bakery **piekarnia**
Can I pay with a credit card?
Czy mogę zapłacić kartą kreditową?
Fruit **owoc**
Vegetables **warzywo**

EATING OUT

Menu **jadłospis/menu**
The menu please **Proszę dać mi menu**
Breakfast **śniadanie**
Lunch / Dinner **obiad / kolacja**
Main course **danie główne**
Starter / Soup **przystawka / zupa**
Desert **deser**
The bill please **Proszę o rachunek**
Waiter! **proszę pana/i**
Cheers **na zdrowie**
Bon appetit **smacznego**

MENU READER

barszcz czerwony beetroot soup
befsztyk beefsteak
bigos cabbage/sauerkraut hotchpotch
borowiki porcini mushrooms
chłodnik cold beetroot soup
czekolada chocolate
chleb bread
dodatki side dishes
flaki tripe soup
frytki chips
herbata tea
kaczka pieczona roast duck
karp carp
kawa coffee
kiełbasa sausage
kluski dumplings

kotlet schabowy pork schnitzel
kurczak chicken
kurki chanterelles
lody ice cream
łosoś salmon
makowiec poppy-seed cake
mleko milk
naleśniki pancakes
pierogi Polish dumplings
pieczeń wołowa roast beef
piwo beer
polędwica beef sirloin (often with mushroom sauce)
pstrąg trout
ryba fish
ryż rice
sałatka salad

śledź herring
sok jabłkowy apple juice
sok pomarańczowe orange juice
surówka raw food, side salad
szampan sparkling wine
szarlotka apple strudel
wino białe white wine
wino czerwone red wine
woda mineralne (gazowana/ niegazowana) mineral water (sparkling/still)
ziemniaki potatoes
zupa grzybowa mushroom soup
zupa pomidorowa tomato soup
żurek sour rye soup

Street Atlas

For chapters: See inside front cover

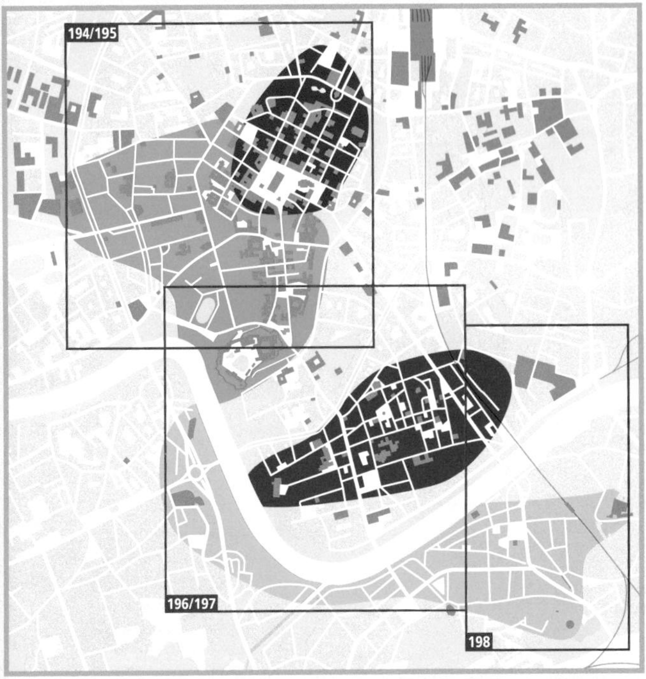

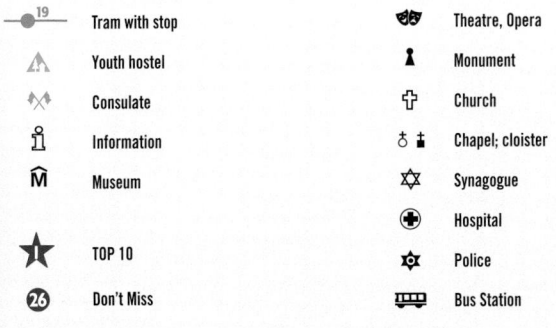

194/195

196/197

198

Key to Street Atlas

—•—19 Tram with stop	🎭 Theatre, Opera
⚠ Youth hostel	🯅 Monument
⚔ Consulate	✝ Church
ℹ Information	Chapel; cloister
Ⓜ Museum	✡ Synagogue
	⊕ Hospital
★ TOP 10	✪ Police
㉖ Don't Miss	🚌 Bus Station
㉒ At Your Leisure	

1 : 7500

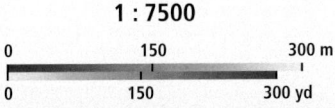

0	150	300 m
0	150	300 yd

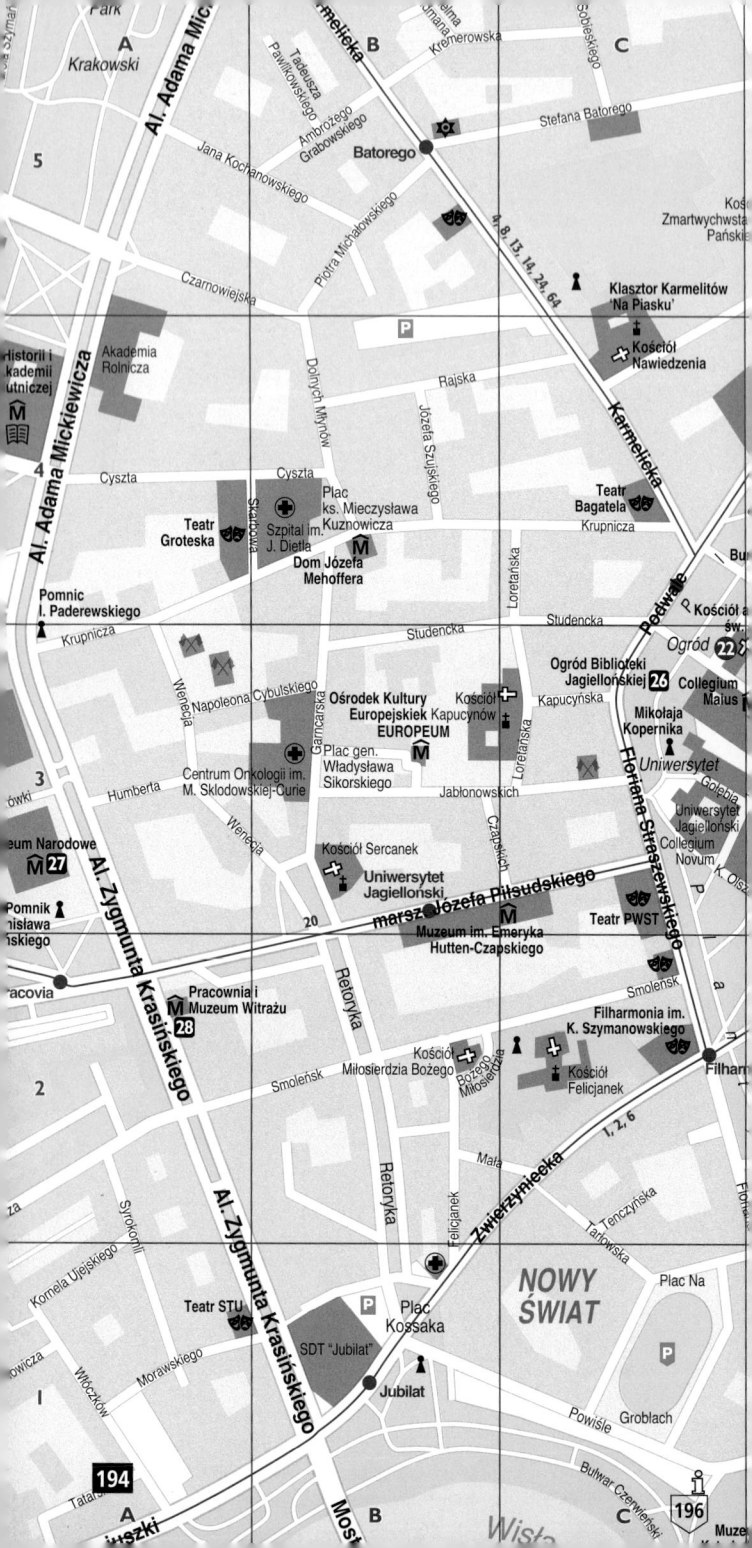

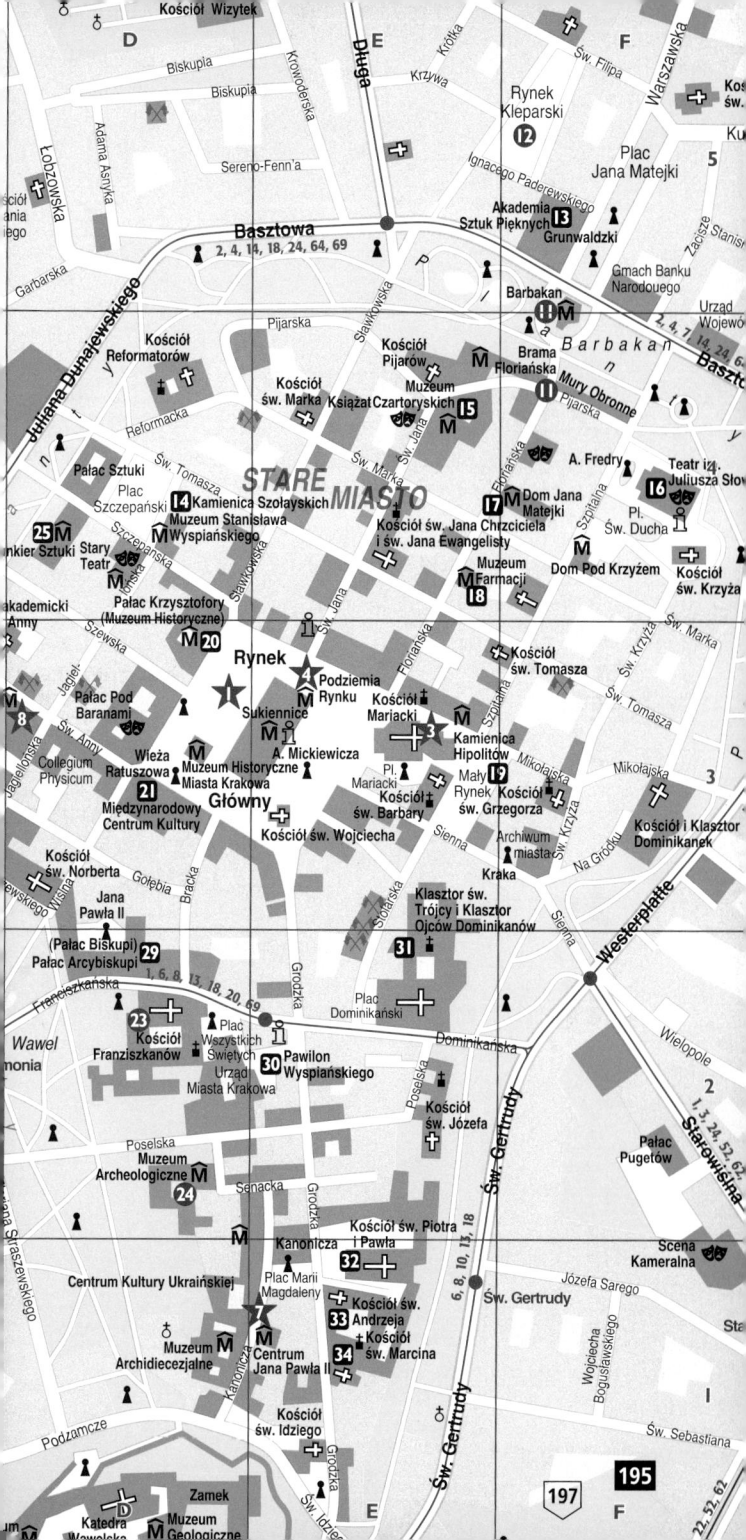

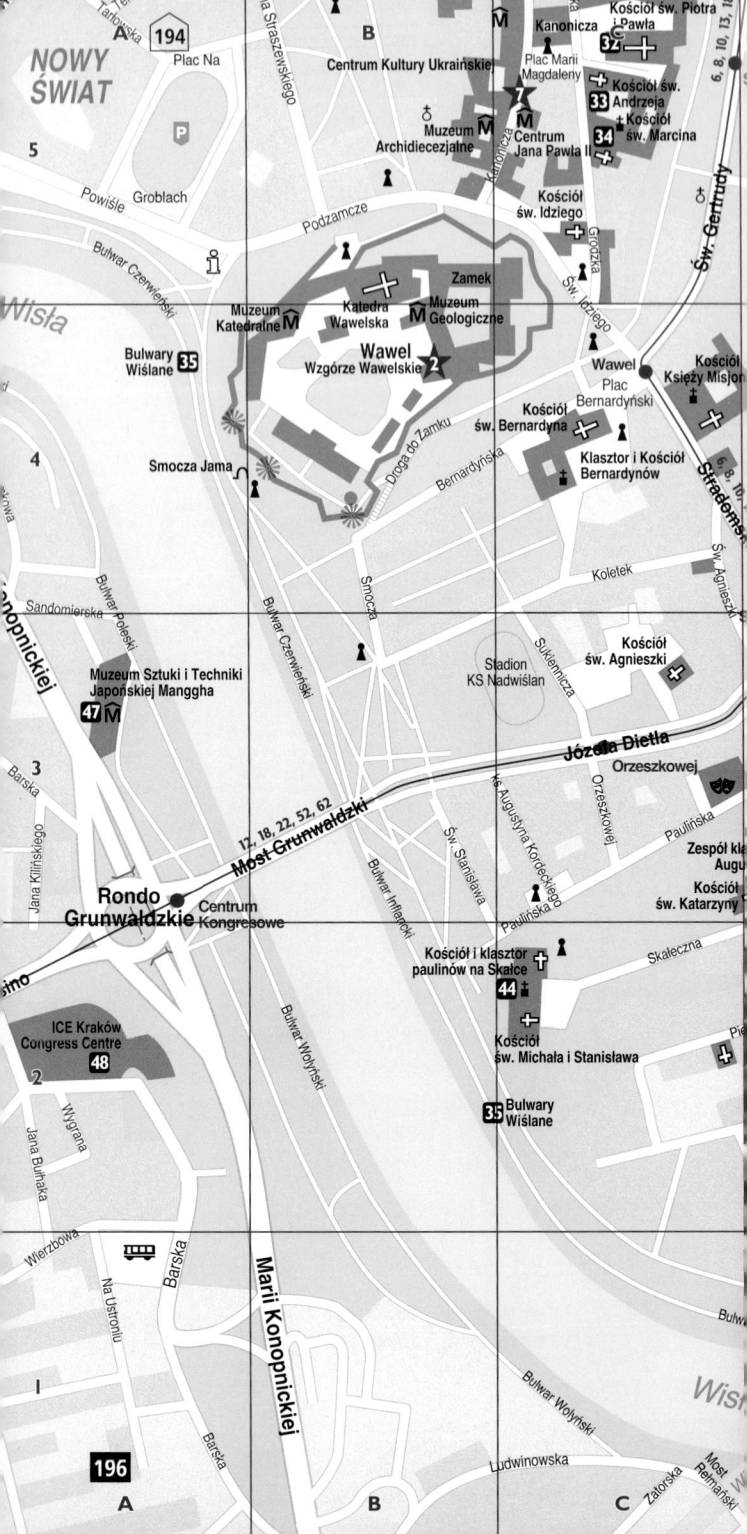

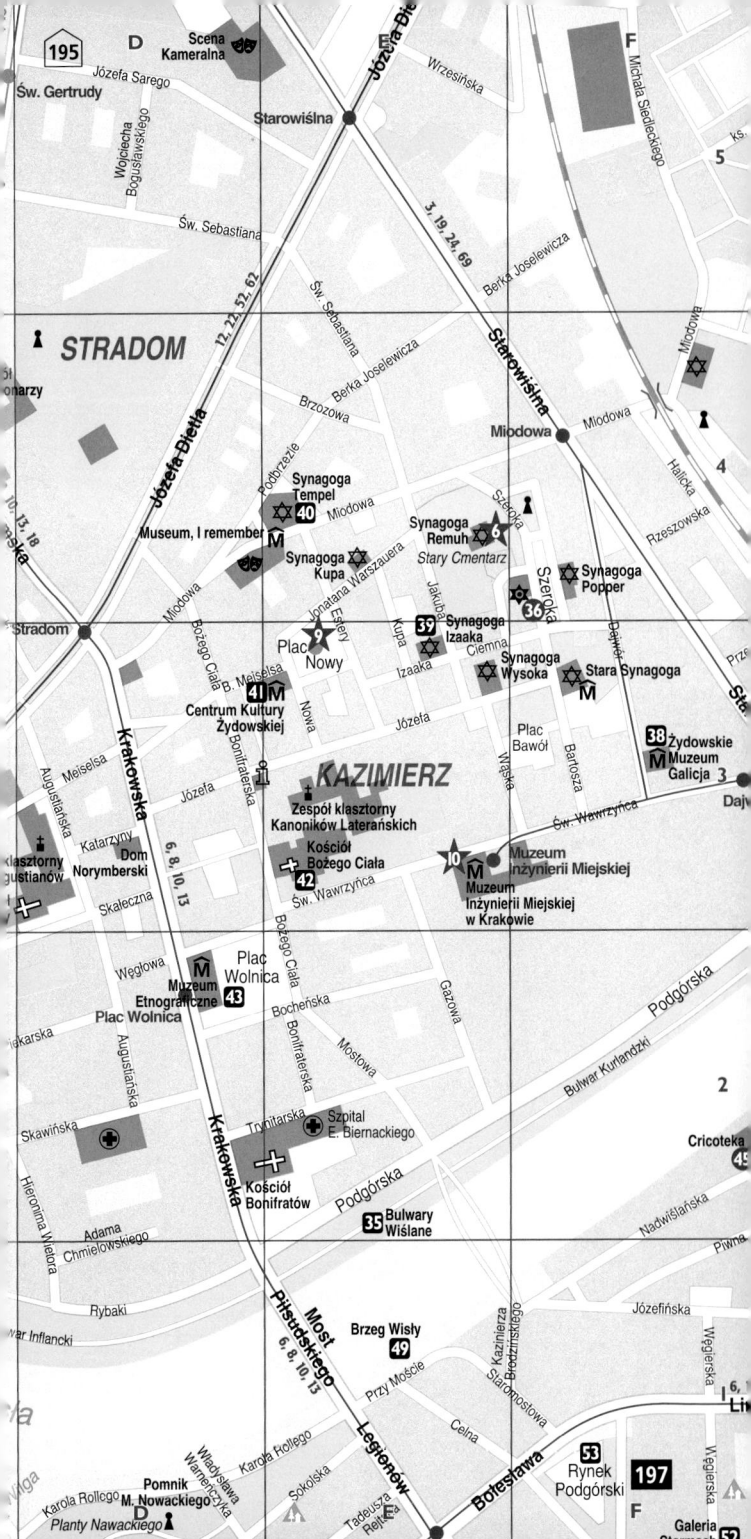

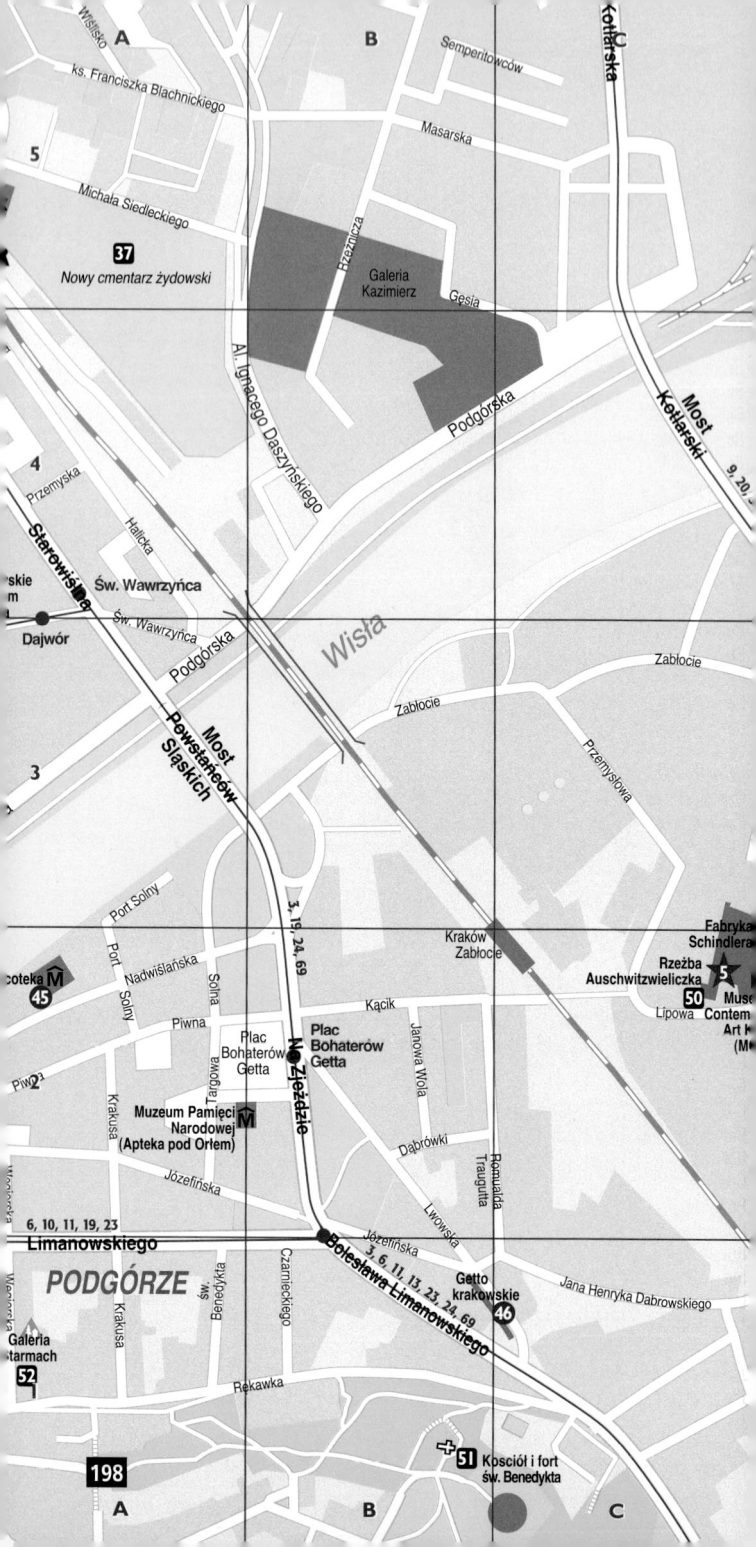

Street Index

Street Index

Index

Index

Index

Index

Index

Picture Credits

akg-images: Album/Prisma 10/11, 17 top; Schütze/Rodemann 11

DuMont Bildarchiv/Peter Hirth: 20, 24 left, 27, 32, 51, 52, 53, 54, 58, 61, 82/83, 85, 92, 93, 120, 121, 127, 129, 147 (© Beat Streuli), 166, 167, 169, 172

Freyer, Ralf: 163

Getty Images: Henryk T. Kaiser 57

Klöppel, Klaus: 124

laif: Christophe Boisvieux 66; Hirsch 26; Peter Hirth 31, 104 left, 117; Malte Jaeger 24/25, 25 centre and right; Pool COCHARD/ GAILLARDE 84; Jean-Baptiste Rabouan 106; Lucas Vallecillos/ VWPics/ReduxRedux 115, 143 top and bottom, 148; Gerhard Westrich 6/7, 29

LOOK-foto: age fotostock 80, 90, 130; Kay Maeritz 91

mauritius images: AA World Travel Library/Alamy 98, 100, 155, 180; age/Henryk T. Kaiser 14, 67; Bildarchiv Monheim GmbH/Alamy 59; Wojtek Buss 171; E. Champelovier/Alamy 24 centre; croftsphoto/ Alamy 25 left; Artur Cupak 13 top, 15 bottom left and right; Digital-Fotofusion/Gallery/Alamy 18; Robert Dziewulski/Alamy 15 top right; Endless Travel/Alamy 50 bottom, 95; Urs Flüeler 21; foodfolio/ Alamy 22; Peter Forsberg/Alamy 184; Paul Gapper/Alamy 23; David Gee/Alamy 68; Janusz Gniadek/Alamy 64, 123, 189; Andrzej Gorzowski/Alamy 63; Nick Higham/Alamy 102; imageBROKER/Kurt Amthor 178; imageBROKER/Christian Handt 48; imageBROKER/ Peter Schickert 96; INSADCO Photography/Alamy 119; Slawek Koziol/Alamy 62; Malgorzata Larys/Alamy 176; les polders/Alamy 142; John Norman/Alamy 30; Pegaz/Alamy 8, 17 bottom, 28, 33, 34, 86, 104 right, 116, 152, 179; Photononstop/Alamy 97; Dirk Renckhoff/ Alamy 122; Maurice Savage/Alamy 150; Jakub Siemiaczko/Alamy 15 top left; Daniel Staniszewski/Alamy 19, 22/23 (background); Slawek Staszczuk/Alamy 99; Matthew Taylor/Alamy 13 bottom, 50 top, 182; Wojciech Tchorzewski/Alamy 144; United Archives 4; VCP Photo/Alamy 101; VIEW Pictures Ltd/Alamy 32/33 (background), 34 (background), 149, 153; John Warburton-Lee 164, 168; R. Widmann 81; Hans Winke/Alamy 174; Gregory Wrona/Alamy 24 right; wyrdlight/Alamy 65

picture-alliance: akg-images 12 top; dpa 12 bottom; dpa/dpaweb 87; allOver/TPH 118; ZB 131

On the cover: Getty images/Yoko Aziz (top), mauritius images/ Urs Flüeler (bottom), Getty Images (background)